# Tarot

Origins, Evolution, Esotericism, Divination, and Magic

Matthew Leigh Embleton

Copyright ©2024 Matthew Leigh Embleton. All rights reserved.

# Tarot

1. Origins: Chinese Playing Cards ............................................................................................. 1
2. Origins: Middle Eastern Playing Cards .................................................................................. 4
3. Evolution: Playing Cards in Medieval Europe ........................................................................ 6
4. Evolution: Tarot Cards in Medieval Europe ......................................................................... 10
5. Evolution: Early Tarot Decks ................................................................................................ 13
5.1. The Visconti-Sforza Tarot ............................................................................................... 14
5.2. The Mantegna Tarocchi .................................................................................................. 16
5.3. The Sola Busca Tarot ..................................................................................................... 18
5.4. Minchiate ......................................................................................................................... 20
5.5. Tarot de Marseille ........................................................................................................... 24
6. Esotericism: Ancient Knowledge and Symbols .................................................................... 42
6.1. Esotericism and Tarot .................................................................................................... 48
6.2. The Rider-Waite-Smith Deck ......................................................................................... 55
7. The Tarot Deck ..................................................................................................................... 58
7.1. The Major Arcana ........................................................................................................... 59
7.2. The Minor Arcana ........................................................................................................... 82
7.2.1. Wands ........................................................................................................................ 83
7.2.2. Cups ........................................................................................................................... 97
7.2.3. Swords ..................................................................................................................... 111
7.2.4. Pentacles ................................................................................................................. 125
8. Divination ............................................................................................................................ 139
8.1. One Card Reading: Yes / No Question ....................................................................... 141
8.2. Three Card Spreads ..................................................................................................... 142
8.3. Four Card Spreads ....................................................................................................... 156
8.4. Five Card Spreads ....................................................................................................... 159
8.5. The 'Celtic Cross' Spread ............................................................................................. 164
9. Magic .................................................................................................................................. 165
9.1. General Advice ............................................................................................................. 168

Cover: A circular spread of the Visconti-Sforza, Rider-Waite-Smith, and Tarot de Marseille decks.
Source: Image created by the author
Note: All images are in the Public Domain, unless otherwise specified.

©2024 Matthew Leigh Embleton (Original)
©2025 Matthew Leigh Embleton (This Edition)

# Acknowledgments

I have long been fascinated by history, and I am very grateful to the special people in my life who have supported and encouraged me in my work, and kindly gifted me with special tarot decks. Thank you for believing in me. You know who you are.

I am grateful for the friendships I have had with members of the magical community, through which I have learned much about magic, spiritualism, the occult, and about myself.

# Introduction

**Was Tarot created by Kabbalists who modelled the major 'trump' cards on the 22 letters of the Hebrew Alphabet?**

Some modern esoteric traditions, especially those within the Kabbalistic and mystical realms, suggest that the tarot's Major Arcana (the 'trump' cards) were influenced by the 22 letters of the Hebrew alphabet. This theory was popularised by scholars such as Eliphas Levi and other 19th-century occultists. They argued that each of the 22 Major Arcana cards corresponded to a letter of the Hebrew alphabet and could be mapped onto the Tree of Life in Kabbalah. While there is no definitive historical evidence that tarot was created by Kabbalists or that its cards were directly modelled on the Hebrew alphabet, the association between tarot and Kabbalah became more prominent in the 18th and 19th centuries, especially with the rise of Western esotericism. The connection is more about later mystical interpretations rather than the original creation of tarot cards.

**Is Tarot a hieroglyphic text created by Hermes Trismegistus?**

Another popular esoteric belief is that tarot has roots in ancient Egypt and that it is a 'hieroglyphic' text created by Hermes Trismegistus, a legendary figure who supposedly combined the wisdom of the Egyptian god Thoth and the Greek god Hermes. Some occult traditions argue that tarot contains ancient esoteric knowledge, encrypted in a way similar to hieroglyphs. There is no historical evidence to support the idea that tarot was created by Hermes Trismegistus or that it is a direct descendant of ancient Egyptian hieroglyphs. While tarot cards contain symbols and archetypes that some may link to Egyptian imagery or wisdom, the origins of tarot cards are much more recent and rooted in medieval European traditions.

**Did Tarot come from Ancient Egypt?**

Some proponents of the idea that tarot originates in ancient Egypt claim that the cards are a direct lineage from the Egyptian Book of Thoth, a mythical and legendary text believed to contain divine wisdom. This theory was popularized in the 18th and 19th centuries by occult writers, who saw tarot as a form of ancient Egyptian wisdom. There is no historical evidence that tarot cards originated in Egypt. The earliest known tarot decks appeared in Italy during the 15th century, long after the height of ancient Egyptian civilization. While tarot may use symbols and archetypes that seem similar to those found in Egyptian culture, the cards themselves are more likely a product of European Renaissance culture, influenced by various medieval traditions, including playing cards, alchemy, and mysticism.

**Is Tarot the oldest book in the world created by ancient Egyptian god Thoth who invented writing?**

Some theories suggest that tarot is an ancient 'book' created by the Egyptian god Thoth, who was associated with wisdom, writing, and knowledge. According to this belief, tarot was a sacred book passed down from Egypt and contains mystical teachings about the universe. While Thoth is indeed a god of wisdom and writing in Egyptian mythology, there is no direct connection between the tarot cards and the Egyptian pantheon. Tarot is not the oldest book in the world, and it was not created by Thoth. Tarot cards emerged much later in history, around the 15th century in Europe, and there is no direct evidence that they are a product of ancient Egyptian teachings.

# 1. Origins: Chinese Playing Cards

The evolution of Tarot from a family of card games to a system of divination was shaped by several key events in history. The 'Four Great Inventions of China' are traditionally named as the compass, gunpowder, papermaking, and printing[1]. The history of Tarot begins with the latter two of these.

---

[1] Andrade, Tonio (2016-01-12). The Gunpowder Age: China, Military Innovation, and the Rise of the West in World History. Princeton University Press. doi:10.2307/j.ctvc77j74. ISBN 978-1-4008-7444-6. JSTOR j.ctvc77j74.

A Wine Card depicting Guang Chengzi painted by Ren Xiong, late Qing Dynasty

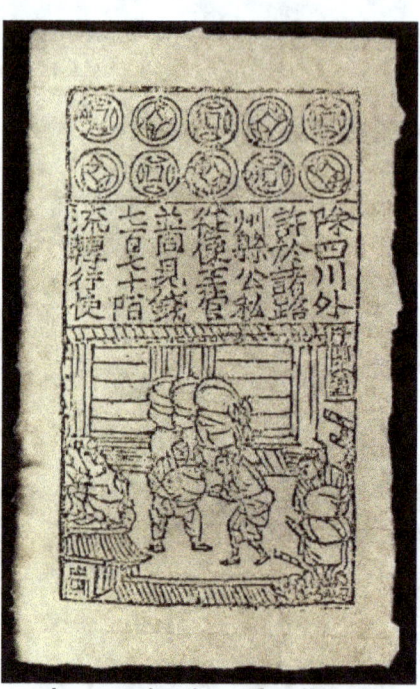
A reproduction of a Jiaozi currency note from the Song Dynasty, c.1023

A Chinese woodblock printed playing card, c. 1400, found near Turpan

The first paper-like plant-based writing material was papyrus, which was used in ancient Egypt as far back as 3000 BCE[2]. In China, hemp paper was used for wrapping, padding, and packaging from around 800 BCE. The invention of paper as we know it, or at least the most significant innovation in its production, has been credited to Cai Lun, a court official during the Han Dynasty (202 BCE – 220 CE). According to tradition his innovation took place in the year 105 CE[3]. Using a pulp made of plant fibres and hemp waste[4][5][6], the costs of production were reduced, and paper became more affordable, widely available, and widespread around the world. Woodblock printing also originated in China during the Han Dynasty. Each image print is created by carving the design into a wooden block, which is then inked and pressed onto the target material. Larger numbers of impressions could then be printed using the same wooden blocks over and over again. This technique was originally used to print patterns onto textiles[7], and by the Tang Dynasty (618-907) it was also being used to print onto paper[8]. The Game of Leaves or the Leaf Game is commonly described as the first card game, originating around the 9th century in the Tang Dynasty. However this is disputed, and some sources describe it as a board game with dice in which players consulted the leaves (pages) of a book, rather than 'leaf' being a synonym for 'card'[9]. It is possible that Wine Cards are the earliest known form of 'playing cards' (in the loosest sense of the term), originating in China also during the Tang Dynasty. However the cards did not have suits or numbers, instead they were printed with instructions or forfeits for whoever drew them during drinking games[10][11]. It can be said with a degree of confidence that the idea

---

[2] Houston, Keith, The Book: A Cover-to-Cover Exploration of the Most Powerful Object of our Time, W. W. Norton & Company, 2016
[3] Hunter, Dard; Hunter, Cornell (1978) [1943]. Papermaking: The History and Technique of an Ancient Craft (2nd ed.). New York: Dover Publications. ISBN 978-0-486-23619-3.
[4] Wilkinson, Endymion (2012), Chinese History: A New Manual, Harvard University Asia Center for the Harvard-Yenching Institute
[5] Papermaking. (2007). In: Encyclopædia Britannica. Retrieved April 9, 2007, from Encyclopædia Britannica Online.
[6] Barrett, Timothy Hugh (2008), The Woman Who Discovered Printing, Great Britain: Yale University Press, ISBN 978-0-300-12728-7
[7] Shelagh Vainker in Anne Farrer (ed), "Caves of the Thousand Buddhas", 1990, British Museum publications, ISBN 0-7141-1447-2
[8] Wilkinson, Endymion (2012), Chinese History: A New Manual, Harvard University Asia Center for the Harvard-Yenching Institute
[9] Lo, Andrew. (2000). The Game of Leaves: An Inquiry into the Origin of Chinese Playing Cards. Bulletin of the School of Oriental and African Studies, University of London, 63(3), 389–406.

of playing games with cards or slips of paper, with designs printed on one side so as not to be visible to other players, was definitely invented in China during the late Tang Dynasty. It is also worth noting that paper money was introduced in China in the year 1023 during the Song Dynasty (960-1279)[12]. The Jiaozi is regarded as the first paper money in history.

By the 11th century papermaking had arrived in Europe, and playing cards were spreading throughout Asia. They also spread west along the Silk Road, through Persia and India, and all the way to Egypt, which at the time was under the rule of the Mamluk Sultanate[13]. The Silk Road was a network of trade routes that were active from c. 114 BCE to c. 1450 CE, spanning over 6,400 kilometres (4,000 miles). It was so called because of the trade in Chinese silk that was widely sought after in Rome, Egypt, and Greece[14]. Other luxury goods included tea, dyes, perfumes, and porcelain. Western exports to China included horses, camels, honey, wine, and gold.

The main routes of the Silk Road

---

[10] Lo, Andrew. (2000). The Game of Leaves: An Inquiry into the Origin of Chinese Playing Cards. Bulletin of the School of Oriental and African Studies, University of London, 63(3), 389–406.
[11] Lo, Andrew (2004) 'China's Passion for Pai: Playing Cards, Dominoes, and Mahjong.' In: Mackenzie, C. and Finkel, I., (eds.), Asian Games: The Art of Contest. New York: Asia Society, pp. 217-231.
[12] "Paper Money in Premodern China.". ChinaKnowledge.de - An Encyclopaedia on Chinese History, Literature and Art. May 10, 2016. Retrieved February 6, 2018.
[13] Needham, Joseph; Tsien, Tsuen-hsuin (1985), Science and Civilization in China: Volume 5, Chemistry and Chemical Technology, Part 1, Paper and Printing, Cambridge University Press, ISBN 0-521-08690-6
[14] "The Silk Road". National Geographic Society. 26 July 2019. Retrieved 25 January 2022.

# 2. Origins: Middle Eastern Playing Cards

With the popularity of Chinese playing cards spreading across Asia, local emulations and variations of these cards soon followed, notably in Mamluk Egypt where the so-called 'Mamluk Cards' are known to have emerged. The oldest surviving playing cards in the world are four fragments found in the Keir Collection and one in the Benaki Museum. They are dated to the 12th and 13th centuries (late Fatimid, Ayyubid, and early Mamluk periods)[15]. Three different packs of 'Mamluk' playing cards similar in

---

[15] Dummett, Michael (1980). The Game of Tarot. London: Duckworth. ISBN 978-0715610145.

appearance to the above and dating to the 15th century were discovered by Leo Aryeh Mayer in the Topkapi Palace in Istanbul in 1939[16][17].

Mamluk '*Kanjifah*' cards, also known as '*Na'ib*'.
From left to right: 6 of Coins, 10 of Polo Sticks, 3 of Cups, 7 of Swords

The original Mamluk deck contained 52 cards in four suits: Coins, Polo Sticks, Cups, and Swords. Each suit contained three court cards: *malik* (king), *na'ib malik* ('lieutenant'), and *thani na'ib* ('second lieutenant'), and ten pip cards.

They were called '*kanjifah*' ('*kan-*' from Persian '*ganj*' = 'treasure' + '*-jifa*' from Chinese '*chepae*', '*chi-p'ai*', or '*zhipai*' = 'paper ticket' or 'playing cards').

Also known in Persia and India as *Ganjifah*, the game ultimately became known as '*Na'ib*' ('Lieutenants') after the court cards. These court cards did not depict any kings or lieutenants in their suits, perhaps due to a strict religious aversion to any kind of iconism or idolatry.

As well as being at the western end of the Silk Road, the Mamluk Sultanate was also perfectly positioned at the shores of the eastern Mediterranean with access to ports across Europe.

This enabled their monopoly in the immensely profitable trade of luxury goods between East and West. Playing cards were exported from Cairo, Alexandria, and Damascus until the fall of the Mamluks in 1517[18].

---

[16] Mayer, Leo Ary (1939), Le Bulletin de l'Institut français d'archéologie orientale, vol. 38, pp. 113–118, retrieved 2008-09-08.
[17] Berry, John (December 2001). "Mamluk Problems". The Playing-Card. 30 (3). The International Playing-Card Society: 139. ISSN 0305-2133.
[18] The Mamluk Cards. (https://l-pollett.tripod.com/cards64.htm). Retrieved on 2024-10-18.

# 3. Evolution: Playing Cards in Medieval Europe

By around 1360-1370, an increasing number of European merchants, diplomats, and sailors were bringing *Na'ib* cards back with them from Islamic territories to ports across Italy and Spain. At the time Spain was still partly occupied by the Emirate of Granada in the south, and there is an earlier reference to card games being banned in Barcelona as far back as 1310 by the *Consejo de Ciento* (Council of One-Hundred)[19]. The name *Na'ib* was borrowed into Italian (*naibi, naibbe, nayb*), Spanish (*naipes*), Catalan (*naip*), and French (*nahipi*)[20]. They were also referred to as 'Saracen Cards', or

---

[19] J. Amades y J. Colomines, "Els Soldats i altres Papers de Rengles" (Barcelona, 1933-1936) vol. II p. 7.

'Moorish Cards' and were associated with Islamic culture in the public consciousness[21]. The cards quickly gained widespread popularity, particularly with the upper classes, aristocracy, and nobility as a leisurely and agreeable pastime. Part of what we know about the rapid spread of these cards is the moral reaction against them in the form of bans and prohibitions, the first of them in Florence in 1377[22][23][24]. The list of bans goes on and on across the many cities of France, Italy, Germany, Switzerland, and Spain well into the 1400s. After the arrival of woodblock printing in Europe, the first Italian and Spanish cards were made based on the 'Mamluk' cards, but the suit of Polo Sticks was replaced by Batons, as the game of Polo was not as well known in the West at that time[25]. The deck had four suits, each with three or four 'court cards' and nine or ten 'pip cards'. The four suits varied by country, region, and even by city. In Italian suits, the Swords (*Spade*) remained curved like the scimitars of the Mamluk cards, helping to distinguish between swords and batons. In Spanish suits the Swords (*Espadas*) were straight, while the Batons (*Bastos*) were drawn less like ceremonial batons, and more like clubs[26].

---

[20] Mamluk cards. Cards.old.no. (https://cards.old.no/1500-mamluk/) Retrieved on 2024-10-19.
[21] The Early History of Playing Cards. wopc.co.uk (https://www.wopc.co.uk/the-history-of-playing-cards/early-history-of-playing-cards) Retrieved on 2024-10-19.
[22] Peter F. Kopp: Die frühesten Spielkarten in der Schweiz. In: Zeitschrift für schweizerische Archäologie und Kunstgeschichte 30 (1973), pp. 130–145, here 130.
[23] Hellmut Rosenfeld: Zu den frühesten Spielkarten in der Schweiz. Eine Entgegnung. In: Zeitschrift für schweizerische Archäologie und Kunstgeschichte 32 (1975), pp. 179–180.
[24] Detlef Hoffmann: Kultur- und Kunstgeschichte der Spielkarte. Marburg: Jonas Verlag 1995, p. 43.
[25] An Introduction at i-p-c-s.org (https://www.i-p-c-s.org/wp/an-introduction/), Retrieved 2024-10-19.
[26] An Introduction at i-p-c-s.org (https://www.i-p-c-s.org/wp/an-introduction/), Retrieved 2024-10-19.

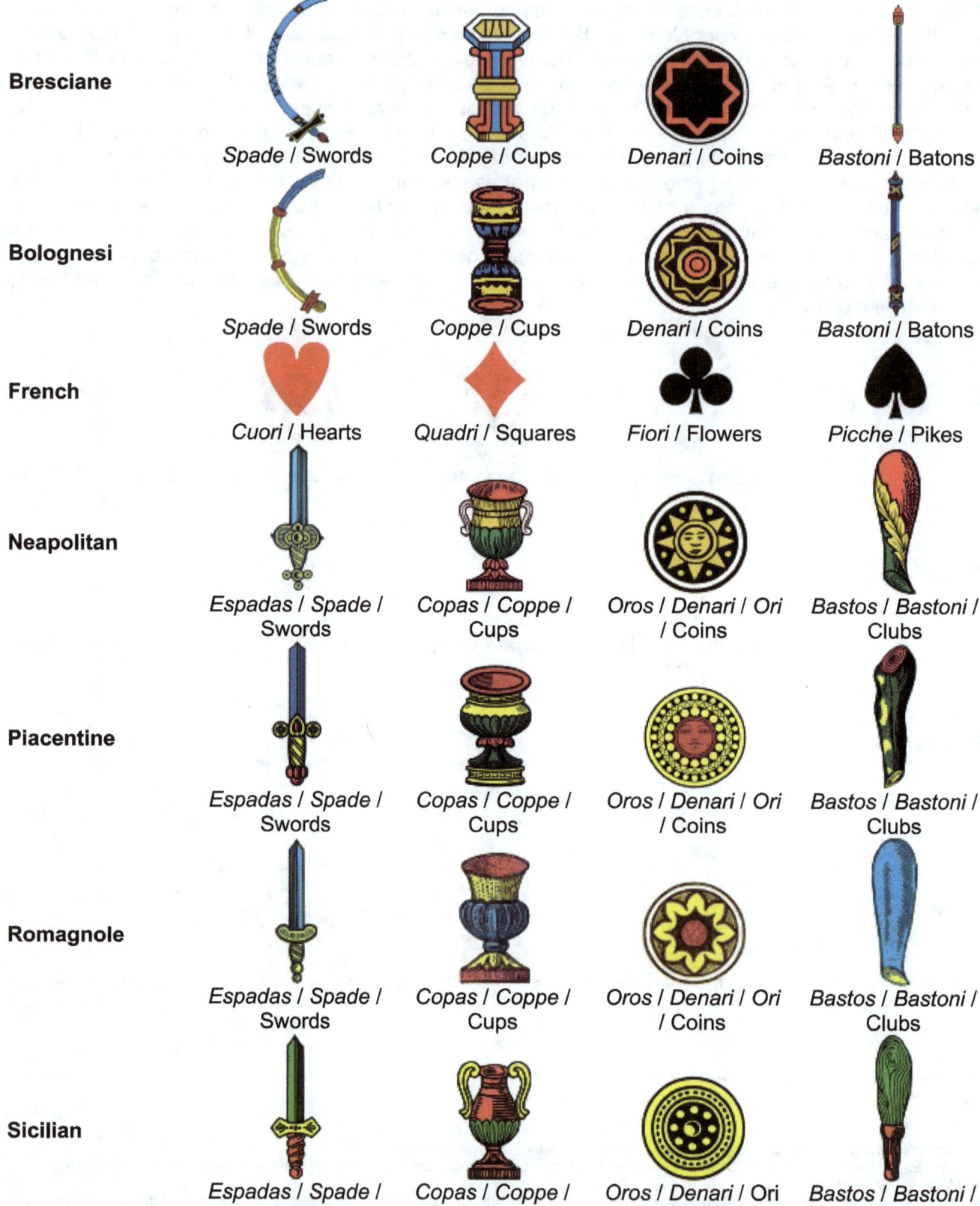

Tarot                                                03 Evolution: Playing Cards in Medieval Europe

| | | | | |
|---|---|---|---|---|
| **Sardinian** | *Espadas / Spade /* Swords | *Copas / Coppe /* Cups | *Oros / Denari / Ori* / Coins | *Bastos / Bastoni /* Clubs |
| **German** | *Eicheln / Ghiande* / Acorns | *Blätter / Foglie /* Leaves | *Herzen / Cuori /* Hearts | *Schellen / Campanelli /* Bells |
| **Castilian** | *Espadas /* Swords | *Copas /* Cups | *Oros /* Coins | *Bastos /* Clubs |
| **Cadiz** | *Espadas /* Swords | *Copas /* Cups | *Oros /* Coins | *Bastos /* Clubs |
| **Catalan** | *Espases / Espadas /* Swords | *Copes / Copas /* Cups | *Oros / Oros /* Coins | *Bastons / Bastos /* Clubs |
| **Aluette** | *Espadas / Épée /* Swords | *Copas / Coupe /* Cups | *Oros / Denier /* Coins | *Bastos / Bâton /* Clubs |
| **Portuguese** | *Espadas / Espadas /* Swords | *Copas / Copas /* Cups | *Ouros / Oros /* Coins | *Paus / Bastos /* Clubs |

# 4. Evolution: Tarot Cards in Medieval Europe

Some card games involved one of the four suits being nominated as a 'trump' suit, where any cards that were dealt from that suit out-ranked all other cards played. The Italian word *trionfi* translates as 'triumphs', related to the Latin word '*triumphus*', which is also where the English word 'trump' comes from. Sometime between 1410 and 1430, the *Trionfi* were created as an additional suit of 21 trump cards, along with 'The Fool' which was not numbered. Each '*trionfo*' card featured a symbolic allegory or a personification of an abstract idea, concept, or an archetype. When these *Trionfi* were added to the traditional deck, the number of cards increased from 56 to 78. This new expanded 78 card deck was used to play a family of games called *Tarocchi* in Italian, *Tarot* in French, and *Tarock* in German. In the French tradition, the trumps were also called '*Atouts*'.

|    | English           | Italian         | Spanish                | French           | German              |
|----|-------------------|-----------------|------------------------|------------------|---------------------|
| 0  | The Fool          | Il Matto        | El Loco                | Le Fol           | Der Narr            |
| 1  | The Magician      | Il Bagatto      | El Mago                | Le Bateleur      | Der Magier          |
| 2  | The Popess        | La Papessa      | La Sacerdotisa         | La Pances        | Die Hohepriesterin  |
| 3  | The Empress       | L'Imperatrice   | La Emperatriz          | Imperatris       | Die Herrscherin     |
| 4  | The Emperor       | L'Imperatore    | El Emperador           | L'Empereur       | Der Herrscher       |
| 5  | The Pope          | Il Papa         | El Sumo Sacerdote      | Le Pape          | Der Hierophant      |
| 6  | The Lovers        | Gli Innamorati  | Los Enamorados         | La Moureu        | Die Liebenden       |
| 7  | The Chariot       | Il Carro        | El Carro               | Le Charior       | Der Wagen           |
| 8  | Justice           | La Giustizia    | Justicia               | Iustice          | Die Gerechtigkeit   |
| 9  | The Hermit        | L'Eremita       | El Ermitano            | L'Ermite         | Der Eremit          |
| 10 | The Wheel of Fortune | La Ruota     | La Rueda De La Fortuna | La Roue De Fortun | Das Rad des Schicksals |
| 11 | Strength          | La Forza        | Fuerza                 | Force            | Die Kraft           |
| 12 | The Hanged Man    | L'Appeso        | El Colgado             | Le Pandu         | Der Gehängte        |
| 13 | Death             | La Morte        | Muerte                 | La Mort          | Der Tod             |
| 14 | Temperance        | La Temperanza   | Templanza              | Temperance       | Die Mäßigkeit       |
| 15 | The Devil         | Il Diavolo      | El Diablo              | Le Diable        | Der Teufel          |
| 16 | The Tower         | La Torre        | La Torre               | La Maison Dieu   | Der Turm            |
| 17 | The Star          | Le Stelle       | La Estrella            | Le Toille        | Der Stern           |
| 18 | The Moon          | La Luna         | La Luna                | La Lune          | Der Mond            |
| 19 | The Sun           | Il Sole         | El Sol                 | Le Soleil        | Die Sonne           |
| 20 | The Judgement     | Il Giudizio     | El Juicio              | Le Iugement      | Das Gericht         |
| 21 | The World         | Il Mondo        | El Mundo               | Le Monde         | Die Welt            |

The symbolism of these trump cards can be interpreted in many ways. For some, they are a series of archetypes, representations of the stages of life, parts of our inner-self, inner-psyche, subconscious, or representations of other people or forces that affect us in our daily lives in the short-term or long-term. Swiss psychotherapist Carl Jung commented that they seem to be descended from the archetypes of transformation[27].

---

[27] Jung, C. G. (1959). "Archetypes of the Collective Unconscious". In Read, Sir Herbert; Fordham, Michael; Adler, Gerhard (eds.). The Archetypes and the Collective Unconscious. The Collected Works of C. G. Jung. Vol. 9, part 1. Translated by Hall, R. F. C. New York: Pantheon Books. p. 38, paragraph 81. ISBN 978-0691018331.

## The Printing Press and the Stencil

Sometime around 1440-1450 in Mainz, Germany, Johannes Gutenberg invented the moveable-type printing press which completely revolutionised printing. Card sheets could be printed much more quickly and efficiently, and at a lower cost. Once the cards were printed, they were traditionally coloured by hand or using stencils. Within several decades the printing press had spread to over 200 cities in a dozen European countries[28].

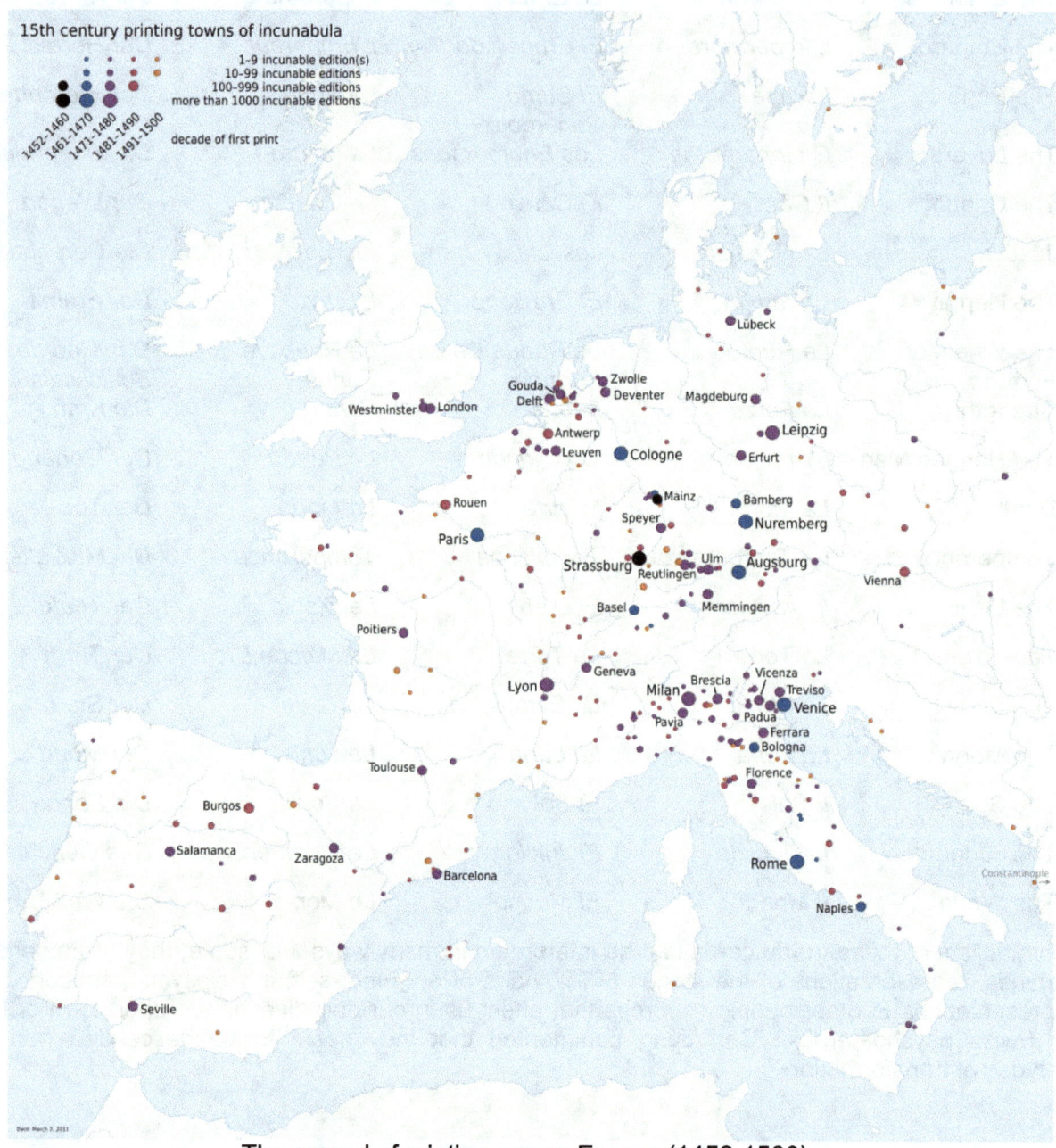

The spread of printing across Europe (1452-1500).

---

[28] Febvre, Lucien; Martin, Henri-Jean (1976). The Coming of the Book: The Impact of Printing 1450–1800. London: New Left Books. Quoted in: Anderson, Benedict. Comunidades Imaginadas. Reflexiones sobre el origen y la difusión del nacionalismo. Fondo de cultura económica, Mexico, 1993. ISBN 978-968-16-3867-2. pp. 58f.

# 5. Evolution: Early Tarot Decks

Expensive hand-painted and gilded custom-made decks made for wealthy clients have been preserved in greater numbers than mass-produced decks, because of their high value. Mass-produced Tarot decks were inexpensive and easily replaced when they became too worn out to be useable, with the old decks probably being tossed on the fire.

## 5.1. The Visconti-Sforza Tarot

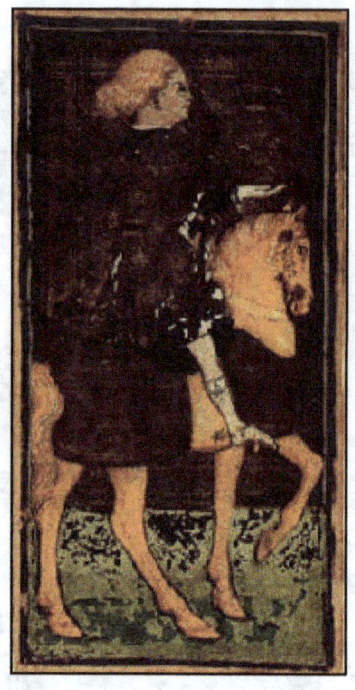

#47 'Il Cavaliere Di Coppe'
The Knight of Cups, c.1452, Milan
(Pierpont-Morgan-Bergamo Deck)

A modern restoration by A.A. Atanassov
Published by Lo Scarabeo, Turin, 2013
Author's collection

The oldest surviving examples of specially commissioned custom made Tarot cards are the collection of 15 or so decks painted for the rulers of the Duchy of Milan, Filippo Maria Visconti and his son-in-law Francesco Sforza.

No complete deck has survived; rather, some collections have a few face cards, while some consist of a single card. They date back to a period when tarot was still called Trionfi (Trumps), and were used for everyday playing[29][30].

These card decks have been variously dated from 1451 to 1466, and are collectively known as the Visconti-Sforza Tarot. They had a significant impact on the visual composition, card numbering, and interpretation of modern decks[31].

The cards that survive are of particular historical interest because of the beauty and detail of the design, which was often executed in precious materials. Some of the cards feature depictions of members of the Visconti and Sforza families in period garments and settings, which offers a glimpse of the life of the nobility in Renaissance Milan.

---

[29] Emily E. Auger. Tarot and Other Meditation Decks: History, Theory, Aesthetics, Typology, McFarland, 2003, ISBN 0-7864-1674-2, ISBN 978-0-7864-1674-5, pages 145, 164, 195, 212-3.
[30] Giordano Berti & Tiberio Gonard. Visconti-tarot. Buch und Karten.: Das älteste Tarot der Welt., Königsfurt Verlag, 1999, ISBN 3-933939-11-9, ISBN 978-3-933939-11-1, 120 pages.
[31] Sandra A. Thomson. Pictures from the Heart: A Tarot Dictionary, St. Martin's Griffin, 2003, ISBN 0-312-29128-0, ISBN 978-0-312-29128-0, 544 pages.

A print of the Visconti-Sforza tarot deck by Lo Scarabeo in 2013, author's collection.

The Pierpont Mergan Bergamo version of the deck (also known as the *Colleoni-Baglioni* and *Francesco Sforza* deck), was produced around 1451[32]. The Morgan Library & Museum in New York City has 35 of the cards, the Accademia Carrara in Bergamo, Lombardy, has 26 in its catalogue, and the remaining 13 are in the private collection of the Colleoni family in Bergamo.

The Cary-Yale deck version of the deck (also known as the *Visconti di Modrone* set) is named after the Cary Collection of Playing Cards, which was absorbed into the Yale University Library in 1967, and it has been dated to around 1466[33]. This version of the deck has six 'court cards' (knave, knight, queen, and king) with an additional 'damsel' (a female counter-part of the knave), and the 'lady on the horse' (a female counterpart to the knight), which means that the total number of cards in this deck would have been 86 rather than 78.

The Brera-Brambilla set is named after Giovanni Brambilla, who acquired the cards in Venice in 1900[34]. Since 1971 the deck has been in the catalogue of the Brera Gallery in Milan.

---

[32] Janina Renée. Tarot for a New Generation, Llewellyn Worldwide, 2001, ISBN 0-7387-0160-2, ISBN 978-0-7387-0160-8, page 6.
[33] Naomi Ozaniec. The Watkins Tarot Handbook: The Practical System of Self-Discovery, Sterling Publishing Company, Inc., 2005, ISBN 1-84293-114-8, ISBN 978-1-84293-114-1, pages 5, 174, 179.
[34] Robert M. Place. The Tarot: History, Symbolism, and Divination, Jeremy P. Tarcher/Penguin, 2005, ISBN 1-58542-349-1, ISBN 978-1-58542-349-1, pages 16 ff.

## 5.2. The Mantegna Tarocchi

The so-called Mantegna Tarocchi are two different sets of fifty picture cards produced in Ferrara, Italy by two different artists dated to around 1465-1485. They were originally thought to have been engraved by the artist Andrea Mantegna, but this is no longer the case. The name Mantegna is still used as 'the *so-called* Mantegna Tarocchi'.

They are also referred to as Baldini cards after Baccio Baldini, a Florentine engraver who was considered as the possible author. It is now believed that due to the similarities with the style of the Salone de Mesi of Palazzo Schifanoia in Ferrara, the engravings were made by artists working with Francesco del Cossa at the Estensi court[35]. The first of the two is referred to as Series E or E-series, and is dated to around 1465. The second set is referred to as Series S or S-series, and is dated to around 1470 or possibly as late as 1485. When both sets are compared side by side, many of the pictures are mirror images of each other.

Mantegna Tarocchi were believed to be a form of Tarocchi cards for playing games, but they are also likely to have been used for the teaching of children undergoing a classical education, as an educational aid in much the same way that 'flash cards' are used today. Altogether they are a snapshot of the Renaissance humanistic view of life and the cosmos.

#23 '*Rhetorica*' Rhetoric, c.1465, Ferrara
(Master of the E-Series Tarocchi)

A modern restoration by Pietro Alligo
Published by Lo Scarabeo, Turin, 2013
Author's collection

The cards contain allegorical images of the following:

- The Conditions of Man: 1 *Misero* (The Beggar), 2 *Fameio* (The Servant), 3 *Artixan* (The Craftsman), 4 *Merchadante* (The Merchant), 5 *Zintilomo* (The Gentleman), 6 *Chavalier* (The Knight), 7 *Doxe* (The Doge), 8 *Re* (The King), 9 *Imperator* (The Emperor), 10 *Papa* (The Pope)

---

[35] Frank & Shanti, EXSTATICA, 2021, ISBN 978-0578842783

- The Nine Muses and Apollo: 11 *Calliope* (epic poetry), 12 *Urania* (astronomy), 13 *Terpsichore* (light verse and dance), 14 *Erato* (lyrical choral poetry), 15 *Polimnia* (hymn), 16 *Talia* (comedy), 17 *Melpomene* (tragedy), 18 *Euterpe* (the flute, music), 19 *Clio* (history), 20 *Apollo* (oracles, healing, archery, music and arts, light, knowledge, herds and flocks, and the protection of the young)

- The Seven Liberal Arts and Fields of Study: 21 *Grammatica* (Grammar), 22 *Loica* (Logic), 23 *Rhetorica* (Rhetoric), 24 *Geometria* (Geometry), 25 *Aritmetricha* (Arithmetic), 26 *Musicha* (Music), 27 *Poesia* (Poetry), 28 *Philosofia* (Philosophy), 29 *Astrologia* (Astrology), 30 *Theologia* (Theology)

- Three Genia of Light and the Seven Virtues: 31 *Iliaco* (The Sun), 32 *Chronico* (Time), 33 *Cosmico* (The World), 34 *Temperancia* (Temperance), 35 *Prudencia* (Prudence), 36 *Forteza* (Fortitude), 37 *Iusticia* (Justice), 38 *Charita* (Charity), 39 *Speranza* (Hope), 40 *Fede* (Faith)

- The Seven Spheres: 41 *Luna* (The Moon), 42 *Mercurio* (Mercury), 43 *Venus*, 44 *Sol* (The Sun), 45 *Marte* (Mars), 46 *Iupiter* (Jupiter), 47 *Saturno* (Saturn), 48 *Octavia Spera* (The Upper Heavens), 49 *Primo Mobile* (Celestial Power), 50 *Prima Causa* (Divine Light)

A print of the Mantegna (Series E) deck by Lo Scarabeo in 2013, author's collection.

## 5.3. The Sola Busca Tarot

#75 Knight of Swords
Cronus-Ammon (Baal Hammon), Syncretic Greco-Egyptian God

#76 Queen of Swords
Olympia, Mother of Alexander the Great

#77 King of Swords
Alexander the Great, Macedonian Ruler

The Sola-Busca Tarot is believed to have been engraved in Ferrara in 1490 by an unknown artist[36], and then hand painted in Venice in 1491[37]. It is the first 78 card Tarot deck to have survived in its entirety, and the first in which all the plain suits are fully illustrated[38] [39].

The deck is significant not only for its age, but also because of the quality of its artwork, which contains expressive figures engraved with precise contours and shading[40].

The Sola Busca Tarot is also the earliest deck in which the designs on the trump cards deviate from the classic Tarot iconography. This departure is something that emerged later in tarot decks such as the 'Bourgeouis Tarot' which originaged in Germany around 1865, and the 'Industrie und Gluck Tarock' (Diligence and Fortune) Tarock which appeared in the Austro-Hungarian Empire around 1815.

The Sola Busca trumps feature allegories of notable figures from the Ancient world:

- Figures connected to the story of Alexander the Great: himself, his mother Olympia a.k.a. Polyxena (a sorceress), his father Philip II of Macedon, his tutor Nektanebo (a priest and

---

[36] Bezzone, Francesca (5 April 2019). "Mystery and history of art merge together in the Sola Busca tarots". L'Italo-Americano. Retrieved 11 April 2020.
[37] Hind, Arthur (1938). Early Italian Engravings. pp. 241–247, 370–393.
[38] Berti, Giordano (2013). "History of Sola-Busca Tarot". Sola-Busca Tarot Mayer 1998. Retrieved 10 April 2020.
[39] Kaplan, Stuart (1990). Encyclopedia of Tarot. Vol. 3. U.S. Games Systems. p. 30. ISBN 0880791225.
[40] Zucker, Mark J. (1997). "The Master of the 'Sola-Busca Tarocchi' and the Rediscovery of Some Ferrarese Engravings of the Fifteenth Century". Artibus et Historiae. 18 (35): 181–194. doi:10.2307/1483546.

magician) who was an Egyptian Pharaoh in exile, and the syncretic Greco-Egyptian god Cronus-Ammon).

- Others: Deiotarus of Galatia (Celtic King and ally of the Romans), Hippias of Elis (A Greek teacher), Nimrod (King of Shinar), Nebuchadnezzar (King of Babylon), Apollo (God of oracles, healing, archery, music and arts, light, knowledge, herds and flocks, and the protection of the young), and Pallas (Daughter of Triton and foster-sister of Athena)

The deck also features figures across the history of the rise and fall of the Roman Empire:

- Roman generals: Lucius Postumius Albinus ('Flamen Martialis' = Keeper of the flame of Mars), Gaius Marius , Gaius Lutatius Catulus, Sextus Pompey, and Lucius Caecilius Metellus

- Roman politicians: Quintus Pompeius Sosius Falco, Marcus Tullius Cicero, Gaius Papirius Carbo Arvina, Cato the Younger, and Marcus Livius Drusus

- Roman emperor: Nero

A single complete hand-painted deck is known to exist, along with 35 uncoloured cards held by various museums. Unlike the earlier Visconti-Sforza tarot decks, the cards of the Sola Busca are numbered. The trump cards have Roman numerals, whereas the pip cards of the plain suits have Arabic numerals[41].

Like the Mantegna Tarocchi before it, the Sola Busca Tarot appears to resemble a set of instructive 'flash cards', championing ancient heroes and their achievements, and reminding the player or owner of the necessary qualities and virtues needed in order to survive and thrive, such as strength, honour, valour, and so it would seem in the constantly warring states of Renaissance Italy... a ruthlessness greater than one's enemies.

The imagery and symbolism woven throughout the Sola Busca Tarot deck is visibly connected with that of Western Esotericism[42], a tradition full of symbols representing celestial bodies, astrological and mythological figures, chemical elements, and scientific and magical processes, in the form of: birds of prey, crows, daggers, dragons, feathers, fire, garlands, gourds, griffins, lamps, laurel wreaths, nesting doves, orbs, purses, ribbons, severed heads, the skull & crossbones, skulls, stars, torches, wands, and waning moons, etc.

The deck traces its provenance to the noble Busca-Serbelloni family, and in the 19th century the deck was owned by Marchioness Busca (The Duchess of Serbelloni) in Milan. In 1907, the Busca-Serbelloni family donated black and white photographs of all 78 cards to the British Museum, where they were inspirational to a whole generation of occultists.

From 1948 the deck was owned by the Sola-Busca family, from which it received its name. In 2009, the deck was purchased for €800,000 by the Italian Ministry of Cultural Heritage and Activities and delivered to the Brera Museum in Milan[43][44].

---

[41] "Collection online". British Museum. Retrieved 23 March 2020.
[42] Various, authors (2012). Il Segreto dei Segreti - I Tarocchi Sola Busca e la cultura ermetico-alchemica tra Marche e Veneto alla fine del Quattrocento. Milan: Skira. ISBN 978-88-572-1764-2.
[43] Berti, Giordano (2013). "History of Sola-Busca Tarot". Sola-Busca Tarot Mayer 1998. Retrieved 10 April 2020.
[44] Panza, Pierluigi (16 February 2010). "I tarocchi per rilanciare Brera". Corriere della Sera (in Italian). p. 39. Archived from the original on 15 June 2015

## 5.4. Minchiate

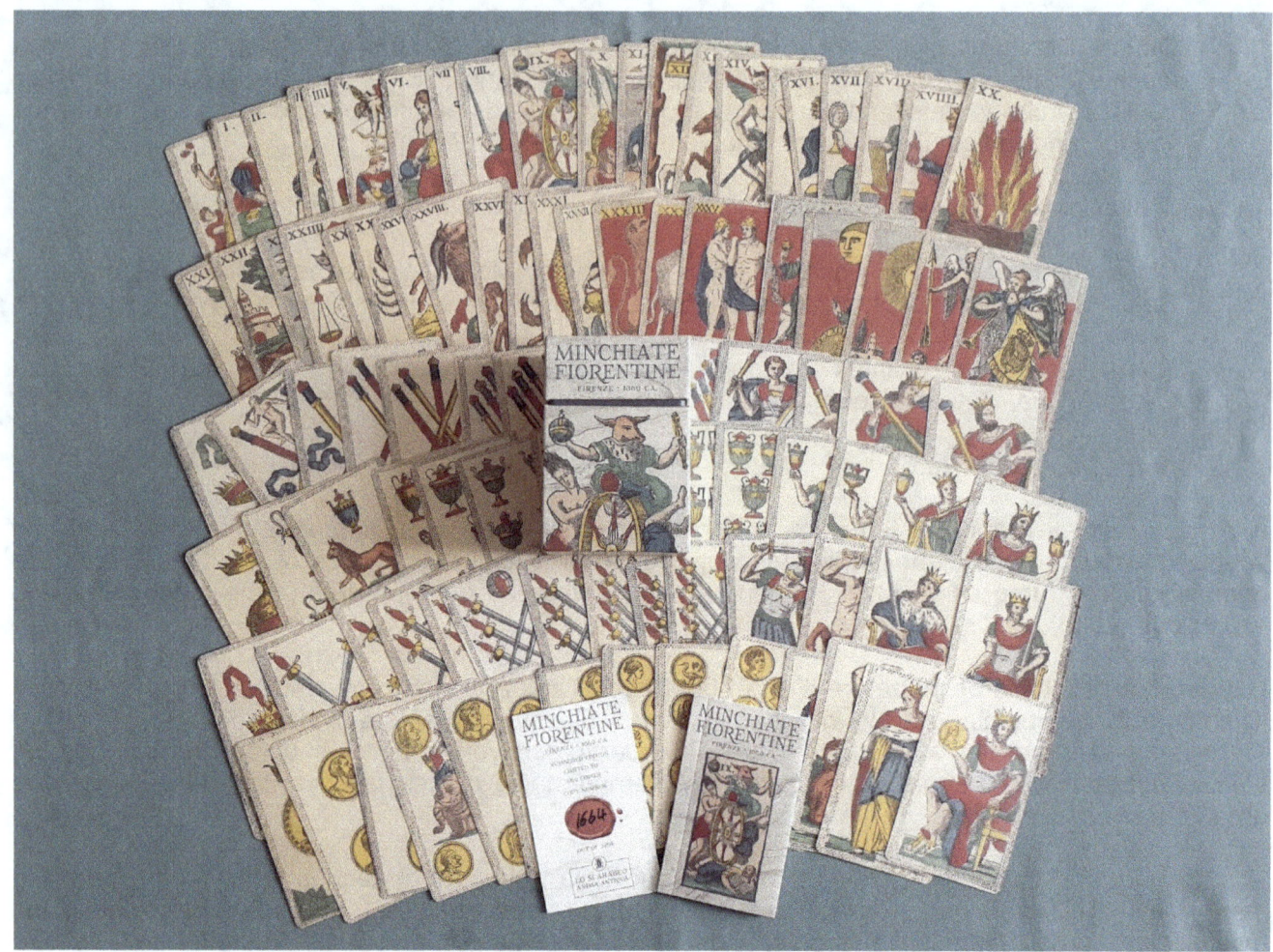

A print of the Minchiate Fiorentine deck, Florence, c. 1860 by Lo Scarabeo, 2024, author's collection.

In Florence, the earliest reference to tarot cards, then known as *trionfi*, is dated to around 1440 when a notary in Florence recorded the transfer of two decks to Sigismondo Pandolfo Malatesta[45]. Evolving from the *trionfi* or tarot in a slightly different direction is the Minchiate deck, which became distinct from tarot in its recognisable form by 1530-1550.

The name *Minchiate* comes from a dialect word originally meaning 'nonsense' or 'trifle', related to the word '*minchione*' meaning 'fool', and '*minchionare*' meaning 'to laugh at' someone'. The name can be problematic in some dialects, especially in Italian, where it has evolved over time from being a relatively neutral word into an impolitely informal word, crude slang, or even a vulgar swear word or expletive. Alternative names used include 'Florentine Tarot', 'Tarocchi Fiorentini', 'Germini', 'Galleriini', or 'Ganellini'.

The Minchiate deck had an expanded set of 40 trump cards instead of the traditional 21, taking the total number of cards to 97[46]. Almost all of the trump cards in the traditional tarot deck can be found in

---

[45] Pratesi, F. (2012, July 9). Studies on Giusto Giusti. Retrieved July 7, 2025, from http://trionfi.com/giusto-giusti
[46] Jeu de Minchiate de fantaisie à enseignes françaises at the Bibliothèque nationale de France. Retrieved 2 March 2016.

the Minchiate deck, with the exception of The Popess who appears to have dropped out of use from around 1500 onwards[47].

| | | Minchiate | English Translation | | | Tarot de Marseille |
|---|---|---|---|---|---|---|
| 0 | | Il Matto | The Madman | 0 | | Le Mat |
| 1 | I | Papa Uno / L'Uno / Il Papino / Ganellino | Pope One | 1 | I | Le Bateleur |
| 2 | II | Papa Due / l'Imperatrice | Pope Two / The Empress | 3 | III | L'Impératrice |
| 3 | III | Papa Tre / L'Imperatore | Pope Three / The Emperor | 4 | IIII | L'Empereur |
| 4 | IIII | Papa Quattro / Il Papa | Pope Four / The Pope | 5 | V | Le Pape |
| 5 | V | Papa Cinque / L'Amore | Pope Five / Love | 6 | VI | L'Amoureux |
| 6 | VI | La Temperanza | Temperance | 14 | XIIII | Temperance |
| 7 | VII | La Fortezza | Fortitude | 11 | XI | La Force |
| 8 | VIII | La Giustizia | Justice | 8 | VIII | La Justice |
| 9 | IX | La Ruota della Fortuna | The Wheel of Fortune | 10 | X | La Roue de Fortune |
| 10 | X | Il Carro | The Chariot | 7 | VII | Le Chariot |
| 11 | XI | Il Gobo / Il Tempo | The Hunchback / Time | 9 | VIIII | L'Ermite |
| 12 | XII | L'Impiccato / Il Traditore | The Hanged Man / The Traitor | 12 | XII | Le Pendu |
| 13 | XIII | La Morte | Death | 13 | XIII | (La Mort) |
| 14 | XIV | Il Diavolo / Il Demonio | The Devil | 15 | XV | Le Diable |
| 15 | XV | La Casa del Diavolo | The House of the Devil | 16 | XVI | La Maison Dieu |
| 16 | XVI | La Speranza | Hope | | | - |
| 17 | XVII | La Prudenza | Prudence | | | - |
| 18 | XVIII | La Fede | Faith | | | - |
| 19 | XVIIII | La Carità | Charity | | | - |
| 20 | XX | Il Fuoco | Fire | | | - |
| 21 | XXI | L'Acqua | Water | | | - |
| 22 | XXII | La Terra | Earth | | | - |
| 23 | XXIII | L'Aria | Air | | | - |
| 24 | XXIIII | La Bilancia | Libra | | | - |
| 25 | XXV | La Vergine | Virgo | | | - |
| 26 | XXVI | Lo Scorpione | Scorpio | | | - |
| 27 | XXVII | L'Ariete | Aries | | | - |
| 28 | XXVIII | Il Capricorno | Capricorn | | | - |
| 29 | XXVIIII | Il Sagittario | Sagittarius | | | - |
| 30 | XXX | Il Cancro | Cancer | | | - |
| 31 | XXXI | I Pesci | Pisces | | | - |
| 32 | XXXII | L'Acquario | Aquarius | | | - |
| 33 | XXXIII | Il Leone | Leo | | | - |
| 34 | XXXIIII | Il Toro | Taurus | | | - |
| 35 | XXXV | I Gemelli | Gemini | | | - |

---

[47] Depaulis, Thierry (2007). "Early Italian Lists of Tarot Trumps". The Playing-Card. 36 (1): 39–47.

|    |         | Minchiate   | English Translation |    |       | Tarot de Marseille |
|----|---------|-------------|---------------------|----|-------|--------------------|
| 36 | XXXVI   | *La Stella* | The Star            | 17 | XVII  | *L'Étoile*         |
| 37 | XXXVII  | *La Luna*   | The Moon            | 18 | XVIII | *La Lune*          |
| 38 | XXXVIII | *Il Sole*   | The Sun             | 19 | XVIIII| *Le Soleil*        |
| 39 | XXXVIIII| *Il Mondo*  | The World           | 21 | XXI   | *Le Monde*         |
| 40 | XL      | *Le Trombe* | The Trumpets        | 20 | XX    | *Le Jugement*      |

Minchiate spread throughout Italy and parts of Germany in the 18th century, but its popularity gradually declined in the late 19th and early 20th century. There has however been a revival of interest in Minchiate in recent times, both as a playable historical card game, and as a collectible historical tarot deck.

What makes the Minchiate deck interesting for use in divination is that the extra trump cards add an expanded set of symbols to readings (e.g. astrological, ethical, elemental, alchemical, etc.):

**The Four Virtues**

#16  
*La Speranza*  
Hope

#17  
*La Prudenza*  
Prudence

#18  
*La Fede*  
Faith

#19  
*La Carità*  
Charity

**The Four Elements**

#20  
*Il Fuoco*  
Fire

#21  
*L'Acqua*  
Water

#22  
*La Terra*  
Earth

#23  
*L'Aria*  
Air

## The Twelve Signs of the Zodiac

#24
*La Bilancia*
Libra

#25
*La Vergine*
Virgo

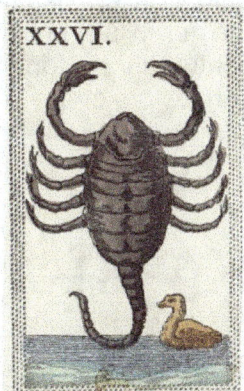

#26
*Il Scorpione*
Scorpio

#27
*L' Ariete*
Aries

#28
*Il Capricorno*
Capricorn

#29
*Il Sagittario*
Sagittarius

#30
*Il Cancro*
Cancer

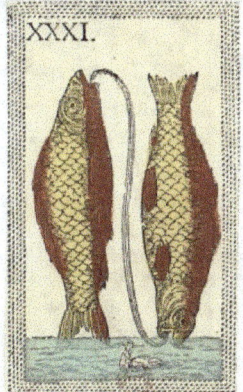

#31
*I Pesci*
Pisces

#32
*L' Acquario*
Aquarius

#33
*Il Leone*
Leo

#34
*Il Toro*
Taurus

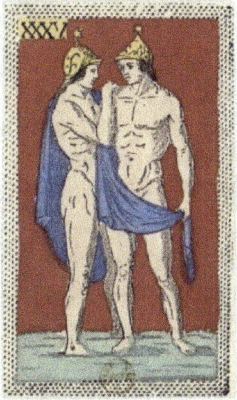

#35
*I Gemelli*
Gemini

## 5.5. Tarot de Marseille

The Tarot de Marseille (Tarot of Marseille), also shortened to the initials *TdM*, is believed to have been created in northern Italy (Florence or Milan) in the early 15th century. The oldest surviving printed tarot cards date from the late 15th century in the form of uncut card sheets such as the Rosenwald Sheet and the Cary Sheet, which are ancestors of the Tarot de Marseille.

'*La Papessa*' from the Rosenwald Sheet, Florence c.1470-1490

The Cary Sheet, Milan c.1500

Tarot de Marseille was introduced to southern France after the French conquest of the Duchy of Milan in the Second Italian War (1499-1501), after which subsequent versions known as the Milan-Marseille type spread throughout France. French exposure to the art, architecture, and humanist ideas flourishing in Italian city-states, especially Florence and Rome, resulted in French nobles, artists, and scholars beginning to adopt and adapt these new ideas, bringing the Renaissance to France.

The earliest known surviving cards of the Tarot de Marseille pattern were produced by Philippe Vachier of Marseilles in 1639. They were recently discovered by Thierry Depaulis[48] and sold at auction at Hôtel Drouot, Paris in March 2023[49][50]. They were purchased by card maker and tarot enthusiast

---

[48] Thierry Depaulis, Un tarot de Marseille de 1639 !, Le Vieux Papier, fasc. 447, janvier 2023, p. 194-200, (https://www.levieuxpapier-asso.org/bulletin/bulletin-janvier-2023/). Retrieved 2024-10-21.
[49] Papon, C., Reyssat, S. - 'Un tarot marseillais de 1639', La Gazette Drouot (https://www.gazette-drouot.com/article/un-tarot-marseillais-de-1639/42894). Retrieved 2024-10-21.
[50] La Gazette Drouot, Past Auctions, Lot No. 187 (https://www.gazette-drouot.com/en/lots/20935914-tarot-de-marseille-type-i--3a---). Retrieved 2024-10-21.

Yves Reynaud of Tarot de Marseille Héritage, who along with the Phillippe Vachier deck has produced many facsimiles of rare historical Tarot de Marseille decks[51] [52].

A print of the Tarot de Marseille of Philippe Vachier, 1639 by Yves Reynaud, Marseille, 2024, author's collection.

The name Tarot de Marseille was given as late as 1856 by historian Romain Merlin, referring to the variety of closely related designs that were being made in the city of Marseilles, a major centre of playing card manufacture.

Tarot de Marseille was very popular in France in the 17th and 18th centuries for playing tarot card games before it was also made popular for cartomancy or divination in the late 18th century. The Marseille pattern became the most successful standard for centuries, the standard from which many tarot decks of the 19th century and later are derived[53]. Tarot de Marseille is divided by historians and playing card researchers into Type I, Type II, and Type III based on specific stylistic and iconographic variations found in early printed decks.

---

[51] Smith, S. E. (2025, January 6). Vachier: The Oldest Documented Tarot de Marseille. Retrieved June 9, 2025, from https://tarot-heritage.com/2025/01/06/vachier-the-oldest-documented-tarot-de-marseille/
[52] Reynaud, Y. (2024, November 28). Vachier Tarot. Retrieved June 9, 2025, from https://tarot-de-marseille-heritage.com/english/blog/2024/11/28/vachier-tarot/
[53] Depaulis, Thierry (2013). "The Tarot de Marseille – Facts and Fallacies part I". The Playing-Card. 42 (1): 23–43.

**Type I**

Often referred to as 'Early Marseille' or 'Original Marseille', Type I decks are dated from the early 17th to early 18th century. Notable examples include those of Jean Noblet (Paris, c.1650), and Jean Dodal (Lyon, c.1701-1715). The overall style of artwork in these decks could be described as more medieval, more rustic, or with more of a folk art feel. Perhaps what gives them a more medieval appearance is the composition of imagery, especially in the trump and court cards, which like Gothic and Romanesque art is largely symbolic and lacks the strict spatial and proportional symmetry of Renaissance art that would appear in later decks. They were of course originally intended to be used for card games by people of all walks of life, and so they were meant to be simple, bright, and fun.

**Type II**

Often referred to as 'Canonical Marseille', Type II decks are dated from the 1730s onwards. Notable examples include those of Claude Burdel (Fribourg, 1751), and Nicolas Conver (Marseille, 1760). The overall style of artwork in these decks is more symmetrical and refined compared to earlier decks. They are visually influenced by Renaissance art and its principles of proportion, harmony, and balance. Improvements in printing technology and techniques resulted in cleaner lines, cleaner typography, and more regular and more consistent lettering (though there are still some quirks in spelling). The depiction of figures, both human and animal, became clearer and more anatomically correct. They became the standard model for later reproductions.

**Type III**

The Tarot de Marseille Type III classification is not as formally standardised as Type I and Type II. It is often based on the work of historians and researchers like Thierry Depaulis and Jean-Claude Flornoy. When the Type III classification is used, it typically refers to a later stage of regional variations and adaptations, particularly outside France (e.g. Switzerland and Italy). While they are clearly derived from the Tarot de Marseille tradition, there are some differences in iconography or structure. Type III decks represent a cultural reframing of the Tarot de Marseille iconography to suit different religious sensitivities, aesthetic tastes, and socio-political contexts of 18th-19th century Europe, while preserving the basic structure of tarot.

**Tarot de Besançon**

The earliest cards of this pattern came from Strasbourg in the early 18th century[54]. Based on the earlier Type I[55], they were made in south Germany, France, and Switzerland, including the town of Besançon where many cardmakers moved their production to in the early 19th century, hence the name.
The most notable difference in Tarot de Besançon is the replacement of two of the trump cards:
- II *'La Pances'* / *'La Papesse'* ('The Popess' or 'Female Pope'), perhaps an allusion to the legendary or mythical 'Pope Joan' (*Ioannes Anglicus*), became *'Juno'* or *'Junon'* after the Roman goddess Juno who was queen of the gods, and whose Greek equivalent was Hera (this card later became 'The High Priestess').
- V *'Le Pape'* ('The Pope') became *'Jupiter'* after the Roman god Jupiter who was king of the gods, and whose Greek equivalent was Zeus (this card later became 'The Hierophant', an ancient Greek term for High Priest).

These changes were made to remove any controversial references to the Catholic Church, and also so as not to offend the Protestant Reformation and Enlightenment sensibilities of the times.

---

[54] Thierry Depaulis, The Cardmakers of Alsace, IPCS, 2023, chapter "The 'Tarot de Besançon', an 'Ecumenical' Tarot?", pp.164-174
[55] For these two types, see Thierry Depaulis, "The 'Tarot de Marseille' – Facts and Fallacies", The Playing-Card, Vol. 42, no. 1, July-Sept. 2013, pp. 23-43 and Vol. 42, no. 2, Oct.-Dec. 2013, pp. 101-120.

During the French Revolution (1789 to 1799), card makers such as François Isnard replaced another two of the trump cards:
- III *'L'Imperatrise'* ('The Empress') became *'La Grande Mere'* ('The Grandmother').
- IIII *'L'Empereur'* ('The Emperor') became *'Le Grand Pere'* ('The Grandfather').

This was to further neutralise regal or authoritarian titles when anti-monarchist sentiment was strong.

A print of the Tarot de Marseille (Besançon) of B P Grimaud, c. 1891 by Lo Scarabeo, 2024, author's collection.

## Swiss 1JJ Tarot

In 19th century Switzerland, versions of the Tarot de Besançon deck emerged with small design updates and gradually became known as Swiss Tarot and later Swiss 1JJ Tarot[56]. The '1' refers to it being a first-quality deck in a graded production system used by cardmakers, and the two initial Js symbolise the replacement trump cards of Junon and Jupiter.

## Other Variations

Other variations of the Tarot de Besançon include Tarot d'Épinal[57] (Imagier Pellerin, Épinal, early 19th century). Tarocco Piemontese[58] also emerged from around 1820 onwards when cardmakers active in

---

[56] Swiss Tarot at the International Playing-Card Society. Retrieved 7 July 2025.
[57] Starling, R. (2023, December 9). Épinal Tarot. Retrieved July 7, 2025, from https://www.wopc.co.uk/france/pellerin/epinal-tarot

Turin began to make Marseille patterned decks. Tarocco Bolognese[59] (Tarocchino) also removed The Popess, The Pope, The Empress, and The Emperor, replacing them with four Moors. Belgian Tarot[60] variants such as Vandenborre Tarot (Brussels, c. 1780) replaced The Popess with 'Spanish Captain', and The Pope with 'Bacchus' (The Roman god of wine, whose Greek equivalent was Dionysus).

A print of the Tarot de Marseille based on Claude Burdel, 1751 by Lo Scarabeo, 2006, author's collection.

## The Fool

The Fool was originally known in Italian as '*Il Matto*', meaning 'the madman', 'the fool', or 'the beggar'. The original purpose of this card was as an 'excuse'. It would be played to avoid following suit or to avoid losing a round. It was originally unnumbered and seen as separate or additional. It either appeared at the very beginning of the deck, between the trumps and the suited cards, or at the very end. Some Belgian decks numbered The Fool as 'XXII'[61]. It has since been numbered as zero and ordered at the beginning. In Tarot de Marseille, The Fool became known as 'Le Fou', 'Le Fol' and 'Le Mat', the latter of which is probably a direct borrowing from the Italian.

---

[58] See. Giordano Berti, Old Italian Tarot. 78 cards engraved by Stefano Vergnano, Turin, 1830 ca. Booklet attached to "Vergnano Tarot 1830", Araba Fenice, Boves 2014.
[59] Starna, Domenico. Tarocco Bolognese at the World Web Playing Card Museum. Retrieved 17 January 2016.
[60] Belgian Tarot at the International Playing-Card Society. Retrieved 7 July 2025.
[61] Pollett, A. (n.d.). The Tarot and other Early Cards: Regional Tarots - 4: The Franco-Belgian Pattern. Retrieved July 7, 2025, from https://l-pollett.tripod.com/cards63.htm

The image of the Fool builds on hundreds of years of allegorical depictions of foolishness. He carries a staff and knapsack over his shoulder. He is accompanied by a dog that is biting at him or tearing at his clothes. He wears ragged or eccentric clothing. He often appears in motion. Visually, he shares thematic similarities with '*Il Misero*' ('The Wretch') in the Tarot of Mantegna[62], but the meanings are very different. The Wretch has hit rock bottom, whereas The Fool is starting his ascent anew. The Fool evolved into the Joker in modern playing cards, taking on the eccentric side of The Fool, like a jester in appearance.

Il Matto
Visconti-Sforza
c.1451

*Il Misero*
Mantegna Tarocchi
c.1465

Le Fou
Jean Noblet
Paris, 1659

Le Fol
Jean Dodal
Lyon, 1701

Le Mat
Claude Burdel
Fribourg, 1751

Le Mat
Nicholas Conver
Marseille, 1760

Le Mat
Baptiste-Paul Grimaud
Paris, 1891

*The Joker*
From a modern playing card deck

---

[62] Wintle, Simon (June 26, 2023) [June 5, 2017]. "Tarocchi di Mantegna, c.1465". The World of Playing Cards. Retrieved May 29, 2024.

**The Trump Cards**

The trump cards are traditionally numbered with additive Roman numerals, e.g. the number 4 is given as '*IIII*' rather than '*IV*'.

*01 - I Le Bateleur* ('The Juggler' or 'The Street Entertainer') later became known as 'The Magician'.

| Jean Noblet<br>Paris, 1659 | Jean Dodal<br>Lyon, 1701 | *Félix-Bernard Schaer<br>Solothurn, 1784* | *Baptiste-Paul Grimaud<br>Paris, 1891* |

*02 - II La Pances / La Papesse* ('The Popess' or 'Female Pope') later became known as '*Junon*' and the 'High Priestess'.

| Jean Noblet<br>Paris, 1659 | Jean Dodal<br>Lyon, 1701 | *Félix-Bernard Schaer<br>Solothurn, 1784* | *Baptiste-Paul Grimaud<br>Paris, 1891* |

03 – III *Imperatris* / *L'Imperatris* / *L'Imperatrise* / *L'Imperatrice* ('The Empress').

Jean Noblet　　　Jean Dodal　　　Félix-Bernard Schaer　　　Baptiste-Paul Grimaud
Paris, 1659　　　Lyon, 1701　　　Solothurn, 1784　　　Paris, 1891

04 – IIII *L'Empereur* ('The Emperor') also became known as '*Le Grand Pere*' ('The Grandfather' or 'The Great Father').

Jean Noblet　　　Jean Dodal　　　Félix-Bernard Schaer　　　Baptiste-Paul Grimaud
Paris, 1659　　　Lyon, 1701　　　Solothurn, 1784　　　Paris, 1891

05 – V *Le Pape* ('The Pope') later became known as '*Jupiter*'.

| Jean Noblet | Jean Dodal | Félix-Bernard Schaer | Baptiste-Paul Grimaud |
| Paris, 1659 | Lyon, 1701 | Solothurn, 1784 | Paris, 1891 |

06 – VI *La Moureu / La Moureux / L'Amoureux / L'Amourex* ('The Lovers'), like many of the cards, is variously spelled across historical decks, perhaps due to variations in language and dialect (*Langue d'Oc* vs *Langue d' Oïl* French, the transition from Middle French to Modern French, regional spelling variations, etc.), or technical and typographic reasons.

| Jean Noblet | Jean Dodal | Félix-Bernard Schaer | Baptiste-Paul Grimaud |
| Paris, 1659 | Lyon, 1701 | Solothurn, 1784 | Paris, 1891 |

07 – VII *Le Chariot / Le Chariot* ('The Chariot') mostly appears in seventh place, but in some decks #7 is '*Iustice*' ('Justice') (such as the early 17th century deck by J Vieville).

| Jean Noblet | Jean Dodal | Félix-Bernard Schaer | Baptiste-Paul Grimaud |
| Paris, 1659 | Lyon, 1701 | Solothurn, 1784 | Paris, 1891 |

08 – VIII *Iustice / La Justice* ('Justice') mostly appears in eighth place, but in some decks #8 is '*Le Chariot*' ('The Chariot') (J Vieville).

| Jean Noblet | Jean Dodal | Félix-Bernard Schaer | Baptiste-Paul Grimaud |
| Paris, 1659 | Lyon, 1701 | Solothurn, 1784 | Paris, 1891 |

09 – VIIII *L'Hermite* / *L'Ermite* / *L'Ernite* ('The Hermit') also appears in some decks as '*Le Capucin*' or '*Le Capuchin*' (a friar of the Franciscan order) or '*Le Pauvre*' ('The Poor Man'). In some decks #9 is '*Force*' ('Strength') (J Vieville).

Jean Noblet
Paris, 1659

Jean Dodal
Lyon, 1701

Félix-Bernard Schaer
Solothurn, 1784

Baptiste-Paul Grimaud
Paris, 1891

10 – X *La Roue De Fortun* / *La Roue De Fortune* / *La Roux De Fortune* ('The Wheel of Fortune').

Jean Noblet
Paris, 1659

Jean Dodal
Lyon, 1701

Félix-Bernard Schaer
Solothurn, 1784

Baptiste-Paul Grimaud
Paris, 1891

11 – XI *Force* / *La Force* ('Strength'), but in some cases #11 is *L'Ermite* ('The Hermit') (J Vieville).

| Jean Noblet | Jean Dodal | Félix-Bernard Schaer | Baptiste-Paul Grimaud |
| Paris, 1659 | Lyon, 1701 | Solothurn, 1784 | Paris, 1891 |

12 – XII *Le Pandu* / *Le Pendu* ('The Hanged Man').

| Jean Noblet | Jean Dodal | Félix-Bernard Schaer | Baptiste-Paul Grimaud |
| Paris, 1659 | Lyon, 1701 | Solothurn, 1784 | Paris, 1891 |

13 – XIII La Mort ('Death'). In several of the decks that emerged after the Jean Noblet deck of 1659, card #13 La Mort was no longer named at the bottom of the card, perhaps because the image was striking enough to be recognised, and perhaps because of a superstitious aversion to mentioning the card by name.

  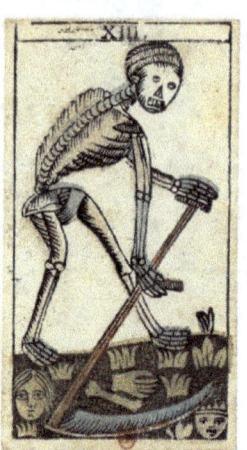 

| Jean Noblet | Jean Dodal | Félix-Bernard Schaer | Baptiste-Paul Grimaud |
| Paris, 1659 | Lyon, 1701 | Solothurn, 1784 | Paris, 1891 |

14 – XIIII *Tenperance / Temperance* ('Temperance'). Like other cards, sometimes their name is spelled with an 'n' where an 'm' might be expected. This is possibly due to language and dialect, or technical or typographic reasons.

| Jean Noblet | Jean Dodal | Félix-Bernard Schaer | Baptiste-Paul Grimaud |
| Paris, 1659 | Lyon, 1701 | Solothurn, 1784 | Paris, 1891 |

15 – XV *Le Diable* ('The Devil').

| Jean Noblet | Jean Dodal | Félix-Bernard Schaer | Baptiste-Paul Grimaud |
| Paris, 1659 | Lyon, 1701 | Solothurn, 1784 | Paris, 1891 |

16 – XVI *La Maison Dieu* ('The House of God') later became known as 'The Tower'. In some decks #16 is *L'Estoille* ('The Star') (J Vieville).

Jean Noblet
Paris, 1659

Jean Dodal
Lyon, 1701

Félix-Bernard Schaer
Solothurn, 1784

Baptiste-Paul Grimaud
Paris, 1891

17 – XVII *Le Toille / L'Estoille / L'Estoile / L'Etoilee* ('The Star'). In some decks #17 is *La Maison Dieu* ('The House of God') (J Vieville).

Jean Noblet　　　Jean Dodal　　　Félix-Bernard Schaer　　　Baptiste-Paul Grimaud
Paris, 1659　　　Lyon, 1701　　　Solothurn, 1784　　　Paris, 1891

18 – XVIII *La Lune* ('The Moon').

Jean Noblet　　　Jean Dodal　　　Félix-Bernard Schaer　　　Baptiste-Paul Grimaud
Paris, 1659　　　Lyon, 1701　　　Solothurn, 1784　　　Paris, 1891

19 – XVIIII *Le Soleil* ('The Sun').

Jean Noblet
Paris, 1659

Jean Dodal
Lyon, 1701

Félix-Bernard Schaer
Solothurn, 1784

Baptiste-Paul Grimaud
Paris, 1891

20 – XX *Le Iugement / Le Jugemant / Le Jugement* ('The Judgement') is also known in some decks as '*La Trompete*' ('The Trumpet') symbolising the trumpet that according to legend will sound to mark Judgement Day and the beginning of the End of Days.

Jean Noblet
Paris, 1659

Jean Dodal
Lyon, 1701

Félix-Bernard Schaer
Solothurn, 1784

Baptiste-Paul Grimaud
Paris, 1891

21 – XXI Le Monde ('The World').

Jean Noblet
Paris, 1659

Jean Dodal
Lyon, 1701

Félix-Bernard Schaer
Solothurn, 1784

Baptiste-Paul Grimaud
Paris, 1891

**The Court Cards**

In each suit are *Valet* (Knave or Page), *Cavalier* or *Chevalier* (Knight), *Reyne*, *Reine*, or *Dame* (Queen), and *Roy* or *Roi* (King). They are sometimes referred to as *'les honneurs'* ('the honours') or *'les laimes[63] mineurs de figures'* ('the minor figures of fortune').

*Valet de Bastons*
(Page of Wands)
Jean Noblet
Paris, 1659

*Chevalier de Coupe*
(Knight of Cups)
Jean Dodal
Lyon, 1701

*Reine De Spee*
(Queen of Swords)
Félix-Bernard Schaer
Solothurn, 1784

*Roy de Deniers*
(King of Coins)
Baptiste-Paul Grimaud
Paris, 1891

---

[63] Wiktionary (2024, April 6). Laimes. Retrieved June 9, 2025, from https://en.wiktionary.org/wiki/laimes

**The Suits of the Tarot de Marseille**

| | | | | |
|---|---|---|---|---|
| **French** | Épées | Coupes | Deniers | Bâtons |
| **Italian** | Spade | Coppe | Denari | Bastoni |
| **Spanish** | Espadas | Copas | Oros | Bastos |
| **English** | Swords | Cups | Coins | Batons |

In the suit of swords, the swords are drawn curved similar to the scimitars of the earlier Mamluk playing cards, perhaps to avoid confusion with the suit of wands or batons.

**The Two of Coins**

In traditional Tarot de Marseille, the '*Deux de Deniers*' ('Two of Coins' or 'Two of Pentacles') was often used by the cardmaker or printer to display their name, city, or business details.

In many regions of France, Switzerland, and Belgium, playing cards were regulated by law. Printers had to mark their cards with their name and sometimes location to identify the manufacturer in case of disputes, taxes, or quality control.

The Two of Coins was an ideal place for this because it had a large open central area between the two coins, the space being used for a banner or ribbon, often drawn looping between the coins.

For collectors and users, the Two of Coins became a signature card, like a business card for the deck. It helped distinguish between decks made by different artisans or companies in various cities like Marseille, Lyon, Solothurn, etc. Historians and researchers have been identifying antique decks based on the Two of Coins.

| Jean Noblet | Jean Dodal | Félix-Bernard Schaer | Baptiste-Paul Grimaud |
|---|---|---|---|
| Paris, 1659 | Lyon, 1701 | Solothurn, 1784 | Paris, 1891 * |

\* Note: The card bears the name 'Arnoult' and the year 1748. Around 1880, the Lequart company published a facsimile of the Arnoult 1748 deck using the original Arnoult woodblocks. In 1891, Lequart was acquired by the major card-maker Grimaud, who continued to publish the same deck, sometimes referred to as the Grimaud-Arnoult or Lequart-Arnoult deck.

# 6. Esotericism: Ancient Knowledge and Symbols

Esotericism is the name given to a wide range of ideas that emerged around the Eastern Mediterranean during Late Antiquity[64]. According to scholars it can be identified as a combination of several key concepts:

---

[64] Eddy, Glenys (19 September 2008). "The Ritual Dimension of Western Esotericism: The Rebirth Motif and the Transformation of Human Consciousness". Sydney Studies in Religion. Archived from the original on 25 October 2022. Retrieved 21 July 2020.

- **Correspondences** - There are real and symbolic correspondences that exist between all things in the universe. For example, the concept of Macrocosm (The Universe) and Microcosm (Humankind), and the phrase 'as above, so below'.
- **Living Nature** - The natural universe has its own life force, also known as Anima Mundi (the Soul of the World).
- **Imagination and Mediations** - Rituals and symbolic images are the tools that provide access to worlds and levels of reality existing between the material world and the divine.
- **Transmutation** - Self-transformation through practise, spiritual transformation, and the attainment of knowledge.
- **Concordance** - There is a fundamental unifying principle or root from which all world religions and spiritual practices emerge. Attaining this unifying principle can bring the world's different belief systems together in unity.
- **Transmission** - The transmission of esoteric teachings and secrets from a master to their disciple, through a process of initiation.

The city of **Alexandria** (founded by Alexander the Great in 331 BCE) became the capital city of the Ptolemaic kingdom of Egypt. It was a Hellenistic state (organised and ruled in the Classical Greek fashion), and it became a major centre of Greek culture, learning, and trade for the next three centuries. This final and longest lasting dynasty of ancient Egypt brought about a new era of syncretism between Greek and Egyptian culture.

The **Library of Alexandria** was one of the largest and most significant libraries of the ancient world. It is estimated that it contained 40,000 to 400,000 scrolls at its height. Alexandria came to be regarded as the capital of knowledge and learning, and many important and influential scholars worked there during the third and second centuries BCE. After a period of gradual decline from the reign of Ptolemy VIII Physcon to the Roman rule of Egypt, scholars and intellectuals took the knowledge with them and continued to teach and practice scholarship elsewhere. The knowledge collected and disseminated during this period became widely influential in western philosophy for centuries afterwards.

**Astrology** is the interpretation of humankind's relationship with the earth and the cosmos, and the relationship between celestial and terrestrial events. This interpretation increased in sophistication over three thousand years of history as it passed from the Sumerians, Akkadians, Assyrians, and Babylonians to the Egyptians, Persians, Greeks, and Romans. Celestial bodies and their patterns of behaviour and characteristics were linked with those of gods, goddesses, and other mythological figures in the heavens. As Rome and its population expanded, so did its pantheon of gods and goddesses, several of which had the same or similar roles as their foreign counterparts, but with different names or spellings. A language of symbols emerged to represent these celestial bodies and deities.

**Alchemy** is an ancient tradition of natural philosophy and a precursor to modern science. As a natural philosophy, it sought to examine and understand the nature of the physical universe. Among its many goals were the transmutation of base metals such as lead and copper into gold and silver, the creation of an elixir of immortality[65], the creation of panaceas able to cure any disease[66], the perfection of the human body and soul, and the *magnum opus* ('great work') in the creation of the 'philosopher's stone' to achieve all of the above. The work of alchemists was often cloaked in a labyrinth of codes and symbols with multiple layers of meaning that would only have been known and fully understood by

---

[65] Pereira, Michela (2018). "Alchemy". In Craig, Edward (ed.). Routledge Encyclopedia of Philosophy. Routledge. doi:10.4324/9780415249126-Q001-1. ISBN 978-0-415-25069-6.
[66] "Alchemy". Dictionary.com. Archived from the original on 18 August 2007. Retrieved 21 August 2007.

those who had been initiated. Many of the symbols corresponded with the symbols of astrology representing primes, elements, planetary metals, compounds, and processes[67].

**The Three Primes**

Sulphur
Soul
Combustibility
Minerva (Pallas / Athena)

Mercury
Spirit
Fusibility and Volatility
Mercury (Hermes)

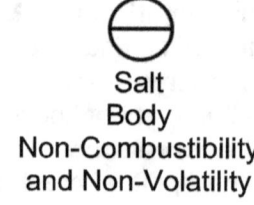
Salt
Body
Non-Combustibility
and Non-Volatility

**The Classical Elements**

| Air | Earth | Fire | Water |
|---|---|---|---|
| △ (with bar) | ▽ (with bar) | △ | ▽ |

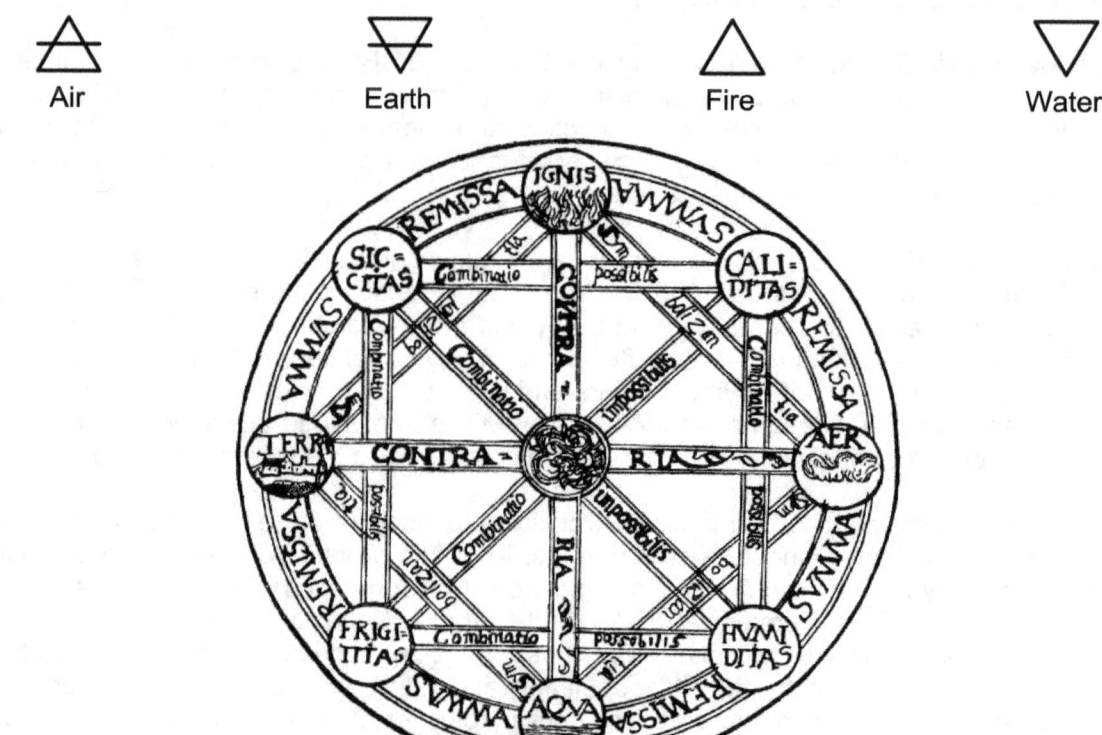

Gottfried Wilhelm Leibniz's representation of the universe resulting by a combination of the four Classical Elements, *Dissertatio de Arte Combinatoria*, 1666

| Four Elements: | | | Properties: | | |
|---|---|---|---|---|---|
| Ignis | = | Fire | Siccitas | = | Dryness; |
| Aer | = | Air | Caliditas | = | Warmth; |
| Terra | = | Earth | Frīgiditas | = | Cold; |
| Aqua | = | Water | Hūmiditas | = | Humidity. |
| | | | Combīnatio [im]possibilis | = | [Im]possible union |
| | | | Contraria | = | Opposites |

---

[67] Fritz Lüdy-Tenger (1928) Alchemistische und chemische Zeichen. Wolfgang Schneider (1962) Lexicon alchemistisch-pharmazeutischer Symbole covers many of the same symbols with a cross-index and indicates synonyms.

## The Seven Planetary Metals and the Classical Planets

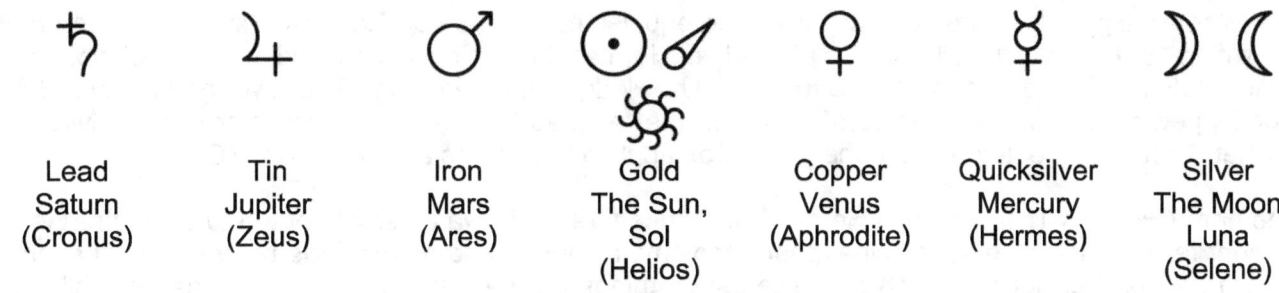

| Lead | Tin | Iron | Gold | Copper | Quicksilver | Silver |
| --- | --- | --- | --- | --- | --- | --- |
| Saturn | Jupiter | Mars | The Sun, Sol | Venus | Mercury | The Moon Luna |
| (Cronus) | (Zeus) | (Ares) | (Helios) | (Aphrodite) | (Hermes) | (Selene) |

## Alchemical Processes and the Signs of the Zodiac

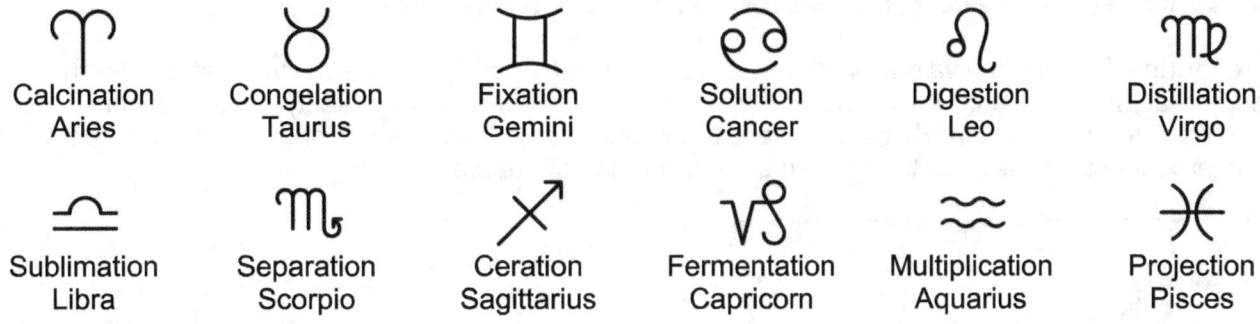

| Calcination | Congelation | Fixation | Solution | Digestion | Distillation |
| --- | --- | --- | --- | --- | --- |
| Aries | Taurus | Gemini | Cancer | Leo | Virgo |

| Sublimation | Separation | Ceration | Fermentation | Multiplication | Projection |
| --- | --- | --- | --- | --- | --- |
| Libra | Scorpio | Sagittarius | Capricorn | Aquarius | Pisces |

## The Four Humours

Humorism was an ancient Egyptian system of medicine practised by ancient Greek and Roman physicians. It is primarily concerned the balance of the four humours within the human body.

The Four Humours (and their concordances) are:

- Blood ('Sanguin', Spring, Infancy, Air, Liver, Warm and moist, Sanguine)

- Yellow bile ('Coleric', Summer, Youth, Fire, Gallbladder, Warm and dry, Choleric)

- Black bile ('Melanc', 'Flegmat', Autumn, Adulthood, Earth, Spleen, Cold and dry, Melancholic)

- Phlegm (Winter, Old age, Water, Brain/Lungs, Cold and moist, Phlegmatic)

Left: The Four Humours, divided between, male and female, the four elements, and the signs of the Zodiac, from 'Quinta Essentia' by Leonhart Thurneisser, 1574.

## Hermes Trismegistus, Hermeticism, and the *Hermetica*

In Ptolemaic Egypt, the Greeks recognised the equivalence of the god Hermes with the Egyptian god of writing and knowledge Thoth[68]. This led to Hermes becoming associated with translation and interpretation, or more generally a god of knowledge and learning. The two gods were then worshipped as one in the temples of Thoth. In the temple at Esna on the west bank of the Nile the epithet 'Thoth the great, the great, the great' was applied to Hermes at around 172 BCE.

The name Hermes Trismegistus ('Hermes the Thrice-Greatest') was then attributed to a wide range of ancient texts on astrology, medicine, pharmacology, alchemy, and magic. This body of texts became known as the '*Hermetica*', which discusses such things as the true nature of God, the possibility of humans transcending rational thought and worldly desires, finding salvation, and being reborn into a spiritual unity with the divine[69]. Similarly, a group of ancient Egyptian texts discussing the gods, sacred animals, the realm of the dead, etc. was referred to as the 'Book of Thoth'.

Mercury (the Roman equivalent of Hermes) was referred to as *Mercurius Trismegistus* (Mercury the thrice-greatest) and *Mercurius ter Maximus* (Mercury the three-times greatest). The core principles of Mercurianism or Mercurian Philosophy were the importance of communication, the power of the mind, the interconnectedness of all things, and the importance of adaptability.

Hermes Trismegistus by Pierre Mussard, Historia Deorum fatidicorum, Venice, 1675

Thoth by Léon Jean Joseph Duboi, c. 1823-1825

---

[68] Bull, Christian H. (2018). The Tradition of Hermes Trismegistus: The Egyptian Priestly Figure as a Teacher of Hellenized Wisdom. Leiden: Brill. doi:10.1163/9789004370845. ISBN 978-90-04-37084-5. S2CID 165266222.
[69] Goodrick-Clarke, Nicholas (2008). The Western Esoteric Traditions: A Historical Introduction. Oxford: Oxford University Press. ISBN 978-0-19-532099-2.

# Kabbalah

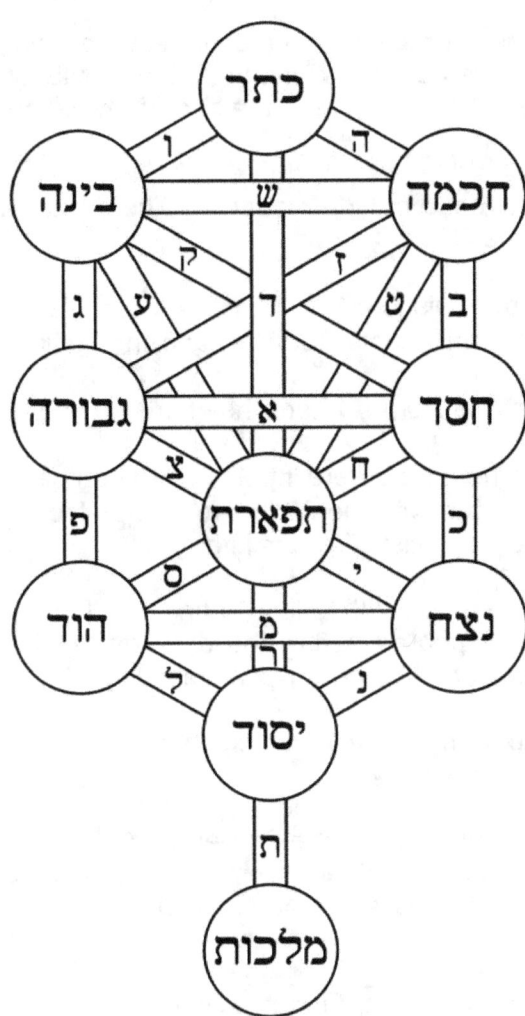

The Kabbalistic Tree of Life

The Kabbalah is a school of thought in Jewish mysticism which originated in Spain, Southern France, and southern Italy in the 12th-13th centuries[70].

The Kabbalistic tradition seeks to symbolically explain the inner meanings of the Hebrew Bible, traditional rabbinic literature, and the significance of Jewish religious observances[71].

Students and practitioners of the Kabbalah aim to achieve a direct and intimate knowledge of the divine on a level beyond that of the intellect.

Perhaps the most iconic visual element of Kabbalah is the Kabbalistic Tree of life, a diagram representing a series of spheres or nodes known as 'sefirot' arranged in three columns or categories, with a pattern of 'branches' between them.

The ten spheres represent ten different archetypes, emanations, or aspects of a single concept (e.g. the ten manifestations of God, the ten powers or faculties of the soul, or the ten structural forces of nature).

The 22 'branches' between the spheres on the tree represent the relationships between each sphere. They are also represented by the 22 letters of the Hebrew alphabet.

The form of Kabbalah adopted by western esotericism and the Hermetic tradition is known as 'Hermetic Kabbalah'.

## Preservation and Translation

During the Islamic Golden Age (8th-13th centuries), texts and their associated symbols were preserved in many astrological and alchemical manuscripts in the Grand Library of Baghdad (also known as the 'House of Wisdom') until its destruction by the Mongol siege of Baghdad in 1258. The texts were also preserved in the Imperial Library of Constantinople at the heart of the Byzantine Empire, until the Ottoman siege of Constantinople in 1453[72][73]. This preserved knowledge then spread across Europe during the Renaissance where the symbols also found their way into art in the form of allegorical paintings sketches, engravings.

---

[70] Bubello, Juan Pablo (2015). "Arte separatoria e hijos del arte en las prácticas y representaciones de Diego de Santiago (Sevilla, 1598) y el lugar de España en el Esoterismo Occidental". Anales de historia antigua, medieval y moderna (49): 79–103. ISSN 1514-9927. Archived from the original on 2019-11-06. Retrieved 2019-11-06.
[71] "Imbued with Holiness" Archived 2010-10-12 at the Wayback Machine – The relationship of the esoteric to the exoteric in the fourfold Pardes interpretation of Torah and existence. From www.kabbalaonline.org
[72] Neugebauer, Otto (1975). *A history of ancient mathematical astronomy*. pp. 788–789.
[73] Neugebauer, Otto; Van Hoesen, H. B. (1987). Greek Horoscopes. American Philosophical Society. pp. 1, 159, 163. ISBN 9780871690487.

## 6.1. Esotericism and Tarot

**Antoine Court de Gébelin**, born Antoine Court, was a Protestant pastor, Freemason, and occultist, born in Nîmes in the Occitaine region of Southern France. He was a learned man of good reputation who is credited with the beginnings of Tarot becoming widely thought of as a method of divination, fortune-telling, or 'cartomancy'.

In his essay of 1781, *Le Monde primitif, analysé et comparé avec le monde moderne* ("The Primeval World, Analysed and Compared to the Modern World"), Court de Gébelin argues:

- The Tarot deck is an arcane repository of timeless esoteric wisdom[74].
- It contains a hidden code of secrets distilled by Egyptian priests from the ancient Book of Thoth.
- These encoded symbols and secrets were later brought to Rome, where they became known to the popes.
- They were later brought to Avignon in the 14th century where they were introduced to France.
- The 22 trump cards (21 trumps and 'The Fool') correspond with the 22 letters of the Hebrew alphabet, and the 22 paths between the spheres on the Kabbalistic Tree of Life.

Scholars have been sceptical or even critical of Court de Gébelin's theories, noting the lack of historical evidence used to support them. *Le Monde primitif* appeared before the discovery of the Rosetta Stone in 1799 and the subsequent breakthroughs in deciphering the Egyptian language.

His confidence and conviction would no doubt have come from his experience in the study of language, symbolism and meaning, and the origins of allegory in antiquity.

The esoteric mind is trained to recognise the symbolic correspondences that exist between all things in the universe, and his fellow occultists, esotericists, colleagues, peers, other Freemasons, etc. would have been keen to readily accept and embrace his theories. He has since been described as the intellectual grandfather of much of modern occultism.

**Jean-Baptiste Alliette**, also known by his pseudonym **Etteilla**, was a French occultist and tarot researcher who was the first to develop and publish a structured concept for the interpretation of tarot cards for divination.

In his 1783-1785 work *Manière de se récréer avec le jeu de cartes nommées tarots* ('The way to recreate yourself with the deck of cards called tarots'), Etteilla published his ideas about the correspondences between Tarot, Astrology, the Four Classical Elements, and the Four Humours. This significant development in Tarot and divination found a wide audience, and Etteilla was the first professional tarot occultist known to history who made his living by card divination[75].

In 1788 Etteilla formed the *Société des Interprètes du Livre de Thot* ('Society of Interpreters of the Book of Thoth), and in 1789 he published his Tarot deck specifically designed for divination[76]. In 1790 he founded the *Nouvelle Ecolle de Magie* ('New School of Magic') and published *Cours théorique et pratique du Livre du Thot* ('Theoretical and practical course from the Book of Thoth').

---

[74] Chisholm, Hugh, ed. (1911). "Court de Gebelin, Antoine". Encyclopædia Britannica. Vol. 7 (11th ed.). Cambridge University Press. p. 324.
[75] John Michael Greer, The new encyclopedia of the occult, pg. 162, Llewellyn Publications (2003), ISBN 1-56718-336-0
[76] Decker, Ronald, Thierry Depaulis and Michael Dummett. A Wicked Pack of Cards: The Origins of the Occult Tarot. London: Gerald Duckworth & Co. Ltd., 1996

The 'trump' cards are described as the 'Superior Lames'[77], the court cards are the 'Median Lames', and the pip cards are the 'Inferior Lames'. Gradually, the Superior Lames would become known as the Major Arcana ('Major Secrets'), and the Median and Inferior Lames would together become known as the Minor Arcana ('Minor Secrets').

A print of the Grand Etteilla (or 'Book of Thoth' Etteilla) (Type 3) deck by Lo Scarabeo, 2003, author's collection.

About half the cards of Major Arcana in the Etteilla deck match with those of the traditional Marseille Tarot deck, but with some differences in the ordering:
- #9 *La Justice* ('Justice') is #11 Justice.
- #10 *Temperance* ('Temperance') is #14 Temperance.
- #11 *La Force* ('Strength') is #8 Strength.
- #13 *Le Grand Pretre* ('The Grand Priest') is #5 The High Priest / The Hierophant.
- #14 *Le Diable* ('The Devil') is #15 The Devil.
- #15 *Le Magicien Ou Le Bateleur* ('The Magician or The Juggler') is #1 The Magician.
- #16 *Le Jugement Dernier* ('The Last Judgement') is #20 Judgment.
- #17 *La Mort* ('Death') is #13 Death.
- #20 *La Roue De Fortune* ('The Wheel of Fortune') is #10 Wheel of Fortune.
- #78 *La Folie Ou L'Alchemiste* ('The Fool or the Alchemist') is #0 The Fool.

---

[77] Wiktionary (2024, April 6). Laimes. Retrieved June 9, 2025, from https://en.wiktionary.org/wiki/laimes

Other cards in the Major Arcana of the Etteilla deck can be matched with those of the Marseille with similar names or imagery:

- #2 *La Lumiere* ('The Light') is comparable with #19 *Le Soleil* ('The Sun').

| Traditional Marseille | Etteilla Type I | Etteilla Type II | Etteilla Type III |
|---|---|---|---|
|  |  |  |  |
| #19 *Le Soleil* ('The Sun') Jean Dodal, Lyon, 1701 | #2 *La Lumiere* ('The Light') Etteilla, Paris, 1790 | #2 *La Lumiere* ('The Light') Z Limson, Paris, 1840 | #2 *La Lumiere* ('The Light') Delarue, Paris, 1870 |

- #3 *Les Plants* ('The Plants') is recognisable with #18 *La Lune* ('The Moon') by the moon, with the two towers in the background, and the three animals in the foreground in Type I and II.

| Traditional Marseille | Etteilla Type I | Etteilla Type II | Etteilla Type III |
|---|---|---|---|
|  |  |  |  |
| #18 *La Lune* ('The Moon') Jean Dodal, Lyon, 1701 | #3 *Les Plants* ('The Plants') Etteilla, Paris, 1790 | #3 *Les Plants* ('The Plants') Z Limson, Paris, 1840 | #3 *Les Plants* ('The Plants') Delarue, Paris, 1870 |

- #4 *Le Ciel* ('The Sky') is recognisable with #17 *L'Etoille* ('The Star') by the star in the sky, and the woman emptying a jug of water in Type I and II.

| Traditional Marseille | Etteilla Type I | Etteilla Type II | Etteilla Type III |
|---|---|---|---|
|  |  |  | 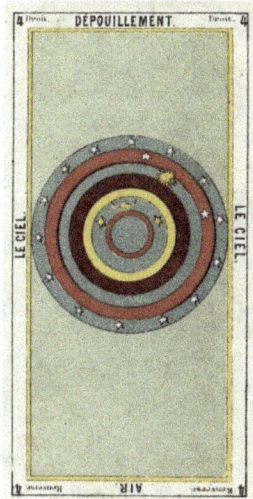 |
| #17 *L'Etoille* ('The Star') Jean Dodal, Lyon, 1701 | #4 *Le Ciel* ('The Sky') Etteilla, Paris, 1790 | #4 *Le Ciel* ('The Sky') Z Limson, Paris, 1840 | #4 *Le Ciel* ('The Sky') Delarue, Paris, 1870 |

- #5 *L'Homme Et Les Quadrupeds* ('The Man and The Quadrupeds') is recognisable with #21 *Le Monde* ('The World') by the woman in the centre encircled by an ouroboros (a symbolic serpent with its tail in its mouth) which is a garland in the traditional Marseille pattern. Also evident are the angel, eagle, lion, and bull in each corner.

| Traditional Marseille | Etteilla Type I | Etteilla Type II | Etteilla Type III |
|---|---|---|---|
|  |  |  |  |
| #21 *Le Monde* ('The World') Jean Dodal, Lyon, 1701 | #5 *L'Homme Et Les Quadrupeds* ('The Man and The Quadrupeds') Etteilla, Paris, 1790 | #5 *L'Homme Et Les Quadrupeds* ('The Man and The Quadrupeds') Z Limson, Paris, 1840 | #5 *L'Homme Et Les Quadrupeds* ('The Man and The Quadrupeds') Delarue, Paris, 1870 |

- #6 *Les Astres* ('The Stars') is comparable with #17 *L'Etoille* ('The Star') Type I and II.

| Traditional Marseille | Etteilla Type I | Etteilla Type II | Etteilla Type III |
|---|---|---|---|
|  |  |  | 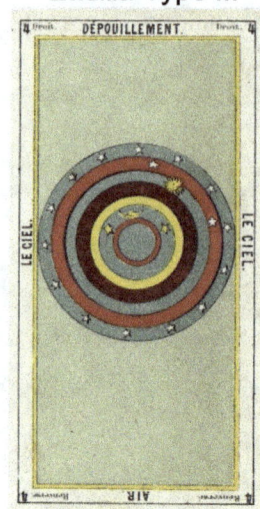 |
| #17 *L'Etoille* ('The Star') Jean Dodal, Lyon, 1701 | #6 *Les Astres* ('The Stars') Etteilla, Paris, 1790 | #6 *Les Astres* ('The Stars') Z Limson, Paris, 1840 | #6 *Les Astres* ('The Stars') Delarue, Paris, 1870 |

- #18 *Le Capucin* ('The Friar') is recognisable with #9 *L'Hermite* ('The Hermit') by the cloaked monk holding a torch.

| Traditional Marseille | Etteilla Type I | Etteilla Type II | Etteilla Type III |
|---|---|---|---|
|  |  |  |  |
| #9 *L'Hermite* ('The Hermit') Jean Dodal, Lyon, 1701 | #18 *Le Capucin* ('The Friar') Etteilla, Paris, 1790 | #18 *Le Capucin* ('The Friar') Z Limson, Paris, 1840 | #18 *Le Capucin* ('The Friar') Delarue, Paris, 1870 |

- #19 *Le Temple Foudroye* ('The Thunderstruck Temple') is recognisable with #16 *La Maison Dieu* ('The House of God' or 'The Tower').

| Traditional Marseille | Etteilla Type I | Etteilla Type II | Etteilla Type III |
|---|---|---|---|
|  |  |  |  |
| #16 *La Maison Dieu* ('The House of God' or 'The Tower') | #19 *Le Temple Foudroye* ('The Thunderstruck Temple') | #19 *Le Temple Foudroye* ('The Thunderstruck Temple') | #19 *Le Temple Foudroye* ('The Thunderstruck Temple') |

Five of the cards in the Etteilla deck are a departure from the traditional Tarot deck:

- #1 *Le Chaos* ('Chaos'), the Primordial personification of the gap or chasm out of which emerged the earth, the underworld below it, and the heavens above it.
- #7 *Les Oiseaux Et Les Poissons* ('Birds and Fishes')
- #8 *Repos* ('Rest')
- #12 *La Prudence* ('Prudence'), which is found in the Minchiate deck as #17 *La Prudenza*
- #21 *Le Despote Africain* ('The African Despot'), which does have a chariot in the image however this does not link it to #7 *Le Chariot*

**Marie Anne Lenormand** was a French bookseller, fortune-teller, and cartomancer who achieved considerable fame in France in the late 18th century and early 19th century.

She claimed to have given cartomantic advice to many famous people including Tsar Alexander I and prominent leaders of the French Revolution such as Jean-Paul Marat, Maximilien Robespierre, Louis Antoine de Saint-Just, and Napoleon and Josephine Bonaparte[78].

**Éliphas Lévi Zahed**, born Alphonse Louis Constant, was a French esotericist, poet, writer, and occultist. He initially pursued a career in the Catholic Church, but abandoned the priesthood in his mid-twenties and became interested in esotericism and the occult[79].

His pen name Éliphas Lévi Zahed was an anagram of his given name 'Alphonse Louis' in Hebrew. He wrote books on magic, Kabbalah, alchemical studies, and occultism, which gained him recognition among the romantic and symbolist artists and esotericists of Paris and London[80][81].

---

[78] Dummett, Michael (1980). The Game of Tarot. London: Duckworth. ISBN 0715631225.
[79] McIntosh, Christopher (1972). Éliphas Lévi and the French Occult Revival.

Éliphas Lévi was briefly a member of the Freemasons of the Grand Orient de France, but left the organisation in the belief that the original meanings of its symbols and rituals had been lost[82].

He incorporated the Tarot cards into his system of magic, which further influenced and inspired other practitioners, and Tarot became an important part of the paraphernalia of the Western tradition of magic[83].

**Joseph Paul Oswald Wirth** was a Swiss occultist, Freemason, artist, astrology enthusiast, and author. He studied esotericism and symbolism with Stanislas de Guaita.

In 1889, with de Guaita's guidance, he created a Tarot of twenty-two Major Arcana known as *Les 22 Arcanes du Tarot Kabbalistique* ('The 22 Arcana of the Kabbalistic Tarot')[84].

The designs were similar to the Tarot de Marseille but with additional incorporated occult symbolism, including the letters of the Hebrew alphabet.

Card #1 *'Le Bateleur'* ('The Magician') from Oswald Wirth's Tarot deck of 1889

---

[80] Juin, Hubert (1972). Écrivains de l'avant-siècle (in French). Paris: Seghers.
[81] Mercier, Alain (1969). Les Sources ésotériques et occultes de la poésie symboliste (1870-1914) (in French). Vol. 1: Le symbolisme français. A.-G. Nizet.
[82] Chacornac Frères (2001) [1926]. "Éliphas Lévi was a freemason - briefly". Éliphas Lévi, rénovateur de l'occultisme en France (1810-1875), Paul Chacornac (1884-1964) (in French). Translated by Trevor W. McKeown. Paris: Librairie Génerale des Sciences Occultes. Archived from the original on 18 December 2001 – via Grand Lodge of British Columbia and Yukon.
[83] Josephson, Jason Ānanda (May 2013). "God's Shadow: Occluded Possibilities in the Genealogy of Religion". History of Religions. 52 (4): 321. doi:10.1086/669644. JSTOR 10.1086/669644. S2CID 170485577.
[84] Decker, Ronald; Dummett, Michael (2002). History of the Occult Tarot. London: Gerald Duckworth & Co. pp. 177–185. ISBN 0715631225.

## 6.2. The Rider-Waite-Smith Deck

A print of the Rider-Waite-Smith deck of 1909 by Rider, 1999, author's collection.

**Arthur Edward Waite** was a British poet, Freemason, and scholarly mystic who wrote extensively on the occult and esotericism. According to his biographer R. A. Gilbert, he was the first to attempt a systematic study of the history of Western occultism as a spiritual tradition rather than a protoscience or a religion[85].

Waite translated the works of Éliphas Lévi from French into English and published them under the title *The Mysteries of Magic* in 1886[86]. He joined the Hermetic Order of the Golden Dawn in 1891[87], but left in 1893. In 1896 he joined the Outer Order of the Golden Dawn, and the Second Order of the Golden Dawn in 1899. In 1901 he became a Freemason[88][89], and in 1902 he entered the *Societas Rosicruciana in Anglia*, a society of Christian esotericism.

---

[85] Gilbert, R. A. (1987). A. E. Waite: Magician of Many Parts (1st ed.). Wellingborough, Northamptonshire: Crucible. ISBN 185274023X.
[86] Decker, Ronald; Dummett, Michael (2002). A History of the Occult Tarot: 1870–1970. London: Duckworth. ISBN 0715631225.
[87] King, Francis X. (1989). Modern Ritual Magic: The Rise of Western Occultism. Prism. ISBN 978-1853270321.
[88] Anon (n.d.). "Arthur E. Waite". Freemasonry.bcy.ca. Grand Lodge of British Columbia and Yukon. Retrieved 30 November 2022.
[89] Gilbert, R. A. (1986). "The Masonic Career of A. E. Waite". Ars Quatuor Coronatorum. 99. Archived from the original on 5 September 2010. Retrieved 23 May 2010 – via MasterMason.com.

**Pamela Colman Smith** was a British artist, illustrator, theatrical designer, writer, publisher, and occultist. She wrote and illustrated two books of Jamaican folklore, Annancy Stories (1899) and Chim-Chim, Folk Stories from Jamaica (1905). These books included Jamaican versions of tales involving the traditional African folk figure Anansi the Spider[90].

Smith provided the illustrations for *The Illustrated Verses of William Butler Yeats*, a book about actress Dame Ellen Terry by Bram Stoker. William Butler Yeats introduced Smith to the Hermetic Order of the Golden Dawn in 1901 where she met Waite.

In December of 1909, William Rider & Son of London published the first limited edition of the Rider-Waite-Smith Tarot. The Rider-Waite-Smith deck is arguably the most popular and most widely known and used of all Tarot decks[91,92,93]. What makes the deck so effective is that the illustrations are deceptively simple, and yet they contain a wealth of symbolism.

The Fool is placed before the 21 trumps in order to determine the correspondences with the Major Arcana, the Hebrew alphabet, and the Kabbalistic Tree of Life.

In the Major Arcana the 'Papess' became the 'High Priestess' pictured without a papal tiara. The 'Lovers' had previously depicted a medieval scene of a man and a woman being blessed by a cleric, which became a naked Adam and Eve in the Garden of Eden.

In order to accommodate the astrological correspondences taught by the Hermetic order of the Golden Dawn, the 'Justice' (#8) and 'Strength' (#11)) cards are swapped around in order for Strength (#8) to correspond with Leo (the mighty lion) and for Justice (#11) to correspond with Libra (the balancing scales of law and justice).

All of the suit cards in the Minor Arcana have their own allegorical images which further help to guide interpretation, where earlier decks (with a few rare exceptions) had simple designs and arrangements of Wands, cups, swords, coins, etc. The suit of Batons was renamed as Wands, and the suit of Coins was renamed as Pentacles.

As well as the traditional allegorical images of Tarot, some of the images appear to have been especially inspired by those of the Sola Busca Tarot of 1491. This theory is made probable by the fact that black and white photographs of all 78 Sola Busca cards were donated by the Busca-Serbelloni family to the British Museum in 1907, where it was likely to have been seen by Waite and Smith two years before their deck was published.

---

[90] Kaplan, Stuart R. (2009). The Artwork & Times of Pamela Colman Smith. Stamford, Connecticut: U.S. Game Systems.
[91] Decker, Ronald; Dummett, Michael (2019). A History of the Occult Tarot. London: Duckworth. p. 291. ISBN 9780715645727.
[92] Giles, Cynthia (1994). The Tarot: History, Mystery, and Lore. New York: Simon & Schuster. p. 46. ISBN 0671891014.
[93] Visions and Prophecies. Alexandria, Virginia: Time-Life Books. 1988. p. 142.

#48 Queen of Cups
Rider-Waite-Smith, London, 1909

#52 Three of Swords
Rider-Waite-Smith, London, 1909

#31 Ten of Wands
Rider-Waite-Smith, London, 1909

#34 Queen of Chalices
Sola Busca, Ferrara, 1491

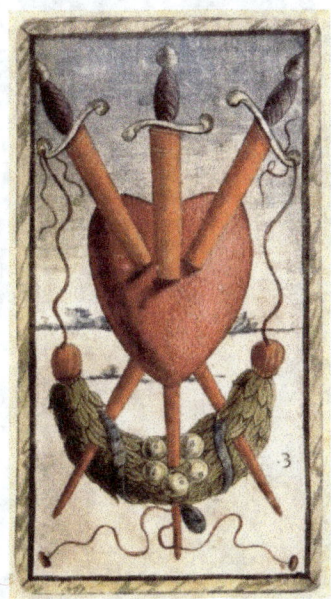
#66 Three of Swords
Sola Busca, Ferrara, 1491

#73 Ten of Swords
Sola Busca, Ferrara, 1491

# 7. The Tarot Deck

This is an overview of the cards of the Tarot deck, which is designed to give a simple description and summary of the meanings and symbolisms of each card. It is by no means exhaustive as it is such a broad subject that no-one will ever have the 'last word' on it. The reader is encouraged to familiarise themselves with these meanings, and to use their own intuition to interpret them and how they fit into the 'bigger picture' of the reading.

## 7.1. The Major Arcana

The Major Arcana represent the headline events in the big picture, the key moments in the grand scheme of things, the life lessons along the whole journey, the big chapters in the great narrative, the high-level markers in the master plan of life. They also represent the structure of human consciousness, the archetypes of the people we are, the people we become, the people we meet along the way, the people that influence us, and the people that we influence.

**0 The Fool**

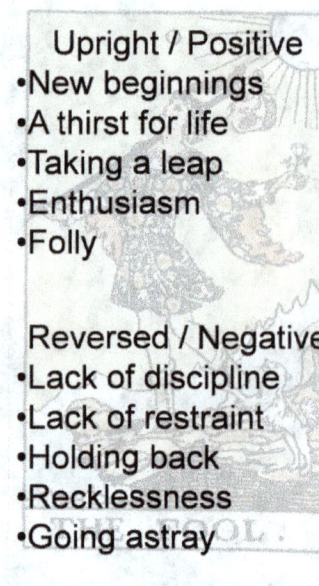
Upright / Positive
- New beginnings
- A thirst for life
- Taking a leap
- Enthusiasm
- Folly

Reversed / Negative
- Lack of discipline
- Lack of restraint
- Holding back
- Recklessness
- Going astray

Hebrew Letter Aleph

Astrological Sign Uranus

**Description:** The Fool is the main character of the story. The cards of the Major Arcana are the path that the Fool travels through the great mysteries of life, which is traditionally described as 'The Fool's Journey'.

**Upright**: The Fool represents setting out on a new journey, new beginnings, optimism, trusting in life, being spontaneous, leaping into the unknown, and making a leap of faith.

You may be taking a risk or making a leap of faith, or you may be encouraged to do so to avoid missing out on an opportunity. Great things rarely, if ever, materialise from within one's comfort zone. You are on the verge of an exciting new adventure, which will bring you along a path where you will need to take a leap of faith. This leap of faith will enable you to grow as a result.

**Reversed:** The Fool represents taking risks, recklessness, holding back, or unknowingly going astray. You may be aware of the risks being taken, but embrace your decision nonetheless.

The Fool is generally a positive card, and the change it can bring is usually welcome change, but its appearance in some readings in the reversed position can signify a need to take time out to look before you leap.

**Symbolism:** The rising sun indicates the start of a journey and the beginning of ascension towards the divine. The red feather represents life force or the flame of life. The small bag represents travelling light. The white rose represents purity and innocence.

The white dog represents man's evolution from beast. The cliff represents the unknown ahead. The mountains represent obstacles to be overcome, and the ascension into higher consciousness and enlightenment.

The Fool's legs indicate forward momentum with self confidence, and his yellow tights and boots represent the energy of the sun. His undershirt is white representing purity and innocence, and his top shirt is floral and flamboyant, indicating an interest in aesthetics rather than utility. The black wand represents the carrying of past experiences and the subconscious.

## 1 The Magician

**Upright / Positive**
- Increase in skill
- Skill used for good
- Manifestation
- Originality
- Achievement

**Reversed / Negative**
- Deception
- Sleight of hand
- Misuse of skills
- Trickery
- Fooling oneself

**Hebrew Letter**
Bet

**Astrological Sign**
Mercury

The Magician is a skilled person with the initiative, resourcefulness, and willpower to achieve his ambitions. He is connected to the spiritual realm and the material realm, and he uses this connection to focus on the creation and manifestation of his goals.

**Upright:** If the Magician represents you, then it is *you* who possess the tools and the skills you need to achieve your ambitions. If the Magician represents someone else, then it represents you encountering and being influenced by the Magician, a figure who will appear to be diplomatic, eloquent, self-confident, and persuasive.

**Reversed:** Take care however, because you also have the ability to fool yourself, or to allow yourself to be fooled by others if your focus is drawn away from any finer details that may be hidden or lacking. Take care not to allow yourself to be fooled or manipulated by the Magician, who with a sleight of hand may divert your attention away from the grey areas of what has *not* been said, what has *not* been clarified, and what has been left open to assumption, creating room for misunderstandings later. This may be avoided by seeking clarity at all times.

**Symbolism:** The Magician stands with one arm stretched upwards towards the sky, and the other pointing downwards towards the earth, an allegory of the phrase 'as above, so below'.

The double-headed wand in his hand is also pointing both up and down, repeating the meaning. His robe is white which symbolises purity, and his cloak is red which symbolises worldly experience and knowledge.

On the table in front of the Magician are the four suits of the tarot which represent the four classical elements over which he has achieved mastery, a cup (water), a pentacle (earth), a sword (air), and a wand (fire).

Above his head is the symbol of infinity and around his waist is an ouroboros (an ancient symbol of a snake biting its own tail, representing infinity or eternity). In the foreground are roses and lily of the valley, symbols of the cultivation, manifestation, blossoming, and fruition of his ideas and aspirations.

## 2 The High Priestess

**Upright / Positive**
- An increase in intuition
- Femininity
- Psychic ability
- Spiritual nurturing

**Reversed / Negative**
- Secrets
- Disconnection from intuition
- Answers not revealed
- Doubt

**Hebrew Letter** Gimmel

**Astrological Sign** Moon

**Description:** The High Priestess guards the gateway to the temple of sacred knowledge. She is identified with the *Shekhinah*, a female presence of the divine in a sacred place. In some decks she is known as the Popess, or the Roman goddess Juno (Greek: Hera).

**Upright:** The High Priestess represents the esoteric world, heightened powers of intuition, believing and trusting in one's intuition, a new subject of study, spiritual knowledge, mysticism and the occult, a spiritual quest, journeying inwards, the subconscious, and the unknown.

You may benefit from taking time out for self-healing, gaining knowledge, and spiritual growth. Knowing one's power brings humility, not knowing one's power brings insecurity.

**Reversed:** The High Priestess represents disconnection from intuition, inaction, mysteries, and secrets withheld or not yet revealed. It is time to bring a period of introspection to an end, collating together all that you have learnt. Even if some of the answers you have been looking for have not yet been revealed, move forward, and trust your intuition.

**Symbolism:** The two pillars marked B (*Boaz*, 'in his strength') and J (*Jachin*, 'he will establish') mark the gateway to the Temple of Solomon. The black and white of the pillars symbolise duality, masculine and feminine, and darkness and light.

The thin veil that protects the gateway into the temple is decorated with palm leaves (male), and pomegranates (female), growing on a tree shaped like the Kabbalistic Tree of Life. The crown she is wearing is similar to that of the ancient Egyptian goddess Hathor, which symbolises cow horns and a sun disk, indicating her ancient spiritual authority.

The blue cloak and white robe are a reference to the Virgin Mary, the mother of Jesus. The cross around her neck is equilateral and symbolises the boundaries between the four classical elements. The Torah on her lap represents divine law, which is partly covered, obscure, or hidden, and contains the first five books of the Hebrew Bible.

The crescent moon at her feet is a reference to the Woman of the Apocalypse, who is described in chapter 12 of the Book of Revelation as having "the moon under her feet".

## 3 The Empress

**Upright / Positive**
- Abundance
- Pregnancy and birth
- Good results
- Reassurance
- Support

**Reversed / Negative**
- Creative block
- Dependence on others
- Lack of control or influence
- Loss of power

**Hebrew Letter Dalet**

**Astrological Sign Venus**

**Description:** The Empress is a powerful woman with an aura of authority around her. She sits on her throne of stability with symbols of her power and success around her.

**Upright:** The Empress represents beauty, comfort at home, commitment to people and business transactions, creation, earthly abundance, feeling settled, fertility, good feelings and thoughts, goodness, light, material income, material matters, new life, nurturing, security, and stability in domestic affairs. She also symbolises the divine feminine, nurturing and fertility, pregnancy, motherhood, marriage, the birth of a child, or a creative venture.

You may be the Empress, in which case you are capable of achieving the abundance and stability that you are looking for, which will be useful in times to come as a platform for a new creative venture, relationship, marriage, or birth. Indecision must be overcome, the implementation of all the plans lies ahead.

**Reversed:** The Empress represents a creative block, dependence on others, difficulties, disagreements, illness, and quarrels.

You need to break free from this state of dependence on others, or escape from the creative block, which has been caused by a lack of control, or by the influence of a powerful figure, in order to realise your potential success and stability. Use this delay to find the right path, to discover the truth in any matter.

**Symbolism:** The throne represents stability and power. The crown of twelve stars represents her connection to the celestial realm and the zodiac, highlighting her universal influence. She is holding a sceptre which symbolises her authority and control over the natural world.

The symbol of Venus symbolises her association with the goddess of love, beauty, creativity, harmony, nurturing, and fertility.

The landscape around her includes fields of wheat, rivers, and trees, which symbolise abundance and the nurturing aspects of nature. Her element is earth which symbolises grounding, and the physical and material aspects of life.

**4 The Emperor**

Upright / Positive
- Power
- Stability
- Ambition
- Success
- Achieving goals

Reversed / Negative
- Power struggles
- Excessive control
- Inflexibility
- Domination
- Lack of discipline

Hebrew Letter
He

ה

Astrological Sign
Aries

♈

**Description:** The Emperor is an ambitious, powerful, and successful leader, one who relies heavily upon rules, establishment, structure, strategy and having all the facts. He also represents a father figure who may offer advice and wisdom.

**Upright:** The Emperor represents a father figure, ambition, an older man, authority, decisiveness, dependability, establishment, fatherhood, leadership, logic, power, practicality, protectiveness, rules, stability, strategy, structure, structure, and success.

Emulate the Emperor and take control of a situation, showing leadership, obtaining all of the facts before making decisions, acting decisively with authority, and seeking clarity at all times.

**Reversed:** The Emperor represents abuse of power, an absentee father, domination, domineering behaviour, excessive control, inflexibility, lack of control, lack of discipline, paternity issues, rigidity, and stubbornness.

You should watch out that power and authority does not cause you to be domineering, excessively controlling, lacking discipline, or inflexible. Sticking to old ways because they have worked thus far is the enemy of innovation, adaptation, and improvement.

**Symbolism:** The ram skulls adorning the throne represent the zodiac sign of Aries, whose ruling planet is Mars, the Roman god of war. His long white beard symbolises wisdom. His armour represents security and invulnerability, and his red garments symbolise worldly experience and knowledge.

The sceptre in his right hand symbolises Ankh, an ancient Egyptian hieroglyphic symbol meaning 'life' or 'the key of life'. The globe in his right hand represents the world and the Emperor's absolute rule over the world.

The stark barren mountain top where the Emperor's throne sits represents regulation, unyielding power, the top of the world and worldly hierarchy, and at the height of male ego.

**5 The Hierophant**

Upright / Positive
- Commitments
- Traditions
- Good advice
- Forgiveness
- Teachers and guidance

Reversed / Negative
- Unwanted commitments
- Outdated traditions
- Over-kindness as weakness
- Judgement

Hebrew Letter
Vau

Astrological Sign
Taurus

**Description:** The Hierophant is a teacher of wisdom, a spiritual mentor. The term 'Hierophant' comes from ancient Greek meaning chief priest or high priest. In some decks he is known as the Pope, or the Roman god Jupiter (Greek: Zeus).

**Upright:** The Hierophant represents a contract of marriage, a leader, a pastor, a philosophical quest for answers, authority, beliefs, conformity, conventional wisdom, hierarchical order, institution, morality, orthodoxy, religion, righteousness, sacredness, setting aside time for prayer and meditation, spirituality, and tradition.

If the card represents you, then it is *you* who is representing moral righteousness or who is encouraged to do so, by involvement with a traditional group activity or institution, as a kind of contract (perhaps a contract with oneself), or as an advisor. If the card represents someone else, then it is a figure that you receive instruction or counsel from.

**Reversed:** The Hierophant represents a challenge to power, a rejection of authority, alternative lifestyles, challenging the old ways, gullibility, nonconformity, reversed roles, unorthodoxy, and vulnerability from over-kindness which can be seen as weakness and exploited by others.

You have a choice to make between doing what is expected of you and playing it safe, or following your heart and facing the consequences, whichever is more important for your success.

**Symbolism:** The Hierophant's right hand is raised in blessing or benediction. Two fingers point skyward and two point down, indicating a bridge between heaven and earth. He is holding a triple cross or papal cross and wearing a triple crown or papal crown.

At the top of his crown are three nails, symbolising the crucifixion of Jesus. He is seated on a throne between two pillars representing law and freedom, obedience and disobedience, virtue and sin.

At his feet are the keys to heaven and two priests with their heads partly shaved, a traditional practice of spiritual significance.

## 6 The Lovers

**Upright / Positive**
- Partnerships, relationships, love
- Harmony
- Passion
- Choices to be made
- Alignment of values

**Reversed / Negative**
- Unstable relationships
- Temptation
- Bad choices
- Passions becoming obsessions

**Hebrew Letter** Zayin

**Astrological Sign** Gemini

**Description:** The Lovers depicts Adam and Eve naked in the Garden of Eden. Above them is the angel Raphael, whose name means 'God heals', blessing the man and the woman and reminding them of their union with the divine.

**Upright:** The Lovers represent alignment, an alignment of values, attraction, beauty, good choices, good decisions, harmony, kindred spirits, love, morals, partnerships (personal or professional), passionate feelings, relationships (personal or romantic), romance, soul mates, trials overcome, and true love.

The Lovers can also symbolise temptation, a new opportunity, and life choices to be made. Being part of partnership can require a sacrifice of old ways in favour of new ones, an equal balance between both parties, and an equal balance between head and heart.

**Reversed:** The Lovers represent self-love, disharmony, imbalance, and misalignment of values. Perhaps both parties have different ideas about what the partnership is really about. The alignment of shared values may have been assumed but not fully discussed and understood, resulting in differences which become increasingly apparent.

Finding a balance in a partnership can sometimes be a struggle, and sacrifices have to be made in order to maintain it, or let it go in favour of something else, something new. Either way, the decision should not be taken lightly, as the results will be long-lasting. This situation or dilemma may be avoided by seeking clarity at all times.

**Symbolism:** Behind the woman is a tall apple tree with a snake winding its way up the trunk, representing the temptation of sensual pleasures that take one's focus away from the divine. Behind the man is a tree of flames, which represent passion.

The twelve flames represent the twelve signs of the zodiac, a symbol of time and eternity. The man looks towards the women, and the woman looks towards the angel, which represents the path from conscious, to subconscious, to super-conscious, from physical desire to emotional needs to spiritual concerns. The volcanic mountain in the background represents fertility and passion.

## 7 The Chariot

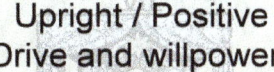

Upright / Positive
- Drive and willpower
- Inspiration
- Determination
- Travel
- Movement

Reversed / Negative
- Conflicts to overcome
- Opposition
- Negativity
- Ostentatiousness

Hebrew Letter Heth

Astrological Sign Cancer

**Description:** The Chariot depicts a charioteer overcoming opposing forces in order to be able to steer the chariot in the direction he wishes to travel.

**Upright:** The Chariot represents action, ambition, being a source of inspiration, being an authority, control, determination to see something through, discipline, drive, fame and fortune, movement, recognition, success, travel, victory, and willpower.

Take control of a situation by overcoming the conflict of opposing forces and moving forward. The Chariot card recommends that you rise above that which is no longer serving any purpose, and then move forward. Action is the key to all success.

**Reversed:** The Chariot represents aggression, conflict, forcefulness, issues with self-discipline, lack of direction, lack of self control, manipulation of others, opposition, ostentatiousness, powerlessness, revenge, and war.

You may be delaying action because of confusion or conflicts, and an uncertainty about which direction to go in. Make a decision on the best way to move forward, and then to go into action, rise above conflicts, stick with it, and see it through, otherwise they will go nowhere.

**Symbolism:** The armour decorated with crescent moons symbolises that which is coming into being. The tunic with a white square represents strength of will. The laurel and star crown indicates victory, success, and spiritual evolution.

The charioteer is not holding reins, but a wand, symbolising that he controls the movement and direction of the chariot through the strength of his will and mind.

The canopy above the charioteer decorated with stars symbolising his connection to the celestial world and the Divine will. The black and white sphinxes pulling the chariot denote duality, positive and negative, opposing forces to be reconciled. The river behind the chariot symbolises flowing movement, which the charioteer aspires to.

## 8 Strength

**Upright / Positive**
- Remaining strong
- You are stronger than you think you are
- A sense of responsibility

**Reversed / Negative**
- Lack of inner strength
- Self-doubt
- Low-energy levels
- Raw emotions, frustrations

Hebrew Letter
Teth

Astrological Sign
Leo

**Description:** A woman calmly tames a lion and gently stroking or holding the lion's forehead and jaw. The lion is well known for its ferocity and strength which is loudly projected outwards with a roar. The woman uses her hidden inner strength and resilience to tame the lion without force. It is the victory of inner strength over outer strength.

**Upright:** The Strength card represents a strong sense of responsibility, action, bravery, caring for others, choosing how to respond in a conflict, compassion, control, courage, finding your inner strength, grace, inner power, instinct, remaining strong, self-confidence, self-worth, taking quiet control, and tolerance.

Trust in yourself, as you are stronger than you think you are. Do not use that strength to be too hard on yourself. Exercise mind over matter, courage, subtle power, channelling and controlling the animal self. Take care and responsibility, applying self-discipline and compassion to achieve transformation. Do not allow your fear to decide your fate.

**Reversed:** The Strength card represents being willing to accept less than you deserve, defeat, fragility, giving up what you want in favour of others, inadequacy, lack of confidence, low self-worth, people trying to bring you down, raw emotions, vulnerability, and weakness. Overcome all of this by believing in yourself.

**Symbolism:** The symbol of infinity over the woman's head represents enlightenment, infinite potential, spiritual powers, wisdom, and higher understanding. The white robe that the woman is wearing represents purity of spirit. The belt and crown of flowers represent an expression of nature.

The lion represents animal passions and earthly cravings. The Lion's fierce roar does not frighten his mistress, as she soothes him with calmly spoken words and a gentle touch. The lion's tail is between its legs, symbolising submission and obedience of wild impulses to the hand of wisdom.

The woman and the lion symbolise the two aspects within each of us, wild and tame, virtue and vice, light and shadow.

## 9 The Hermit

**Upright / Positive**
- Self-discovery
- Solitude
- Soul-searching
- Introspection
- Inner guidance
- Gaining knowledge

**Reversed / Negative**
- Withdrawl
- Loneliness
- Unsociable
- Isolation and paranoia
- Living in the past

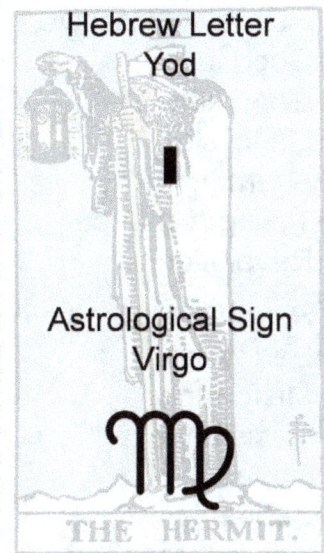

**Hebrew Letter**
Yod

**Astrological Sign**
Virgo

**Description:** The Hermit is a person who has chosen a path of self-discovery and reached a heightened state of awareness. The lantern of truth and light that he carries with him only illuminates his next few steps ahead rather than his full journey. He must step forward to see where to go next, knowing that not everything will be revealed at once. He has patiently put one foot in front of the other in order to reach the top of the mountain. He holds the light up as a beacon of inspiration and hope to the world below. He is a soul-seeker who has moved away from materialism.

**Upright:** The Hermit represents alone time, gaining wisdom, independence, inner guidance, introspection, respite, solitude, soul-searching, spiritual enlightenment, and standing alone.

You are entering a period of self-reflection, spiritual enlightenment, solitude, self-healing, and contemplation. A short time spent alone will lead to a greater understanding of oneself, one's existence, values, and direction in life. Knowing yourself is the beginning of all wisdom. The answers you seek are often found within.

**Reversed:** The Hermit represents being unsociable, betrayal, hiding what you really think, isolation, loneliness rather than solitude, and negative effects of too much withdrawal.

A prolonged withdrawal can lead to feelings of isolation, fear, and paranoia. Do not take too long to reflect on the past, or waiting for something from your past to return, or you will remain trapped in the past and unable to move forward, paralysed by fear and doubt. Don't be too detached or you will end up all alone.

**Symbolism:** The snow-capped mountain top on which the Hermit stands represents spiritual mastery, growth, and accomplishment. Although the Hermit is aware of his surroundings, his gaze is turned inwards. The lantern with the six pointed star inside represents the Seal of Solomon which is a symbol of wisdom.

The staff held in his left hand, the side of the subconscious mind, is a sign of authority, guidance, and power, an axis connecting man and god, which he uses to guide and balance himself. His cloak represents concealment.

**10 Wheel of Fortune**

Upright / Positive
- Good luck
- Good karma
- Life cycles
- A turning point
- Taking a chance
- Revolution

Reversed / Negative
- Bad luck
- Misfortune
- Resistance to change
- Sudden changes
- Unpreparedness

Hebrew Letter
Kaph

Astrological Sign
Jupiter

**Description:** The Wheel of Fortune (*Rota Fortunae*) is an ancient symbol of the capricious nature of fate. The wheel is connected to the Roman goddess Fortuna, and the Greek goddess Tyche, who spin the wheel at random, changing the positions of those upon the wheel, whereby some suffer great misfortune, and others experience good fortune.

**Upright:** The Wheel of Fortune represents a change in the air, a turning point, and the ups and downs of life, chance, change, destiny, fate, karma, life cycles, luck, nothing staying the same for long, taking a chance, and the circle of life.

Hope for the best and / or be prepared to take a gamble. We cannot become what we want by remaining what we are.

**Reversed:** The Wheel of Fortune represents bad luck, breaking cycles, disruption, loss of control, misfortune, not getting anywhere, setbacks, the dangers of resistance to change, things going around in circles, unpleasant change, and upheaval.

Prepare for the worst and / or take control before that change happens, rather than having the wheel thrust change upon you unprepared.

**Symbolism:** The Hebrew letters on the wheel are YHVH (Yahweh, God). There are also the letters TARO (Tarot), TORA (Torah), ROTA (Latin: Wheel), ORAT (Latin: Speak), ATOR (Egyptian goddess of fertility and love). The alchemical symbols for mercury (mind and air), sulphur (soul and fire), water (emotions), and salt (body and earth) represent the building blocks of life and the four alchemical elements which represent formative power.

On the left side of the wheel is the serpent Typhon, the ancient Greek Titan of storms (equated with the Egyptian god Set) which represents life force plunging into the material world. On the right side of the wheel rises Anubis, the Egyptian god of the dead who welcomes souls to the underworld. The Sphinx on top of the wheel represents knowledge and strength. The four winged creatures in each corner are an angel (Aquarius), an eagle (Scorpio), a lion (Leo), and a bull (Taurus). Their wings signify stability during movement and change. Each of the creatures is holding a copy of the Torah, representing wisdom.

## 11 Justice

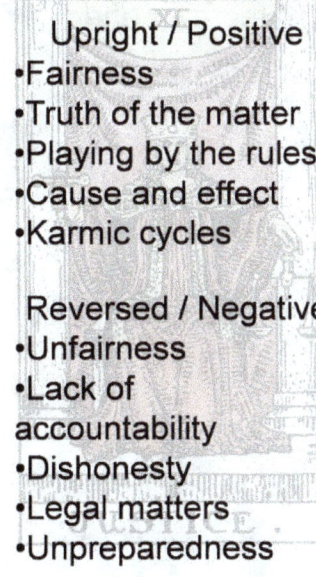
Upright / Positive
- Fairness
- Truth of the matter
- Playing by the rules
- Cause and effect
- Karmic cycles

Reversed / Negative
- Unfairness
- Lack of accountability
- Dishonesty
- Legal matters
- Unpreparedness

Hebrew Letter Lamed

Astrological Sign Libra

**Description:** The personification of Justice, also known as Lady Justice, has her origins in the Roman goddess Justitia (or Iustitia), who is an equivalent of Greek goddess Dike and her mother Themis.

**Upright:** The Justice card symbolises action and consequence, cause and effect, court cases, fairness, getting what you deserve for the better, good commitments, good contracts, honesty, justice, karma, law, life lessons, playing by the rules, positive legal outcomes, and truth.

Legal matters need to be dealt with, to seek clarity on where you stand legally. You may need to weigh up a situation with balancing scales and come to a final decision about something. You may need to attain a greater sense of balance in your life and / or seek out the truth of a matter.

**Reversed:** The Justice card represents bad commitments, corruption, getting what you deserve for the worse, injustice, karmic debt, lack of accountability, negative legal outcomes, and unfairness.

You may be warned of legal matters overtaking or overwhelming you if you are unprepared, and also to beware and protect yourself from dishonesty by having all the evidence and facts. You may be warned against being dishonest towards yourself and thereby to others, which when later found out will require an explanation. What goes around comes around.

**Symbolism:** Two pillars symbolise balance, law, and structure. The purple veil hanging between the two pillars represents authority, wisdom, spirituality, and compassion. The sword in her right hand represents a well ordered mindset in order to be able to give fair judgement (Swords represent the mind and thoughts in Tarot).

The sword points upwards, expressing a firm and final decision, and the double-edged blade signifies our actions having consequences (consider the phrase 'double-edged sword'). The scales in her left hand, the side of the subconscious and of intuition, represent balance and a balanced judgement, logic and impartiality.

The crown with a small square mounted on it represents well-ordered thoughts. The white shoe that appears from under her cloak is a reminded of the spiritual consequences of actions.

# 12 The Hanged Man

**Upright / Positive**
- Different perspectives
- Self-sacrifice
- Suspended in time
- Surrender
- Letting go

**Reversed / Negative**
- Delays
- In a state of suspended animation
- Powerless to act
- Lack of action delaying matters

Hebrew Letter
Mem

Astrological Sign
Neptune

**Description:** The Hanged Man depicts a man suspended from a T-shaped cross of living wood. He is hanging upside down, viewing the world from a completely different perspective. His facial expression is calm, indicating that he is hanging there by his own accord, in a form of self sacrifice in order to gain insight and perspective. This allegory resonates with the legend of the Norse god Odin who hung himself from the World Tree Yggdrasil in order to gain knowledge.

**Upright:** The Hanged Man represents a change of perspective, being suspended in time, improved divination, prophecy, psychic ability, sacrifice for the greater good, spiritual development, surrender, and transitions.

You may be in a moment of pause, surrender, letting go, or seeking new perspectives.

**Reversed:** If the card is reversed, it represents apathy, detachment, delays, disinterest, having to wait, illness, impulsiveness, negative patterns, playing the waiting game, martyrdom, prison sentences, stagnation, stubbornness, suicide, uncertain outcomes, and an unwillingness to sacrifice.

You may be experiencing delays, as if in a state of suspended animation. You may be waiting for the conclusion of events that are outside of your control. While being momentarily upside down may offer a different perspective, a decision or action may be needed to break free from this suspended state.

What you are waiting for may not happen unless you take action first. You may have to sacrifice something in order to be able to break free and move forward, trusting in the unknown.

**Symbolism:** The Hanged Man's red trousers represent human passion, the physical body, vitality, and strength. His blue shirt symbolises knowledge, truth, confidence, and faith.

The living wood represents nature, hope, renewal, and growth, in contrast with manmade nature of the T-shaped cross upon which he is suspended, indicating man's interaction with nature or a surrender to the forces of nature.

The top beam of the T-shaped cross represents the meeting place between the earth and the sky. The halo around the Hanged Man's head represents compassion and wisdom.

## 13 Death

**Upright / Positive**
- Death and rebirth
- Transitions
- Personal transformation
- Releasing the old in favour of the new

**Reversed / Negative**
- Resistance to change
- Unexpected ending
- Unstoppable change
- The temporal nature of all things

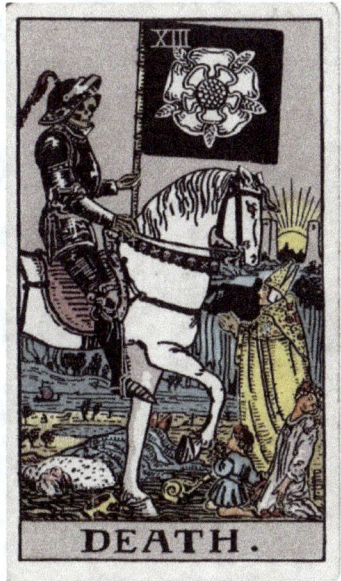

**Hebrew Letter**
Nun

**Astrological Sign**
Scorpio
♏

**Description:** The Death card shows the messenger of Death in the form of a skeleton dressed in black armour riding a white horse.

**Upright:** The Death card does not literally symbolise death as such, but rather the end of one thing and the beginning of another, a transition, a symbolic death and rebirth, fundamental changes, life changing events, new starts, and a reminder of the temporal nature of all things.

The Death card can even represent a change for the better, or blessings in disguise. Release the old in order to accept the new. Old ways will not open new doors.

**Reversed:** The Death card represents break ups, death of a relative or loved one, depression, divorce, inevitable endings, inner purging, life changing events, past lives, personal transformation, reincarnation, repeating negative patterns, resistance to change, sadness, and stagnation.

Now is a time of unavoidable change and transformation that will bring you to the next level in life. It is not always easy, but trust that it will be worth it. Resistance will only delay and prolong the situation.

**Symbolism:** The skeleton represents the part of the body which survives long after life has left it. The red feather on the helmet of the skeleton represents the flame of life and a transformative moment in the Fool's Journey. The armour symbolises invincibility and the inevitability that death will come no matter what. The dark colour of the armour represents mourning and the mysterious. The white horse represents purity, strength, and power.

The sun setting between the two towers in the background represents endings, and the gateway to the kingdom of the dead. A royal figure lies dead on the ground, while a bishop, a woman, and a child plead to be spared, but to no avail. The five petal white rose on the black flag represents beauty, purification, immortality, and emerging life springing forth in the midst of death.

One interpretation suggests that the child kneeling in the foreground is actually the Child of Life, who is not afraid, and can be seen riding on the back of the same pale horse in the Sun card later on in the deck.

## 14 Temperance

**Upright / Positive**
- Moderation
- Self-restraint
- Alchemy, mixing and blending
- New approaches
- A compromise

**Reversed / Negative**
- Imbalance
- Excess
- A need for self-healing
- Re-alignment
- Holding back

Hebrew Letter Samekh

O

Astrological Sign Sagittarius

**Description:** The Temperance card depicts an angel who is both masculine and feminine. The figure of Temperance is the personification of moderation and self-restraint.

**Upright:** The Temperance card represents a balance of situations, blending and alchemy, calmness, change, divine timing, ease, flexibility, harmony, health and healing, managing emotions, moderation, moderation, patience, peace, perspective, planning and preparing for the future, staying calm, and staying grounded.

Find moderation and exercise a personal alchemy of mixing and blending different ideas and approaches. Try something new, a sensible compromise, a moderate balance, a kind of harmony, which may produce a surprising outcome. Everything in moderation, even moderation itself. A state of balance is possible and achievable where you feel everything will be ok.

**Reversed:** The Temperance card represents a need for self-healing or re-alignment, avoidance of conflict, being manipulated, clashes, excess, hastiness, imbalance, lack of perspective, outside issues coming into the home, overlooking problems, recklessness, tolerance to a fault, and self-indulgence.

Let go of various trappings which may be holding you back, in order to self-heal, re-align, and go forwards.

**Symbolism:** The white robe represents purity. Mounted on the robe are a yellow triangle enclosed in a square which represents humans and the earth (the triangle) being bound by natural law (the square). The angel balances between one foot on the rocks, expressing the need to stay grounded, and the other foot in the water, showing the need to connect with dreams, hopes, and desires.

The pouring of water between two cups symbolises the symbolic flow and alchemy of life between the ethereal and the material world. The mountain path in the background leading up a mountain range symbolises the journey through life.

The golden crown above the mountains encased in glowing light represents taking the higher path, staying true to one's life purpose and meaning, and the attainment of a goal, mastery, mastery of oneself.

## 15 The Devil

**Upright / Positive**
- Raw animal instincts
- The base side of human nature
- Self-interest
- Indulgence
- Self-absorbtion

**Reversed / Negative**
- Dark thoughts
- Detachment
- Selfishness
- Temptation
- Self-destruction

Hebrew Letter
Ayin

Astrological Sign
Capricorn

**Description:** The Devil is represented by Baphomet, or the Horned Goat of Mendes, a creature who is half man, half goat. Originally Baphomet symbolised the balance between good and evil, male and female, human and animal.

**Upright:** The Devil card represents the base side of human nature, raw animal instincts, excesses, addiction, selfishness, and self-absorption. Examine your role in what has happened that has led you to this place or situation, and break free from addictive self-defeating attitudes.

Giving in to addiction gives away your power. Temptation manipulates you into self-destructive patterns of behaviour, and you may become imprisoned in dark thoughts and ideas. Do not share your weaknesses, as others will use them against you.

**Reversed:** The Devil card represents releasing limiting beliefs, exploring dark thoughts, and detachment.

You are warned of the dangers of taking too much time out for yourself, too much time alone with dark thoughts which may lead to dark places, temptation, and self-destruction.

**Symbolism:** The wings are those of a vampire bat, which sucks the lifeblood out of its prey, symbolic of surrender to raw desires. The Devil has a hypnotic stare which hypnotises those who come near him, bringing them under his influence.

Above the Devil's head is an inverted pentagram, a sign of the darker side of magic and occultism. He salutes with his right hand, and holds a flaming torch pointing down with his left hand, symbolising a descent into darkness.

At the Devil's feet are a man and a woman with horns on their head who are chained to the Devil's throne. A closer look reveals that the chains around their neck are loose and could be escaped from.

The man and the woman both have tails, which symbolises their animal and raw instincts, the grapes and the fire on the ends of their tails signify pleasure and lust. The longer they stay with the Devil, the more they become like him.

## 16 The Tower

**Upright / Positive**
- A sudden revelation
- A ground-shaking event
- Unstable foundations
- Collapse
- Rebuilding

**Reversed / Negative**
- Destruction
- Fear of change
- Disaster
- Personal collapse
- Unavoidable fundamental change

Hebrew Letter
Pe

Astrological Sign
Mars

**Description:** The Tower represents a building that appears to be secure but is actually built on assumptions and uncertainties which have been overlooked and ignored for a long time. A sudden revelation like a lightning bolt causes disruption and destruction to all that stands, shaking everything to the ground, an event for which the stage has been set for a long time.

**Upright:** The Tower card represents confusion, destruction, disaster, divorce, loss, pain, revelations, tragedy, trauma, upheaval, and violence.

The collapse of the tower brings about a change of lifestyle, or a need to re-organise your life, taking time to rebuild and recover. The tower will fall, but how you deal with it determines how difficult or painful it will be. Use the stone blocks of the collapsed tower to build something new, taking into account all that you have learned. Not all storms come to disrupt your life, some come to clear your path.

**Reversed:** The Tower card represents a personal collapse, transformation, averting disaster, avoiding loss, avoiding tragedy, delaying the inevitable, and resisting change.

Your own fear of change may be bringing about a collapse within yourself. You may be averting or mitigating the disaster, but you may also be only delaying the inevitable. Accept the change, re-organise yourself, and rebuild.

**Symbolism:** The tower is a solid structure, but it has been built on shaky foundations, and it only takes one bolt of lightning to bring it down. The lightning bolt represents a sudden surge of energy, a disruptive revelation, which brings potentially destructive change. The crown at the top of the tower has been knocked over by the lightning, which represents energy flowing down from the universe, through the crown (head) into the figurative body of the tower.

The two people are so desperate to escape the tower that they have thrown themselves from the tower, not knowing where they are going or what awaits them as they fall. The twenty two flames represent the twelve signs of the zodiac, and the ten points on the Kabbalistic Tree of Life, suggesting that even in times of destruction and disaster, there is either divine involvement, divine intervention, or it serves a divine plan.

**17 The Star**

**Description:** The Star card depicts a maiden who is both grounded and able to nurture her hopes and dreams with the water of life.

**Upright:** The Star card represents beauty, calm, contentment, creativity, dreams coming true, dreams fulfilled, faith, good prospects, health improvements, hope, hope for the future, inspiration, opportunity, peace, purpose, reassurances, renewal, spirituality, tranquillity, and wishes granted.

It is possible to achieve your dreams and improve your health, with hope for the future. Make a wish, keep dreaming.

**Reversed:** The Star card represents boredom, despair, focusing on the negative, hopelessness, lack of creativity, lack of faith, lack of inspiration, loss and theft, monotony, and the jealousy of others disrupting your life and plans.

Guard against the negative actions of others who are acting out of jealousy and the hatred of those who are doing well for themselves. Protect your dreams and your wishes.

**Symbolism:** The naked maiden represents a creative soul, divine, innocent, with nothing to hide. She has one foot on the land which keeps her grounded, and one foot in the water which represents her hopes and dreams.

The jug in her left hand represents the subconscious, and the jug in her right hand represents the conscious. The water represents the nourishing of the earth and the continuation of the cycle of fertility.

The pouring of water represents the act of gently calming strong emotions. The water poured on the land split into five streams represents the five senses. The bird perched on top of the tree in the background is an Ibis, which is associated with the Egyptian god Thoth, the god of wisdom, magic, and writing.

The stars represent direction, divine guidance, hope, and wisdom. The budding flowers represent hope, renewal, growth, and rejuvenation.

## 18 The Moon

**Upright / Positive**
- Intuition
- Dreams
- Emotions
- Knowing what you want
- Trusting yourself

**Reversed / Negative**
- Illusion
- Fears and anxieties
- Unsure how to get what you want
- Inner confusion
- Repressed emotions

Hebrew Letter
Qoph

Astrological Sign
Pisces

**Description:** The Moon has 16 major and 16 minor rays of emanating around it, shedding dew drops of moisture on the land. A domesticated dog and a wild wolf are both howling at the moon, and a crayfish is emerging from the water.

**Upright:** The Moon card represents anxiety, deception, dreams, fear, illusion, instability, intuition, misconception, the subconscious, and vagueness.

You may know what you want, but you are not able to trust your judgement in how to go about achieving it, or you may be worried about the future. Worries and fears may be bringing about self-deception or may be holding you back. Fears that are not being dealt with are rising up from the subconscious.

You have made it through similar situations, and you should trust that you will make it through this situation too. Rely on your senses, as there is not enough clarity available to rely on logical decisions. Allow your intuition to guide you, knowing that it is ok not to have all the answers and to surrender a degree of trust to the universe.

**Reversed:** The Moon card represents blocked intuition, regaining composure, releasing fear, self-deception, subsiding anxiety, truth, and unveiling secrets.

You cannot see the whole truth or the whole picture, and so things may not be what they seem. Take care to find out as much as you can, and put the rest down to trusting in the universe to send you signs that you can use your intuition to interpret for guidance.

**Symbolism:** The Moon is a symbol of intuition, dreams, and the subconscious. It dimly lights the path to higher consciousness in the background between the two towers. The pool in the foreground represents the subconscious mind.

The crayfish crawling out of the pool symbolises the early stages of consciousness unfolding. The dog and the wolf howling at the moon represent the tamed and wild aspects of our minds, and the traditional versus the unorthodox.

## 19 The Sun

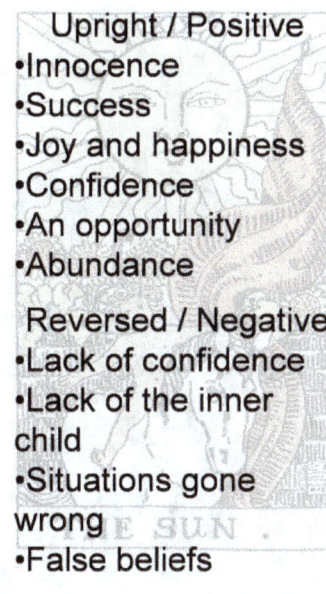

**Upright / Positive**
- Innocence
- Success
- Joy and happiness
- Confidence
- An opportunity
- Abundance

**Reversed / Negative**
- Lack of confidence
- Lack of the inner child
- Situations gone wrong
- False beliefs

Hebrew Letter
Resh

Astrological Sign
Sun

**Description:** The Sun card shows an infant riding on a white horse basking in the light of an anthropomorphised sun with sunflowers in the background. The conscious mind prevails over the fears and illusions of the subconscious. Innocence is renewed through discovery, bringing hope for the future.

**Upright:** The sun card represents energy, enthusiasm, fun, good luck, happiness, joy, light, openness, optimism, pregnancy, success, truth, and vitality.

Enjoy your success. No matter where you go or what you do, positive and radiant energy will follow. Things will get better. Trust what you are seeing. You are entering a period of positivity, playfulness, light, and joy.

You can manifest anything you want now. You can trust that you have the facts. You have clarity. Your positive energy will attract other positive energies. Enjoy this time and make the most of it.

**Reversed:** The Sun card represents a lack of confidence, a lack of the inner child, an exciting event or situation gone wrong, an opportunity on the horizon, anticipating celebration, conceitedness, disappointment, ego, emotional abundance, excessive excitement, false beliefs getting in the way, feeling weak, financial abundance, grandiose expectations, lack of joy, oppression, over-optimism to a fault, pessimism, pretending to be happy, and temporary pessimism.

Overcome negative feelings. Negativity repels positive energies away from you, which is the opposite of what you need. Hold on to positive energy and use it to repel negative energies away from you. Seek clarity in gaining all the facts. Trust that things can get better.

**Symbolism:** The Sun represents accomplishment, clarity, confidence, creative life force, energy, faith, happiness, a happy home, illumination, instinct, life, a new venture or project, self-expression, strength, and willpower. The child represents life, simplicity, innocence, purity, and wholeness.

The horse represents freedom, movement, and power. The sunflowers represent growth, beauty, strength, loyalty, and longevity. The red flag represents the blood of renewal. The wall in the background represents boundaries, security, and protection.

## 20 Judgment

**Upright / Positive**
- Wake-up call
- Crossroads in life
- Life-changing decision to be made
- A calling that cannot be ignored

**Reversed / Negative**
- Self-doubt
- Ignoring your inner calling
- Loss of opportunity
- Something not meant to be

**Hebrew Letter Shin**

**Astrological Sign Pluto**

**Description:** The Judgement card depicts a scene based on imagery of the Last Judgement, a concept found across the Abrahamic religions and Zoroastrianism, also known as the Final Judgement, the Day of Reckoning, Doomsday, etc.

**Upright:** The Judgement card represents a calling that cannot be ignored, a change of status, a final judgement, a fresh start, a great opportunity, a life-changing transformative decision to be made based on the past, a wake-up call, absolution, awakening, coming to a crossroads in life, decisiveness, forgiveness, homesickness, inner calling, rebirth, renewal, resurrection, rewards for past efforts whether good or bad, self-evaluation, and snap judgements.

You are learning from karmic lessons of the past. You now understand how to live to your fullest potential. Ignore gossip about you, and make sure you don't judge others. Focus on constructively and purposefully being the best version of yourself. A rebirth is taking place within you. A wider perspective becomes available.

**Reversed:** The Judgement card represents self-doubt, ignoring your inner calling, the loss of an opportunity, something that is not meant to be, or an outcome that is outside of one's control.

Do not ignore the call for change. Make the ultimate decision that needs to be made in order to be able to move forward. Know that it is never too late for chance, destiny, and fate to turn things around. Every day brings new opportunities for change for the better.

**Symbolism:** The Archangel Gabriel appears from the clouds blowing a great horn with a flag of St George the warrior saint hanging from it.

A group of people in the foreground are resurrected and standing with their arms up, looking up at the Archangel Gabriel in awe.

The coffins of those who are resurrected appear to be floating on waves of the sea, which is a reference to the Book of Revelation 20:13 in which the sea gives up its dead to be judged according to their deeds.

## 21 The World

**Upright / Positive**
- Completion
- Integration
- Accomplishment
- Full cycle
- Conclusion

**Reversed / Negative**
- Lack of personal closure
- Short-cuts
- Delays
- An unwelcome new beginning

**Hebrew Letter**
Taw

**Astrological Sign**
Saturn

**Description:** The World shows a woman in the centre wrapped in a purple cloth, encircled by a wreath. Like the Wheel of Fortune, the four creatures in each corner are an angel (Aquarius), an eagle (Scorpio), a lion (Leo), and a bull (Taurus).

**Upright:** The World card represents a desirable outcome, a sense of belonging, accomplishment, achievement, beginnings, completion, fulfilment, integration, physical or mental change, positive results, success, the end of a cycle and the beginning of a new one, travel, travel around the world, and wholeness.

Celebrate your achievements and prepare for what follows. Have faith in yourself, but do not set yourself goals that are impossible to achieve. The end of one thing is the beginning of something else. You have gone through lessons and are ready to graduate to the next level. You have the world at your feet.

**Reversed:** The World card represents an unwelcome new beginning, burden, disappointment, lack of achievement, lack of completion, lack of success, and stagnation.

As a cycle ends, focus your mind and energy on the new cycle that will follow, keeping in mind the lessons that you have learned along the way.

**Symbolism:** The woman at the centre of the card is Sophia, an ancient Hellenistic personification of wisdom, the sacred centre, and the Fifth Element. The purple cloth symbolises royalty and the authority of wisdom.

The wreath symbolises a continual cycle of successful completion. The wands represent the channelling of energy into manifestation, like the wand held by the Magician, the wands symbolise that what was manifested has now come to completion.

The woman steps through the wreath symbolising the completion of one phase and the beginning of another. The angel, eagle, lion, and bull in each corner symbolise the four classic elements, the four suits of Tarot, the four compass points, the four seasons, and the four corners of the universe.

## 7.2. The Minor Arcana

The Minor Arcana represent the trials and tribulations, the ups and downs, and the successes and setbacks that we experience on a daily basis. Although they are named as 'Minor', they can still have a significant impact. They provide insight into your present situation and what steps you may take in order to achieve your goals. The cards of the Minor Arcana have a temporal meaning that represents the energy moving through your life at the present moment, and this energy can change or be changed depending on the actions you take.

## 7.2.1. Wands

The Suit of Wands (also known as Staves etc.) is associated with the element of Fire, which symbolises action, passion, creativity, energy, and inspiration. This suit is often linked to career, ambition, personal growth, drive, and spiritual quests. Wands represent the spark of inspiration, the desire to create, and the courage to take action on one's goals and dreams.

**The Ace of Wands**

**Description:** A hand emerges from a cloud holding a wand, offering a new opportunity or idea and potential for growth.

**Upright:** The Ace of Wands represents a new opportunity, action, birth, bold ventures, boldness, conception, creativity, energy, enthusiasm, fertility, fertility of ideas, fun, good news, growth, inspiration, leadership, luck, new beginnings, new possibilities, passion, potential, renewal, talent, and travel.

Seize any creative ideas you have, and trust that you will manifest you desires. Move with passion, authenticity, and conviction, and you can achieve great things.

**Reversed:** The Ace of Wands represents boredom, delays, disappointments, feeling stuck, impotence, infertility, lack of passion, missed opportunity, slow movement, and sluggishness.

Do not miss out on the opportunity to begin something new. Find energy in a new project. Harness your creativity to make changes. If you are feeling stuck in a rut, getting excited about a new idea or a new beginning offers a way out. The pursuit of a new venture will bring growth.

**Symbolism:** The rich landscape symbolises growth. The wand symbolises the harnessing of vitality and willpower to manifest desires on the physical plane. The tiny branches and leaves on the wand symbolise growth.

The cloud symbolises the divine ether, from which inspiration springs forth. The castle in the distance represents the promise of opportunities to come. The hills and rolling peaks on the horizon represent challenges along the way, which can be overcome with effort.

## The Two of Wands

**Upright / Positive**
- Planning your next move
- Weighing up your options
- Choices to be made

**Reversed / Negative**
- More planning is needed
- Taking into account additional information
- Inner alignment needed

Element: Fire

Time: Days
Spiritual Action

Aries, Leo, Sagittarius

**Description:** A man dressed in a red robe and hat holds a small globe. The world is in his hands, with enormous potential in front of him if he expands his horizons. He stands within the grounds of his castle, contemplating opportunities and deciding on his next move. He has not yet left his comfort zone, still in the planning phases. The land in the background is fertile but rocky, promising a good chance for success, as long as he can overcome the challenges that will arise.

**Upright:** The Two of Wands represents anticipation, assessing one's life direction, balance, choices, contemplation, decisions, detachment, discovery, duality, future planning, inspiration, looking at your world and considering moving on, options, partnership (love or business), planning, progress, restlessness, the whole world opening up, waiting, and wanderlust.

You have two options to choose from. The grass is not always greener on the other side. Weigh everything into account before making decisions and avoid hasty actions. To make plans come true, hard work is needed.

**Reversed:** The Two of Wands represents cancelled travel, deciding against movement, fear of the unknown, indecisiveness, inner alignment, lack of planning, personal goals, restricted options, and staying put.

Now might not be the right time to make your next move, a little more planning may be needed to take into account all of the information that is available to you.

**Symbolism:** The wands either side of the man indicate two choices. The globe in the man's hand represents the world opening up to him, and charting his course and making plans for movement. The landscape in the background represents the vast potential that lies ahead, waiting to be explored and discovered. The red cloak symbolises energy, passion, and action.

In the foreground, on the bottom left of the card, the lily represents purity, while the rose represents passion. The tiny branches and leaves on the wands represent new growth. The wand on the right is anchored in position indicating a desire to stay put. The wand on the left is held by the man indicating a choice to break free.

**The Three of Wands**

Upright / Positive
- Groundwork
- Preparation
- Alliances and partnerships
- Planning the next stage

Reversed / Negative
- Overcoming fear and introversion
- Waiting for clarity
- Waiting for help
- Waiting for movement

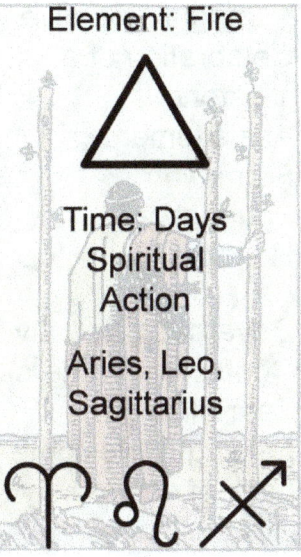

Element: Fire

Time: Days
Spiritual Action

Aries, Leo, Sagittarius

**Description:** The man in a red and green robe stands on a cliff with his back turned. Three wands stand planted firmly in the ground. He has left the comfort of his castle and is now looking over the vast open sea and mountains. From his high vantage point he can see all that lies ahead, including any challenges and opportunities.

**Upright:** The Three of Wands represents big plans, community, creativity, expansion, finding peace, groundwork, groups, growth, inspiration, luck, opportunities, patience, peace across the water, reaping the rewards of your efforts, teamwork, travelling, waiting and looking out for something, waiting for ships to come in, and waiting for someone or something that will help you on the next part of your journey.

Your plans are made and you have done the groundwork, but you may need to form alliances and work with others on your journey to achieving what you want.

**Reversed:** The Three of Wands represents bad leadership, having to work with others, lack of foresight, plans failing, unexpected delays, waiting for clarity, waiting for help, and waiting for movement.

Working with others or relying on others to help you may not seem like an ideal situation, particularly if you are introverted or struggle to form bonds and partnerships with others, but this is the only way you will be able to get to where you want to be. Overcome doubt by being honest about who you are and what you want.

**Symbolism:** The cliff represents a firm foundation, and a high vantage point, a strategic place from which to see all that lies ahead. The three tiny ships in the foreground represent movement and progression. The wands standing firmly in the ground symbolise important preparation and groundwork that has been laid leading up to this moment.

The green cloak suggests that the man and his endeavours are grounded. The man symbolises someone who has prepared and is now ready to explore new horizons and opportunities. The red cloak symbolises energy, passion, and action.

**The Four of Wands**

Upright / Positive
- Celebration of a milestone
- Achievement
- Formation
- Foundations
- Harmony

Reversed / Negative
- Conflict with others
- Fear of failure
- Feeling unwelcome
- Lack of community spirit

Element: Fire

Time: Days
Spiritual Action

Aries, Leo, Sagittarius

**Description:** Two happy people are dancing with flowers in their hands and celebrating an important milestone. In the foreground a wreath with blossom and grapes hangs between the four wands. In the background a group of people are standing in front of a large castle.

**Upright:** The Four of Wands represents belonging, celebration, formation, foundations, harmony, home celebration, inspiration, institutions, manifestation, order, peace, relocation, safety, satisfaction, security, stability, structure, success, and the home.

Celebrate what you have achieved with those who have helped you achieve it. You are reaching a milestone, physically, practically, or spiritually.

**Reversed:** The Four of Wands represents a need for belonging, attachment is holding you back, cancelled celebration or reunion, conflict with others, failure, feeling unwelcome, introversion holding you back, lack of community spirit, lack of success, leaving home, problems with teamwork, self doubt, the status quo, transition, and unhappy families.

Avoid conflicts as much as possible by making sure that those who have helped you reach this milestone are valued and appreciated

**Symbolism:** The four wands symbolise the foundation of a secure structure, like the four legs of a table. The roses hanging over the four wands represent passion, and are symbols of the cultivation, manifestation, blossoming, and fruition of ideas and aspirations.

The structure created by the four wands and the roses represent a passageway to protection, transition, success, and union. The castle in the background represents structure, strategy, security, and success on a grand scale.

The two people dancing represent the partnership that has been formed in order to achieve this milestone and success. The flowers they are holding represent beauty and happiness. The other group of people in the background represent friends and family who are celebrating their success with them. The two people have taken a moment out from the larger celebration to reflect on their achievements.

**The Five of Wands**

Upright / Positive
- Conflict
- Tension
- Disagreements
- Fights
- Competition

Reversed / Negative
- Avoidance of conflict
- Being overworked
- Dishonest tactics
- Inner conflict
- Drained energy after a struggle

Element: Fire

Time: Days
Spiritual Action

Aries, Leo, Sagittarius

**Description:** Five figures are entangled in a violent confrontation, each of them having a wand, stave, or staff that they are using as a weapon. There is no clear winner, and so the conflict rages on and on.

**Upright:** The Five of Wands represents challenges, change, chaos, competition, conflict, creative tension, destabilisation, disagreements, fights, instability, loss of balance, struggles, obstacles, petty squabbles, spontaneity, uncertainty, and vying for attention.

Active competition, conflict, or tension has made you feel challenged, and you are having to fight to keep your position or standing. Standing firm, fighting your corner, and speaking up for yourself may actually help you grow. Engage constructively with the challenge rather than avoiding it.

**Reversed:** The Five of Wands represents a favourable solution, an avoidance of conflict, being overworked, dishonest tactics, envy, feeling unworthy, fighting for affection, inner conflict, jealousy, lack of faith, major quarrels, tension, and the end of a struggle.

The conflict may be over, but all energies are drained, and the cause of the conflict has not been fully resolved. A retreat from conflict may also be a retreat from competition in which you have the potential to grow.

**Symbolism:** The five fighting figures represent movement and collision, conflict and competition, challenge and struggle, creative tension, disorganisation and disruption.

They are representative of either multiple persons in a conflict or multiple aspects of one person who is experiencing a conflict within themselves.

The clashing of staves symbolises the clashing together of opposing ambitions, creative ideas, dreams, emotions, expressions, feelings, primal energies, and relationships.

The ground around the five people has been disturbed and muddied by the conflict, indicating how the conflict has affected foundations around them.

**The Six of Wands**

Upright / Positive
- Achievement
- Glory
- Harmony
- Reward
- Success

Reversed / Negative
- Delays
- Validation not forthcoming
- Feeling unsupported
- Frustration
- Insecurity

Element: Fire

Time: Days
Spiritual Action

Aries, Leo, Sagittarius

**Description:** A man in a red robe triumphantly rides a white through a victory parade, holding aloft a wand decorated by a wreath or laurel of recognition. Other figures in the background are holding aloft wands in support.

**Upright:** The Six of Wands represents accolades, achievement, communication, consistency, cooperation, equality, glory, harmony, healing, peace, progress, recovery, a reward for good work, sincerity, solving, success, victory, and winning an award.

The Six of Wands is a highly positive and uplifting card which symbolises the achievement of a goal or triumph after overcoming challenges and obstacles. This is a time of success, recognition, and achievement. Success is in reach or is already happening.

Take pride in your accomplishments and savour the rewards of your hard work. You are on the right path and others notice and appreciate your efforts. Celebrate your victory, but remain humble and focused on your next steps.

**Reversed:** The Six of Wands represents delays, a dip in confidence, external validation not forthcoming, feeling overlooked, feeling unsupported, frustration, insecurity, lack of recognition, recognition may not come as expected, self doubt, and success not yet fully realised.

You feel overlooked, unrecognised, or less confident than you would like. This could be a temporary setback, a lack of external validation, or doubts about your achievements.

Reassess your focus on external praise and find satisfaction in your internal journey and progress. You may be putting too much value on external approval. Do not be tempted to give in to false pride or overconfidence.

**Symbolism:** The laurel wreath represents recognition and reward for achievements. The wands that are held aloft in the background represent the recognition and support of others. The horse's covering is green, which represents flourishing energy. The man's red cloak symbolises energy, passion, and action.

**The Seven of Wands**

Upright / Positive
- Standing your ground
- Defensiveness
- Being on your guard
- Overcoming obstacles

Reversed / Negative
- Avoiding conflict
- Fear of failure
- Feeling overwhelmed
- Reassessing your approach

Element: Fire

Time: Days
Spiritual Action

Aries, Leo, Sagittarius

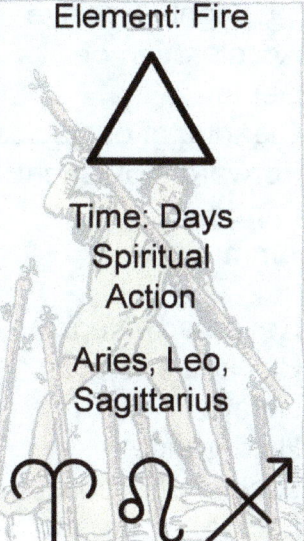

**Description:** A man is standing on higher ground, holding a staff or stave in a defensive stance. Six other wands are pointed at him from the lower ground. He is being attacked on all sides.. The man appears ready to defend his position.

**Upright:** The Seven of Wands represents being in control, being on top of the situation, being on your guard, challenges, competition and rivalry, conflicts, defence, defending your position, defiance, determination and perseverance, feeling defensive, knowing where you want to go, opposition, overcoming challenges, overcoming obstacles, and standing your ground.

Stay firm and stand your ground. You are in a situation where you must defend your ideas, goals, or boundaries. Be courageous and assertive. Fight for what matters to you.

You may be facing challenges or opposition, but with persistence you can prevail. Be strong and keep pushing forward, even when it seems like the odds are against you. Defend what you have earned and what you believe in.

**Reversed:** The Seven of Wands represents avoiding conflict for fear of failure, challenges too great to overcome, defences not being strong enough, feeling overwhelmed, giving up, lack of confidence, pressure of competition, pressure of opposition, self-doubt.

You feel overwhelmed, outnumbered and unsupported, needing to gather strength and resources to regain control. You may need to reassess whether or not it is worth maintaining your stance, continuing to fight, or whether a different approach altogether is needed.

It may be time to let go or shift your approach. Alternatively, you may be the person who is being too defensive or too aggressive.

**Symbolism:** The man's shirt is green, which represents flourishing energy. His tights are orange, which represents initiative and pride. His defensive posture suggests he is in a position of vulnerability. His elevated position suggests that he has an advantage over his attackers or competitors, but that he must remain vigilant and maintain his ground.

**The Eight of Wands**

| Upright / Positive | | Element: Fire |
|---|---|---|
| •Acceleration of events | VIII | △ |
| •Clearing of obstacles | | Time: Days |
| •Forward movement | | Spiritual Action |
| •Important communication | | |
| Reversed / Negative | | Aries, Leo, Sagittarius |
| •Blocked energy | | |
| •Delays | | ♈ ♌ ♐ |
| •Hinderance | | |
| •Lack of direction | | |
| •Lack of progress | | |

**Description:** Eight wands are depicted flying through the air with great speed. The landscape is vast and open and there appear to be no obstructions.

**Upright:** The Eight of Wands represents acceleration of events, clearing of obstacles, enthusiasm, enthusiastic energy, events unfolding faster than expected, excitement, forward movement, being free from hindrances, important communication, increased momentum, rapid exchange of information, rapid movement, speed, swiftness of action, travel, and journeys.

Embrace the momentum and act swiftly. You may be receiving important news or communication that will push things forward. If you have been waiting for something to happen, this card is a sign that things are moving quickly and your goals and projects are progressing. Take advantage of this fast-moving energy and make your next move with confidence.

**Reversed:** The Eight of Wands represents blocked energy, delays, feeling slowed down, feeling stuck, hindrance, lack of direction, lack of progress, miscommunication, missed opportunities, stagnation, things slowing down, unclear communication, and unexpected obstacles.

Things are slowing down or facing delays. You may be feeling frustrated because things are not progressing as you expected. It might also signify a miscommunication or missed opportunities. Reassess the situation and look for alternative ways to get things back on track.

**Symbolism:** The flying wands represent swift action and movement, momentum is building, events are rapidly accelerating. The background landscape which is mostly open sky represents a path cleared of all obstacles. The tiny branches and leaves on the wand that symbolise growth, symbolise that the wands are all moving in the same direction.

The number eight represents balance, strength, and infinity. It can also symbolise the idea of cyclical motion, the idea that momentum builds and continues, like an endless loop of progress. In this context, the number eight suggests that the current momentum is not a fleeting moment, but that it can continue to grow and accelerate.

**The Nine of Wands**

Upright / Positive
- Perseverance
- Resilience
- Inner strength
- Enduring adversity
- Still standing strong

Reversed / Negative
- Exhaustion
- Feeling overwhelmed
- Letting your guard down
- Lack of boundaries

Element: Fire

Time: Days
Spiritual Action

Aries, Leo, Sagittarius

♈ ♌ ♐

**Description:** The Nine of wands depicts a wounded warrior with a bandage on his head. He is still standing strong and alert, and holding a wand as though ready for a defensive or supportive action.

**Upright:** The Nine of Wands represents: perseverance, staying strong and enduring, resilience, inner strength, and strength in the face of adversity, even when the road has been long and hard.

You may be feeling weary or worn out from ongoing struggles but don't give up just yet. You are nearing the end of the battle, and your continued effort will lead to success.

You are facing challenges or have been through a tough time, but you are in a position to stay strong and finish what you have started. Even if you are tired or feeling defeated, hold firm and continue pushing forward.

You are nearly at the finish line, and your efforts will soon be rewarded. The toughest part of the journey is often right before the breakthrough.

**Reversed:** The Nine of Wands represents: exhaustion, being unable to continue, feeling overwhelmed, and not having the energy to keep going. It may also symbolise letting your guard down and having a lack of boundaries where you may have failed to protect yourself or your achievements.

You may be experiencing a burnout, or a situation where you are fighting battles that are no longer worth fighting.

You may feel like giving up or that you're no longer able to cope with the stress or challenges in your life. You may be overly defensive or struggling with your boundaries, either pushing yourself too hard or being too guarded.

You may need to re-evaluate whether it's worth continuing a particular battle or if it's time to step back, recover, and rest before moving forward.

**Symbolism:** The bandage on the wounded warrior's head symbolises physical hardships. The eight other wands stand behind him, symbolising past battles or struggles overcome.

# The Ten of Wands

**Upright / Positive**
- Burdens
- Excessive commitments
- Taking on too much
- The weight of responsibility

**Reversed / Negative**
- Burnout
- Asking for help
- Taking a break
- Giving up
- Letting go

Element: Fire

Time: Days
Spiritual Action

Aries, Leo, Sagittarius

**Description:** The man is hunched over struggling to carry a heavy burden or weight of responsibility symbolised by ten wands.

**Upright:** The Ten of Wands represents burdens, carrying a heavy load, carrying too much, excessive commitments, exhaustion, feeling oppressed, feeling overwhelmed, hard work, loss of perspective, near completion, procrastination, stress, struggling, taking on too much, the end of a cycle, and the weight of responsibility.

You are feeling overwhelmed, stressed, and exhausted due to taking on too many responsibilities. You have been working hard, but the effort is starting to feel unsustainable. Re-evaluate your commitments, prioritise your tasks, and seek support from others. You are nearing the end of a challenging project or phase, but you must find a way to release some of the burdens you are carrying.

**Reversed:** The Ten of Wands represents burnout, considering asking for help, considering taking a break, delegating responsibilities, giving up on something that has been weighing you down, letting go of burdens, lightening your load, overcoming a burnout, and stress beginning to ease.

You may be beginning to unload or let go of some of the burdens you have been carrying. This can be a positive sign that you are learning to delegate, release stress, or simply live your life. It could also mean that you are avoiding responsibility or neglecting important tasks, and you may need to find a balance between offloading and making sure your commitments are being met.

**Symbolism:**

The ten wands symbolise the weight of responsibility, the many tasks that have been accumulated, excessive obligations, tasks, duties, or personal challenges. The desolate and open landscape represents a sense of isolation, as though the man is alone and shouldering the burden alone.

The path the man is walking on suggests that they are close to the end of the journey, even if they are struggling.

**The Page of Wands**

Upright / Positive
- New location
- New journey
- Ambition
- Creative potential
- Wishful dreaming

Reversed / Negative
- Delays
- Feeling blocked
- Feeling uninspired
- Immaturity
- Recklessness

Element: Fire

Time: Days
Spiritual
Action

Aries, Leo, Sagittarius

**Description:** The Page of Wands is depicted as a young figure holding a staff, standing with an air of excitement and curiosity. High energy is at play, fresh ideas, sparks of inspiration and new adventures are announced.

**Upright:** The Page of Wands represents a new location, a physical journey, ambition, creative potential, drive, energy, excitement about life and work, inspiration, new movement, relocation (work or home), resourcefulness, restlessness, wanting change, wishful dreaming, working with nature or earth, youth, and youthful enthusiasm.

You may be feeling inspired or ready to pursue a new path, and the Page encourages you to take action. Embrace your curiosity and be open to new experiences.

It's time to explore new ideas, start a creative project, or take an adventurous leap. Move forward with confidence and excitement.

**Reversed:** The Page of Wands represents delays, feeling blocked, feeling uninspired, immaturity, jumping into something too quickly, lack of direction, lack of enthusiasm, lack of following through, lack of motivation, lack of preparation, recklessness, starting things without finishing them, and struggling to take a first step towards something new.

You are feeling stuck or uninspired and your creative energy and passionate energy is blocked. You may be rushing into something without fully considering the consequences.

Take time to plan and ensure you're moving forward in a grounded way, rather than rushing in without direction. Refocus and rekindle your creative spark and take action with more preparation.

**Symbolism:** The wand represents the page's creative energy, ambition, and drive to explore new opportunities. The desert or open landscape symbolises new horizons and the freedom to explore. It is a space that feels boundless, indicating unlimited possibilities.

**The Knight of Wands**

Upright / Positive
- Hastiness
- Risk taking
- Bold actions
- Confidence
- Drive and ambition

Reversed / Negative
- Acting too quickly
- Impulsiveness
- Inability to finish projects
- Fading enthusiasm
- Restlessness

Element: Fire

Time: Days
Spiritual Action

Aries, Leo, Sagittarius

**Description:** The Knight of Wands is depicted riding a horse, holding aloft a wand. The horse is galloping forward energetically. The vast open landscape appears to be the desert, with three pyramids on the horizon.

**Upright:** The Knight of Wands represents a hasty adult, a person who is inspiring but not reliable, adventurous, an adventurous risk taker, driving too fast, following passions, life on the edge, manual work, motion, movement, new ideas, relocation of work or home, taking chances, total commitment, travel, and working outside.

Take bold action towards your goals. You are full of energy, ready to face new challenges. Now is the time to move forward with enthusiasm. You are motivated and have the drive to pursue new projects, ideas, or adventures. You may feel particularly confident in inspiring others. Harness the energy and charge ahead.

**Reversed:** The Knight of Wands represents acting too quickly, acting without thought, fading enthusiasm, fear of commitment, impulsiveness gone awry, inability to finish what has been started, jumping into things, lack of commitment to a project, lack of direction, lack of follow-through, lack of planning, and loss of energy.

Impulsive decisions are leading to confusion and disruption. Restless energy is scattered amid lack of focus, hastiness, and burnout. You are facing frustration and difficulty in following through on your ambitions. Pause and refocus. Avoid acting in haste. Take time to reflect before committing to new plans or goals. There is a need for more contemplation before taking your next big step.

**Symbolism:** text

The Knight's yellow cloak represents the energy of the sun, transformation, and passion. The horse represents stability and reliability. The stature of the horse represents stamina and strength.

The red feathers on his armour represent the flame of life and passion. The three pyramids in the distance represent goals and obstacles to overcome.

**The Queen of Wands**

Upright / Positive
- Balancing energy
- Wisdom and understanding
- Confidence
- Creativity
- Power

Reversed / Negative
- Difficult asserting oneself
- Exhaustion
- Self-doubt
- Over-extension of oneself

Element: Fire

Time: Days
Spiritual Action

Aries, Leo, Sagittarius

**Description:** The Queen of Wands depicts a Queen on her throne with a regal and commanding presence, holding a staff in her right hand, and a sunflower in her left hand. She has a black cat at her feet. The legs of her throne represent lions. The back of her throne also depicts two lions.

**Upright:** The Queen of Wands represents balancing passionate energy with wisdom and understanding, confidence, creativity, an embracing personality, emotional intelligence, empowerment, feminine energy, fiery energy, inner-strength, inspiration, intuition, leading with compassion, mastery of inner fire, nurturing, and personal power.

Take charge. Be confident. Embrace your passion. Stand in your power. Trust your intuition. Express your creativity and energy freely. Lead with warmth, confidence, and authenticity. You are capable of manifesting your desires and inspiring others along the way.

**Reversed:** The Queen of Wands represents burnout, difficulty asserting yourself, exhaustion, feeling blocked, insecurities, lack of balance, lack of confidence, lack of inspiration, over-extension of oneself, recklessness, self-doubt.

You are not fully tapping into your inner strength. You may be struggling with self-esteem and confidence. You have a sense of being out of balance. You are over-extended or frustrated by a lack of direction in creative projects or leadership roles.

You may also be feeling disconnected from your passions or unable to express your true self in the way you would like. Take a step back, regain your inner composure, and restore your confidence before moving forward.

**Symbolism:** The sunflower with its tall sturdy stem represents strength, resilience, and vitality. The black cat represents untamed energy and untapped potential. The lions represent the element of fire, courage, leadership, vitality, and justice. The queen's golden robes symbolise strength and inner fire burning with great intensity.

**The King of Wands**

Upright / Positive
- Clear sense of direction
- Bold actions
- Confident leadership
- Creativity
- Drive

Reversed / Negative
- Acting too hastily
- Domineering behaviour
- Impulsive leadership
- Lack of clarity
- Overconfidence

Element: Fire

Time: Days
Spiritual
Action

Aries, Leo, Sagittarius

**Description:** The King of Wands sits on his throne with a strong regal posture. The throne is decorated with lions and lizards. There is also a lizard in the foreground. He holds a staff in his hand.

**Upright:** The King of Wands represents a clear sense of direction, bold action, confident leadership, creativity, drive, fire energy, inspiration, inspiring others, maturity, passion, personal charisma, strategic thinking, visionary leadership, and wisdom.

It is time to step into your power. Take leadership over your life and boldly pursue your goals. Be confident in your decisions and inspire others around you with your vision and energy. You are ready to take on a leadership role.

You are being called to harness your creativity and strategic thinking to manifest your goals. Lead with confidence. Trust in your vision. Move forward without hesitation.

**Reversed:** The King of Wands represents acting too hastily, burnout, disconnection from original vision, domineering behaviour, ego-driven behaviour, impulsive leadership, lack of clarity, lack of direction, lack of focus, lack of guiding wisdom, overconfidence, recklessness, and struggling to regain control.

You may be overestimating your abilities or trying to lead without sufficient planning which could lead to mistakes or setbacks. You are feeling unmotivated and disconnected from your passions, or struggling with impulsiveness and lack of control.

Pause, re-evaluate your plans and ensure that your actions align with your long-term vision. Avoid being too domineering or controlling.

**Symbolism:** The lions decorating the back of the throne represent the element of fire, courage, leadership, vitality, and justice. The lizards biting their tails are versions of the Ouroboros, an ancient symbol representing eternal cyclic renewal.

The lizard at the King's feet represents transformation and renewal. The King's red robe represents earthly wisdom and passion. His crown represents status and honour.

## 7.2.2. Cups

The Suit of Cups (also known as Chalices, etc.) is associated with emotions, relationships, intuition, and the subconscious. Cups are linked to the element of Water, which represents fluidity, change, and the depths of feeling. The Suit of Cups invites exploration of your emotional world, your connections with others, and how you navigate the realms of love, desire, and inner fulfilment.

**The Ace of Cups**

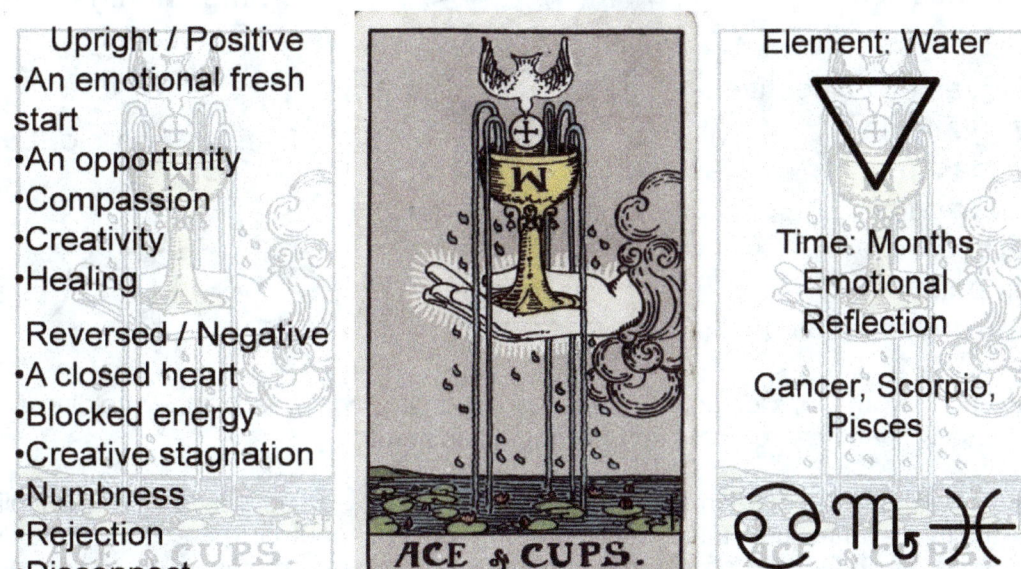

Upright / Positive
- An emotional fresh start
- An opportunity
- Compassion
- Creativity
- Healing

Reversed / Negative
- A closed heart
- Blocked energy
- Creative stagnation
- Numbness
- Rejection
- Disconnect

Element: Water

Time: Months
Emotional Reflection

Cancer, Scorpio, Pisces

**Description:** A hand emerges from a cloud holding a chalice which is overflowing with five streams of water. A dove descends towards the chalice holding in its beak the Eucharist. Below is a pool with water lilies.

**Upright:** The Ace of Cups represents an emotional fresh start, an opportunity, blessings, blossoming of love (familial or romantic), compassion, creativity, deepening connections, growth, healing, inner guidance, inspiration, intuition, loving energy, opening the heart, rejuvenation, and renewal.

An emotional or spiritual breakthrough is on the horizon. Embrace the emotional flow that is coming your way.

**Reversed:** The Ace of Cups represents a closed heart, blocked energy, creative stagnation, difficulty accessing deeper feelings, emotional blockage, emotional numbness, emotional rejection, spiritual disconnect, stifled potential, and unrequited love.

Direct your love and creativity inward. Before you can care for others you need to care for yourself. Find a way to gradually open up emotionally to those around you.

**Symbolism:** The white dove symbolises peace, and the gift of divine inspiration and wisdom. The cup represents the seat of the emotions and the soul. The five streams of water overflowing from the cup represent the five senses. The colour grey represents cosmic wisdom. The 'M' on the chalice represents the divine mother, which upside-down has become the 'W' of the womb, representing a bountiful spring of fertility and inspiration. The cloud from which the hand emerges represents the heavens. The emerging hand represents the giver of the wisdom of the gods. The water lilies symbolise spiritual awakening.

**The Two of Cups**

Upright / Positive
- Balance
- Choices
- Collaborations
- Compatibility
- Friendships
- Harmony

Reversed / Negative
- Arguments
- Breakup
- Separation
- Disharmony
- Imbalance
- Misunderstandings

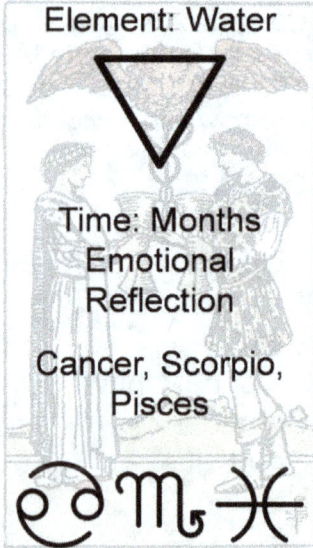

Element: Water

Time: Months
Emotional Reflection

Cancer, Scorpio, Pisces

**Description:** The Two of Cups depicts a man and a woman facing each other holding a cup each. Above them is the winged head of a red lion holding a caduceus.

**Upright:** The Two of Cups represents balance, choices, collaborations, compatibility, deep connection, duality, everlasting, friendships, harmony, love, mutual attraction, mutual respect, partnership (love or business), reciprocated emotions, romance, soul mates, trust, understanding, and union.

You are entering into or currently experiencing a deep and fulfilling connection with someone. Whether it is a romantic relationship, friendship, or business partnership, it is based on mutual respect, understanding, and shared values. It is a time of emotional alignment and harmonious exchanges. The Two of cups is often interpreted as a 'soul mate' card in love readings, indicating that a romantic relationship is blossoming or reaching a new level of harmony. If you are in a relationship, it suggests that both partners are emotionally in tune with one another and that the relationship is likely to be balanced and supportive.

**Reversed:** The Two of Cups represents arguments, breakup or separation, breakups, disconnection, disharmony, emotional breakdown, emotional disconnect, imbalance in a relationship, incompatibility, inequality, lack of emotional connection, misunderstandings, unhappiness, and unhealthy partnerships.

There may be misunderstandings, a breakdown in communication, or a feeling of disconnect between two people who were once in sync. It can also symbolise an imbalance of how emotions are being exchanged or a lack of mutual respect. One partner is giving more than the other or there is a lack of mutual understanding, resulting in emotional distance, unreciprocated feelings, or an unequal power dynamic in a partnership. A partnership is not functioning as it should. This may be resolved by taking time out to discuss the matter, for both sides to be heard and understood, and for emotions to be realigned and resynchronised.

**Symbolism:** The two cups represent emotional exchange. The caduceus is a symbol of healing and transformation. The winged red lion symbolises strength, loyalty, courage, and deep emotional bonds. The background is serene and peaceful, representing calm and balance.

**The Three of Cups**

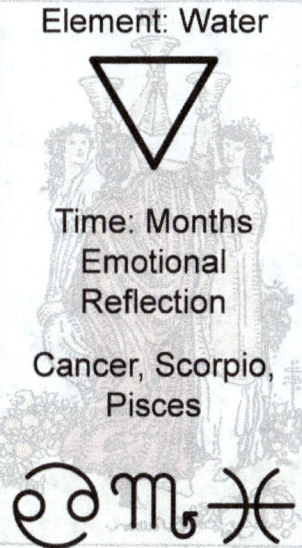

Upright / Positive
- Celebration
- Happiness
- Successful collaboration
- Connection with others

Reversed / Negative
- Conflict
- Disharmony
- Overindulgence
- Tension
- Unhealthy group dynamics

Element: Water

Time: Months
Emotional Reflection

Cancer, Scorpio, Pisces

**Description:** Three women are dancing together in harmony. Their arms are raised holding cups, indicating that they are toasting their success and celebrating together. Around them are many flowers, vines, and fruits.

**Upright:** The Three of Cups represents a sense of community, a time of happiness, celebration, collaboration, connection with others, emotional fulfilment, emotional support, friendship, joy, milestones, shared values, social connections, social opportunities, spiritual celebration, support, and teamwork.

Celebrate and embrace joyful moments. Nurture your friendships and relationships. Embrace community and collective support. Express gratitude and appreciation.

Let go of negative energy and embrace harmony. Share your successes with others. Focus on positive and uplifting energy. Balance individuality and community. Enjoy the present moment.

**Reversed:** The Three of Cups represents blocked energy, conflict, disharmony, excessive partying, isolation, lack of celebration, lack of emotional fulfilment, loneliness, overindulgence, relationship issues, social issues, tension, unhealthy group dynamics.

Pay attention to any imbalances or tensions in your relationships and social circles. Resolve conflicts, re-evaluate unhealthy connections, or avoid excessive socialising that masks deeper emotional issues.

Seek meaningful, supportive connections rather than staying isolated or engaged in unhealthy dynamics. Focus on emotional healing, balancing your social life, and nurturing your true friendships. Restore harmony and joy to your life.

**Symbolism:** The three women symbolise unity, cooperation, and collective joy. They are dancing in a circle, symbolising interconnectedness and equality. The cups symbolise emotional fulfilment, shared love, and the exchange of positive energy. The cups are raised toward one another, symbolising an act of mutual support, celebration, and connection. The lush greenery represents relationships in full bloom, abundance, and vitality.

## The Four of Cups

Upright / Positive
- Apathy
- Disinterest
- Disconnection
- Emotional contemplation
- Numbness

Reversed / Negative
- Opening up
- Emerging from withdrawal
- Gained clarity
- Re-engaging with the world

Element: Water

Time: Months
Emotional Reflection

Cancer, Scorpio, Pisces

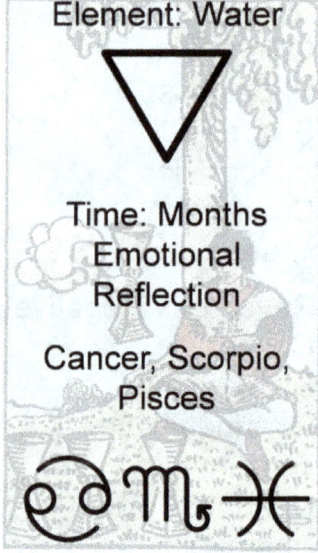

**Description:** A man sits under a tree with arms folded and legs crossed. He appears apathetic, discontent, disengaged, and in a state of emotional contemplation. He appears to be looking at the three cups on the ground in front of him. A hand appears from a cloud and offers the man a fourth cup, but he has either not noticed it yet, or he is disinterested.

**Upright:** The Four of Cups represents apathy, boredom, contemplation, disconnection, discontent, disinterest, dissatisfaction with what is being offered, everyone else is having a better time than you, introspection, missing out, numbness, quiet reflection, rejecting or ignoring offers, self-reflection, solitude, and withdrawal.

You may be feeling emotionally unfulfilled or disconnected. This could be due to boredom, apathy, or a sense that something is missing from your life, but you're unsure what it is. Re-evaluate what you truly want, both from others and from yourself. Take a step back, reflect, and focus inwardly to figure out what will bring you true emotional fulfilment.

**Reversed:** The Four of Cups represents beginning to engage again, beginning to open up, emerging from withdrawal, gained clarity, gratitude and acceptance, letting go of apathy, new opportunities, opening up to new opportunities, and re-engaging with life.

You are beginning to open up to new opportunities or you are starting to emerge from a period of emotional withdrawal. You are beginning to engage with the world around you again, or you have gained clarity about what you truly desire emotionally. Open up to new opportunities. Let go of apathy. Remind yourself to be grateful for what you have and notice blessings around you. Recognise the value of the opportunities or gifts you have received.

**Symbolism:**

The three cups on the ground in front of the man symbolise past emotional experiences which the man is reflecting on. The cloud from which the fourth cup is appearing represents the Ace of Cups, representing a second chance. The tree under which the man is sitting represents a shelter in the wilderness. The hill that the tree and the man are sitting on indicates peace and an opportunity for reflection from a higher perspective.

**The Five of Cups**

Upright / Positive
- Chaos
- Conflict
- Disagreements
- Disappointment
- Sorrow
- Uncertainty

Reversed / Negative
- Acceptance
- Emotional healing
- Recovery
- Forgiveness
- Regaining hope

Element: Water

Time: Months
Emotional Reflection

Cancer, Scorpio, Pisces

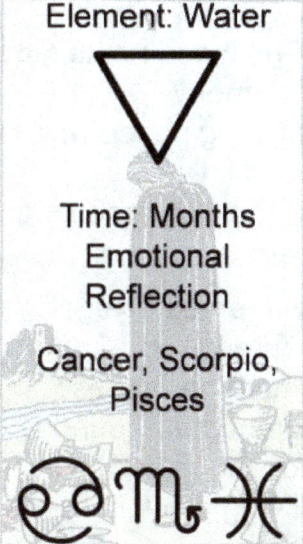

**Description:** A figure wearing a dark cloak stands in the foreground looking mournfully over three cups lying on their side empty, while two cups remain standing upright behind him. In the background there is a bridge over the river leading to a small keep.

**Upright:** The Five of Cups represents changes, chaos, conflict, disagreements, disappointment, dwelling on the negative, feeling let down, instability, loss, obstacles, regret, sadness, self pity, sorrow, tears, and uncertainty.

You may be feeling disappointed or regretful about something that has not worked out as you'd hoped. You may be focused on what has been lost, but two of the cups are still upright. Recognise what you still have.

**Reversed:** The Five of Cups represents a shift in perspective, acceptance of what has happened, emotional healing, emotional recovery, forgiveness, healing, letting go of regret, moving forward after a period of grief or disappointment, recognising what it still available to you, regaining hope, releasing lingering sadness or regret, and shifting focus to the positive.

You are beginning to move past the sorrow or regret that you have been carrying. You are starting to recognise the opportunities that are still available to you, learning how to focus on what remains, rather than what has been lost. Stop ruminating on past mistakes or failures. Instead of continuing to grieve, accept that certain things are out of your control and that it's time to re-evaluate where you are at, and consider moving forward somehow.

**Symbolism:** The person mourning symbolises loss, disappointment, and regret. Their back is turned to the two cups that remain standing, which represent what is still available and untouched. The remaining two cups indicate a sense of hope, new opportunities, or that remaining support that has not yet been lost or forgotten. All is not lost. The three spilled cups represent emotional pain, a sense of loss, disappointment, and unfulfilled expectations. The spilled liquid symbolises emotions that have been wasted or spilled as though they cannot be reclaimed. The liquid in the cups, usually water, symbolises emotions that are flowing, changeable, and capable of being replenished. The river nearby symbolises the potential replenishment of the water.

**The Six of Cups**

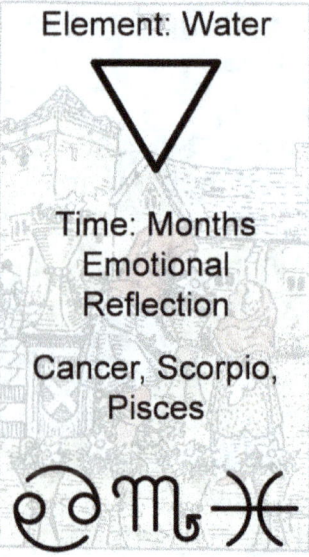

Upright / Positive
- Childhood nostalgia
- Harmony
- Making peace with the past
- Resolving emotional issues

Reversed / Negative
- Unresolved emotional issues
- Emotional wounds not yet healed
- Being stuck in the past

Element: Water

Time: Months
Emotional Reflection

Cancer, Scorpio, Pisces

**Description:** A boy has six large cups full of blossoms. In a gesture of kindness, he gives one of the cups to a young girl. In the background a watchman is walking away.

**Upright:** The Six of Cups represents childhood, communication, consistency, cooperation, focusing on the positive past, harmony, healing, help, kindness, making peace with the past, nostalgia, progress, recovery, remembering the past, resolving emotional issues, sentimentality, sincerity, and the past.

The past is influencing your present emotions. It's time for reflection on past experiences in the form of happy memories, nostalgia, or reconnecting with someone or something from your past.

Reflect on your past but do not become stuck there. If you are longing for 'the good old days' it might be helpful to remember the positive lessons learned from those times. The present is where you can make new memories and experiences.

**Reversed:** The Six of Cups represents being stuck in the past, difficulty finding closure, difficulty in reconnecting, emotional wounds not fully healed, holding on too tightly to the past, missing an opportunity for emotional healing, old ways of thinking, past experiences are hindering your present growth, past relationships or events, refusing to let go of attachments, revisiting past trauma, stuck in nostalgia, the past dominating the present, and unsolved emotional issues.

You are holding on too tightly to the past, and past experiences are hindering your present growth. There may be some unresolved emotional issues related to past relationships or events that need to be resolved before you can move forward.

**Symbolism:** The boy represents our helpful nature, and a display of love and affection. The girl represents the part of us that accepts help from others. Her white mitten represents purity and innocence. The children together represent our childlike qualities as we grow up.

The watchman walking away in the background represents the coming together of the two children is taking place outside of the hustle and bustle of normal adult life. The blossom in the cups represents the affection between the two children, and spiritual growth.

**The Seven of Cups**

**Upright / Positive**
- Assessment
- Choices
- Challenges
- Contemplation
- Lost in fantasy
- Illusions

**Reversed / Negative**
- Breaking free from illusions
- Clarity
- Focus
- Confronting reality
- Realistic choices

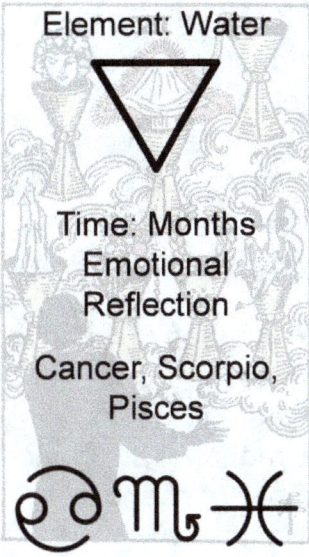

Element: Water

Time: Months
Emotional Reflection

Cancer, Scorpio, Pisces

**Description:** A man looks up at seven cups containing different symbols or objects representing various possibilities or desires, such as wealth, fame, love, and spiritual growth, among others.

**Upright:** The Seven of Cups represents assessment, challenges, choices, conflict, contemplation, distorted view of yourself or others, drugs & alcohol, faith, getting lost in fantasy, ideas, illusions, indecision, individuality, inspiration, knowledge, not feeling things in a clear way, obstacles, opposition, reflection, so many choices, spirituality, study, and wisdom.

While there are many paths ahead, it is important to approach choices with caution and clarity. You might be feeling overwhelmed by many possibilities or decisions, but you need to decide what is right for you.

Do not be influenced by illusions or by unrealistic ideal outcomes. Not all options are as good as they seem. It is tempting to escape your current situation by fantasising about an ideal life or unattainable dreams. While it is good to be optimistic and ambitious, do not become too disconnected from reality. Be wary of choices that are based too much on fantasy or wishful thinking.

**Reversed:** The Seven of Cups represents breaking free from illusions, clarity and focus, confronting reality, disappointment, focusing on practicality, grounding in reality, learning from experience, letting go of illusions, looking for what is feasible and achievable, making a choice, moving past indecision, narrowing down options, regret or letdown, regrets, seeing things more clearly, and taking meaningful action.

The confusion and illusion you have been experiencing is beginning to clear. You are beginning to make more grounded and realistic choices. Let go of any illusions that kept you from taking meaningful action. A choice that seemed appealing at the time turned out to be less fulfilling than expected.

**Symbolism:** The contents of the cups from left to right, top to bottom are: The head of Venus (The Empress), a veiled person (The High Priestess), a snake (representing Mercury or The Magician), a castle (Mars, The Tower), a collection of jewels (Jupiter, The Wheel of Fortune), a wreath (Saturn, The World), a winged dragon (The Sun, symbol of fire and strength).

**The Eight of Cups**

Upright / Positive
- Leaving something behind
- A journey inwards
- A quest for something deeper
- A symbolic journey

Reversed / Negative
- Anxiety
- Afraid to let go
- Emotional avoidance
- Fear of change
- Hesitation

Element: Water

Time: Months
Emotional Reflection

Cancer, Scorpio, Pisces

**Description:** A figure is walking away from eight stacked cups in a desolate and mountainous setting. They are leaving behind emotional attachments or achievements that no longer provide fulfilment, looking towards the horizon, and searching for something new or a desire for personal evolution.

**Upright:** The Eight of Cups represents a decision to leave something behind, a journey inward, a quest for something deeper, a symbolic journey, disappointment, emotional healing, emotional withdrawal, feeling stagnant and unfulfilled, leaving a job, leaving a relationship, leaving behind the familiar to seek out the new, letting go of what you have outgrown, personal growth, realigning with emotional or spiritual needs, realisation that something is no longer working, searching for greater emotional fulfilment, searching for something more authentic, seeking something more, seeking spiritual satisfaction, self discovery, something missing, and the desire to walk away.

You may need to leave behind something emotionally draining or no longer aligned with your values. A period of introspection is necessary, and you are on the verge of making a life change, a decision to move on, looking for something deeper.

**Reversed:** The Eight of Cups represents anxious about seeking something new, being afraid to let go, clinging to something that no longer serves you, emotional avoidance, fear of change, hesitation to move forward, and not confronting necessary changes.

Fear of change is causing you to hesitate. You may be holding on to something that no longer serves you, feeling afraid of letting go to seek something new. You may be avoiding confronting emotional issues that point to a need to re-evaluate your situation and make changes.

**Symbolism:** The sun, which represents conscious and logical thought, is being eclipsed by the moon, which represents deep subconscious emotions. The sun and the moon are aligned in a solar eclipse, symbolising a powerful coming together and unity of the conscious and the subconscious. The red clothes indicate the power and bravery that it takes for the figure to make such a move. The river represents a journey of the emotions, and the depth of emotional changes that the figure needs to go through in order to look for something new. The way the cups are stacked is such that there is a gap along the top row, which visually symbolises that there is something missing.

**The Nine of Cups**

Upright / Positive
- Wishes coming true
- Enjoying success
- Celebrating
- Desires being met
- Emotional balance
- Feeling thankful

Reversed / Negative
- Fleeting satisfaction
- Unsustainable success
- Emotional emptiness
- Unrealistic expectations

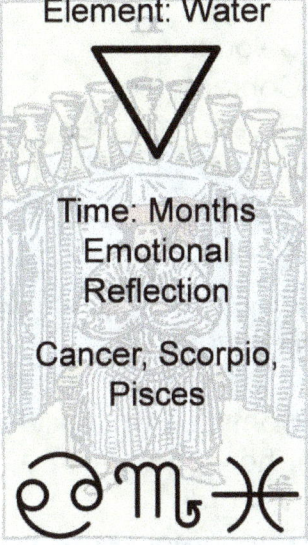

Element: Water

Time: Months
Emotional Reflection

Cancer, Scorpio, Pisces

**Description:** A man sits happy and contented in front of nine cups arranged in an arc. His posture reflects satisfaction, comfort, and success. He is surrounded by emotional or material rewards for all his hard work, and he is able to enjoy them.

**Upright:** The Nine of Cups represents a wish coming true, being able to enjoy success, celebration, desires being met, emotional balance, emotional fulfilment, emotional needs being met, emotional satisfaction, enjoying what you have achieved, feeling thankful, fulfilment, gratitude, happiness, reward for hard work, satisfaction, security, and wish fulfilment.

You are experiencing a time of personal satisfaction or will soon experience a wish coming true. Your emotional needs are being met and you are in a good place in terms of emotional balance. You are feeling emotionally fulfilled, happy, and secure. It's a time to enjoy what you have achieved and feel thankful for it.

**Reversed:** The Nine of Cups represents disappointment, discontentment, dissatisfaction, excess, expectations not met, false sense of fulfilment, fleeting satisfaction, outward success but emotional emptiness, overindulgence, overlooking the deeper aspects of happiness, satisfaction through unhealthy means, something still missing in life, success pursued too intensely, unrealistic expectations, and unsustainable satisfaction.

You may be expecting more than what is realistically achievable, which may lead to dissatisfaction or disappointment if your expectations aren't met. Emotional satisfaction may be present, but it could be fleeting or unsustainable if pursued too intensely, through unhealthy means, or at the expense of other things that are important to you. Although outwardly successful, you feel that there is still something missing. You could be overlooking the deeper aspects of happiness.

**Symbolism:** The man in the Eight of Cups is the opposite of the Seven of Cups, because rather than walking away from his cups, he is proudly displaying them. His crossed arms represent confidence. He embraces the cups given to him. The man's red hat is a symbol of passion and vitality. The man's robe is white which commonly represents purity, but in the case of this man's proud outward display of his cups, it also represents pride and a healthy amount of confidence. The cups arranged in an arc behind the man symbolise a toast to his success.

## The Ten of Cups

**Upright / Positive**
- Belonging
- Contentment
- Dreams realised
- Emotional fulfilment
- Happy family life and home

**Reversed / Negative**
- Relationship challenges
- Conflict with family or household
- Discord
- Temporary setbacks

**Element: Water**

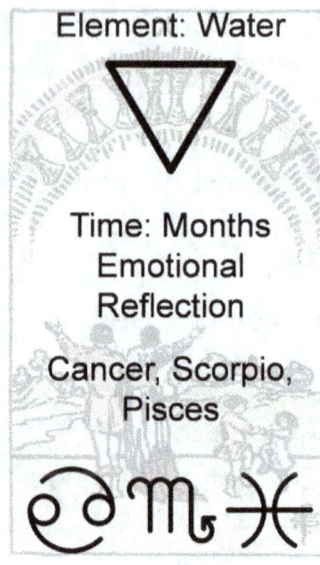

Time: Months
Emotional Reflection

Cancer, Scorpio, Pisces

**Description:** A happy family of a couple and two children stand under a rainbow with ten cups overhead, and everyone appears happy.

**Upright:** The Ten of Cups represents a sense of belonging, contentment, dreams realised, emotional fulfilment, happy family life, harmonious relationships, harmony, lasting joy, long-term happiness, love, love within the home, loving family dynamic, security, the pinnacle of happiness and success, and unity.

You feel secure and fulfilled in your connections with others. There is a sense of unity and love within the home. Your emotional dreams, especially those related to family and relationships, are coming true. You may feel that you have reached the pinnacle of happiness and success in these areas of your life, this kind of happiness is deep and lasting.

**Reversed:** The Ten of Cups represents challenges in relationships, conflict within the family or household, difficulty, dreams not fully manifested yet, emotional isolation, family discord or disharmony, good appearances on the surface, lack of emotional connection, miscommunication, relationship discord or disharmony, something is missing in relationships, temporary setbacks and disruptions, tension, unfulfilled emotional needs, and unresolved issues.

You may feel that something is missing in your relationships, even if things appear to be good on the surface. There may be a lack of emotional connection or satisfaction. More effort or work may be needed to align your current situation with your vision of happiness and fulfilment.

Temporary setbacks may bring about a period of tension or difficulty, but it is not necessarily permanent. There are still challenges to overcome, but the potential for joy and happiness remains as a long-term goal.

**Symbolism:** The rainbow represents emotional promise, renewal, and fulfilment. The red clothes symbolise power, passion. The blue clothes represent tranquillity, intuition, and spirituality. The red and blue clothes combined represent the union and harmony of the heart and the mind. The scene in the background represents happiness and growth.

## The Page of Cups

Upright / Positive
- Creative inspiration
- Outside your comfort zone
- Emotional growth
- Exploring your dreams

Reversed / Negative
- Acting impulsively
- Being taken advantage of
- Difficulties expressing emotion
- Unrealistic dreams

Element: Water

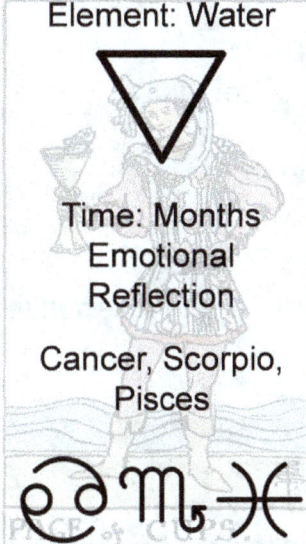

Time: Months
Emotional Reflection

Cancer, Scorpio, Pisces

**Description:** The page of cups is depicted as a young figure holding a cup with a fish emerging from it. He is dressed in a blue tunic decorated with flowers, red tights, and yellow boots.

**Upright:** The Ten of Cups represents creative inspiration, emotional experiences outside your comfort zone, emotional growth and learning, exploring your dreams, listening to your feelings, messages of love or affection from another person or from within yourself, new possibilities, openness to new emotional experiences, self-expression, trusting your intuition.

You are in a place where you are open to exploring and expressing your emotions, or you may encounter someone who is sensitive, caring, and expressive. A period of creative flow or a spark of inspiration may be coming your way, urging you to express yourself through art, music, or some other creative outlet. Trust your intuition and listen to your feelings. Explore your dreams, as they may be providing you with valuable insights or guidance.

**Reversed:** The Ten of Cups represents acting impulsively without considering the consequences, being taken advantage of, challenges with creativity or intuition, difficulties with emotional expression, difficulty accessing creative energy, disconnected from your artistic or imaginative side, emotional blockages, emotional immaturity, emotional manipulation, emotional repression or confusion, emotional vulnerability, finding it hard to express your true feelings, finding it hard to manifest your ideas, ignoring your inner voice, immaturity or naivety, lack of inspiration, lost in unrealistic dreams or fantasies, missing important emotional insights or guidance, and struggling to connect with emotions.

You may be struggling to connect with your emotions, or finding it hard to express how you truly feel. There may be a lack of inspiration or difficulty accessing your creative energy. Avoid acting impulsively without thinking of the consequences. In your emotionally sensitive and vulnerable state, take care not to allow others to take advantage of you.

**Symbolism:** The Page represents light heartedness and a relaxed nature. The fish emerging from the cup symbolises happiness and creativity emerging from the subconscious. The sea in the background represents fluidity, our ranging emotions, and the way in which water nourishes our spirit of creativity and our deepest dreams. The tunic is decorated with water lilies which symbolise beauty emerging from deep, dark, and damp places.

## The Knight of Cups

**Upright / Positive**
- Changes in love
- A shoulder to cry on
- A romantic opportunity
- An idealised romantic hero

**Reversed / Negative**
- Avoiding responsibility
- Unrealistic fantasies
- Creative blockages
- Imbalance of energies

Element: Water

Time: Months
Emotional Reflection

Cancer, Scorpio, Pisces

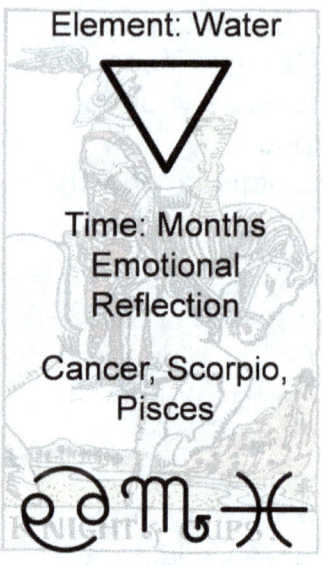

**Description:** The Knight of Cups is riding on horseback holding a cup. The horse is in motion suggesting that the Knight is on a quest or journey driven by his emotions. He is approaching a stream that he is about to cross, leading to a more mountainous landscape on the right. His armour is adorned with red fish, and his helmet and boots are decorated with wings.

**Upright:** The Knight of Cups represents a change in love affairs, a danger of being lost in a dream personality, a good shoulder to cry on, a marriage proposal, a romantic opportunity, addiction of emotions, adventure, an idealised hero of romance and sensuality, being able to play any role, creative love, creative or dramatic activity, difficulty in sustaining new loves, emotional interaction, following one's heart, lost excitement, love, romance, rush of emotions and drama, and the 'knight in shining armour'.

Take steps forward to what you desire the most, whether it relates to love, creative pursuits, or personal growth.

**Reversed:** The Knight of Cups represents avoiding taking responsibility for emotions, being swept away by unrealistic fantasies, creative blockages, distortion or imbalance in energies, emotional confusion, emotional escapism, emotional immaturity, emotional needs not met, emotional unreliability, failing to follow through on romantic gestures or commitments, feeling uninspired, impracticality of emotional pursuits, lack of direction, misunderstandings, not being honest about feelings, offering promises that cannot be kept, over-idealisation, refusal to deal with difficult emotions, running from feelings rather than confronting them, struggling to connect with emotions, and unattainable dreams.

Reassess your emotional approach. Be wary of unrealistic expectations and getting swept away in emotional idealism which may lead to misunderstandings or disappointment.

**Symbolism:** The Knight appears pensive and peaceful, in a dreamy contemplative state. His horse represents motion and movement. The river in the background represents emotional fluidity and intuition.

**The Queen of Cups**

Upright / Positive
- A safe emotional space
- Compassion
- Emotional balance
- Empathy
- Replenishing energy

Reversed / Negative
- Drained emotional energy
- Clouded judgement
- Emotional manipulation
- Lack of self-care

Element: Water

Time: Months
Emotional Reflection

Cancer, Scorpio, Pisces

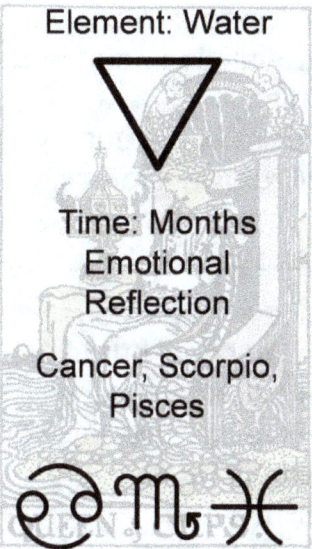

**Description:** The Queen of Cups sits on her throne which is on the shore close to the water. She holds a special ornate cup with two angels guarding the contents.

**Upright:** The Queen of Cups represents a safe emotional space, calm, compassion, creative expression, deep connection to feelings, emotional balance, emotional guidance, emotional intelligence, emotional stability, emotional understanding, empathy, introspection, mastery of one's emotional realm, nurturing, offering support and care to others, replenishing emotional reserves, self-care, self-nurture, serenity, and spiritual healing.

Trust your intuition and emotional insights to guide you in making decisions that align with your heart. You may be called upon to offer emotional support to others. Take care however not to neglect your own emotions and emotional needs. Keep your emotional energy replenished and topped up.

**Reversed:** The Queen of Cups represents absorbing the emotions of others, clouded judgement, confusion, difficulty setting emotional boundaries, drained energy, emotional imbalance, emotional manipulation, emotionally adrift, emotions running high, failure to take time needed to nurture yourself, feeling depleted, feeling emotionally drained, heightened emotional sensitivity, lack of emotional clarity, lack of self-care, out of touch with inner wisdom, overwhelming emotions, putting others first and neglecting yourself, and struggling to manage feelings in a healthy way.

You may be feeling overly sensitive or drained by your emotions. You may be so focused on others that you have neglected your own emotional wellbeing. You may be allowing others to manipulate you emotionally, using your emotional sensitivity to their advantage. Take time out to recharge yourself.

**Symbolism:** The Queen symbolises connection with inner emotions and the subconscious. The Queen's cup is unique in design, larger than normal, and the only cup that is closed, representing the vastness of the soul and the inherent mystery of our inner consciousness. The cup's handles symbolise two angels guarding the cup's contents, this is a reference to the Ark of the Covenant, a divine container guarded by angels, connecting the cup with the mysterious and the divine. The throne is a shade of grey, which symbolises the Queen's unbiased nature. The two figures on the top of the throne are naiads (water nymphs) who symbolise keeping your inner child alive and listening to your dreams and your subconscious.

**The King of Cups**

Upright / Positive
- Balancing heart and mind
- Care and empathy
- Creative expression
- Compassionate leadership

Reversed / Negative
- Emotional burdens
- Lack of compassion
- Overwhelmed by emotions
- Emotional suppression

Element: Water

Time: Months
Emotional Reflection

Cancer, Scorpio, Pisces

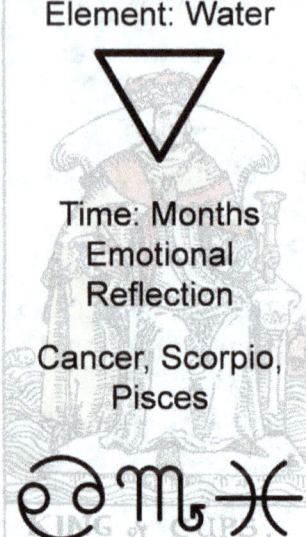

**Description:** The King sits on his throne which is floating on the sea. On the left a fish jumps out of the water. On the right a ship is sailing past in the background. The King is holding an unadorned cup and a shortened sceptre.

**Upright:** The King of Cups represents balancing heart and mind, care and empathy, compassionate leadership, creative expression, emotional calm and understanding, emotional intelligence, emotional maturity, emotional support, emotional support and guidance, harmony, inner wisdom..

You may be called upon to handle complex or difficult emotional situations with calm and understanding. The King represents a compassionate and wise leader, counsellor, mentor who provides emotional support. If the King represents you, then you may be called upon to support others with care and empathy.

**Reversed:** The King of Cups represents challenges to emotional control, difficulty maintaining emotional balance, emotional burdens of others, emotional instability, emotional manipulation, emotional outbursts, lack of compassion or empathy, lack of emotional control, lack of emotional support, overwhelmed by emotions, refusing to acknowledge true feelings, secrecy or deception about feelings, struggling to manage feelings, suppressing emotions, unhealthy emotional boundaries, and withdrawal.

You may be feeling overwhelmed by emotions and struggling to manage feelings in a healthy way. Take care not to allow others to use your emotional sensitivity and compassion to their own advantage.

**Symbolism:** The King is relaxed and level-headed, ruling through compassionate dialogue rather than with an iron fist. The King's throne is miraculously floating on the ocean, symbolising freedom from guilt and virtue floating to the surface. On the left a fish is jumping out of the water symbolising a spark of creativity. On the right in the background there is a ship sailing across the sea, which represents exploring one's emotions, and the manifestation of the creativity embodied by the fish on the left. The King's cup is not ornate like the Queen of Cups, representing humbleness even from a position of power. The King's sceptre is the source of his authority, it is shortened to represent limiting one's power and to avoid ambition, the checks and balances of power.

## 7.2.3. Swords

The Suit of Swords is associated with the mind, intellect, communication, and conflict. Swords are linked to the element of Air, which represents the mind, thoughts, learning, knowledge, and curiosity. The Suit of Swords deals with thoughts, ideas, reasoning, decision-making, and the challenges or struggles that arise in mental and verbal exchanges. Swords are associated with logic, truth, and the ability to cut through illusions or confusion to reach clarity.

**The Ace of Swords**

Upright / Positive
- A breakthrough
- A revelation
- A truth about to come to light
- Cutting through confusion

Reversed / Negative
- Misinformation
- Confusion
- Dishonesty
- Illusions
- Mental blockages
- Miscommunication

Element: Air

Time: Weeks
Intellectual Communication

Gemini, Libra, Aquarius

**Description:** A hand appears from a cloud offering a sword with a crown on top, decorated with leaves. The sword is surrounded by six flames or specks of gold. The hand is glowing and radiant. The background landscape is vast and open.

**Upright:** The Ace of Swords represents a breakthrough, a revelation, a truth about to come to light, an idea, an insight, conflict or challenge, cutting through confusion, cutting away of illusions, defending yourself, important decisions, innovation, intellectual power, justice and righteousness, mental clarity, mental or verbal confrontation, precise thinking, sharp thinking, standing up for what is right, the ability to reason, the arrival of truth, the birth of new ideas or concepts, truth and justice.

You may receive an important piece of information that helps to clear confusion, or gain courage and clarity to speak your truth. A fresh start in intellectual pursuits and communication is needed.

**Reversed:** The Ace of Swords represents being clouded by misinformation, confusion, difficulty in expressing thoughts, dishonesty, illusions, mental blockages, and miscommunication.

There may be mental blockages or difficulty in expressing your thoughts. You may feel clouded by misinformation or illusions. Take time to re-examine matters and come to a clear conclusion.

**Symbolism:** The hand emerging from a cloud represents the giving of a gift. The sword represents intellect and thoughts. The crown at the top of the sword represents the regality of the sword. The plants emerging from the crown are laurels which celebrate the authority of the sword. The six drops of gold around the sword represent the divine spark of the sword. The mountains in the background suggest that even after gaining the sword, the road ahead will still be rough.

# The Two of Swords

**Upright / Positive**
- Balancing thoughts or emotions
- Caught between opposing forces
- Fear of uncertainty
- Mental stalemate

**Reversed / Negative**
- Avoidance of a decision
- Mental confusion
- Overwhelmed by choices
- Resisting decisions

Element: Air

Time: Weeks
Intellectual
Communication

Gemini, Libra, Aquarius

**Description:** The Two of Swords depicts a figure sitting blindfolded with their arms crossed, holding up a sword in each hand. The figure has a small white spot on their forehead.

**Upright:** The Two of Swords represents a need for clear thinking, a need to retreat inwards, avoiding making a decision, balance, balancing thoughts or emotions, being unsure of which path to take, caught between two opposing forces, choices, choosing to ignore a situation out of fear or uncertainty, equilibrium, facing a difficult choice or decision, feeling divided or torn between two opposing options, feeling stuck or uncertain, indecision, inner tension, mental conflict, mental stalemate, reluctance to face the truth, the importance of finding balance.

You are at a crossroads or facing a difficult choice. Weigh the pros and cons carefully before making any decisions. You need mental clarity. Avoiding or procrastinating will not solve the problem. Emotional balance and calm is needed to move forward.

**Reversed:** The Two of Swords represents avoidance of a decision, avoiding making a choice, being forced to make a choice, inability to make a decision, mental confusion, overwhelmed by choices, refusal to acknowledge the truth of a situation, resisting decisions.

You feel overwhelmed by the choices in front of you. There is a refusal to acknowledge the truth of a situation. You are forced to make a choice that you are resisting or avoiding. No one and nothing else can make the choice for you. Take yourself away from the situation and seek a calm mental balance in order to make the choices you need to make.

**Symbolism:** The blindfold represents the power of the mind not being limited to sight and sense perception, and making an unbiased decision. The swords represent the choice being made, each option being weighed up and thought over.

The white spot on the figure's head represents the spiritual third eye which the person is looking from, relying solely on their intelligence. The water in the background represents the subconscious, and the deep psyche that the person's intelligence is rooted in. The crescent moon symbolises the subconscious, hopes and dreams, and the psyche.

# The Three of Swords

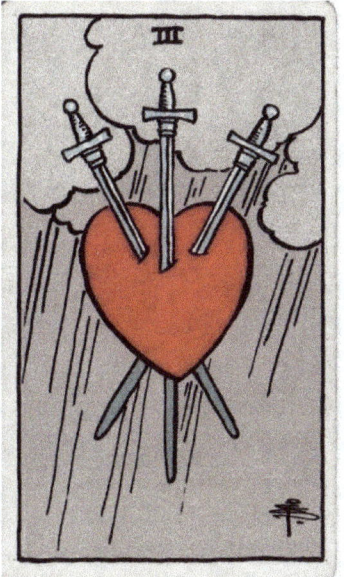
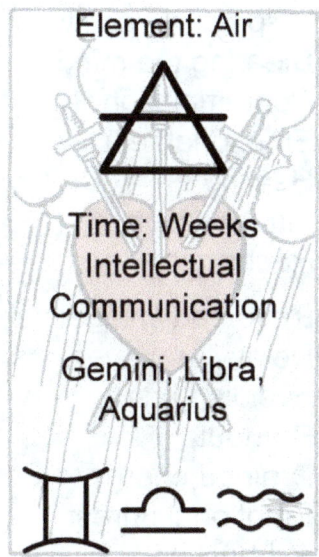

**Upright / Positive**
- Betrayal
- Breakup
- Conflict between heart and mind
- Heartbreak and loss
- Painful experiences

**Reversed / Negative**
- Suppression and denial of emotions
- Beginning emotional recovery
- Lingering emotional wounds

Element: Air

Time: Weeks
Intellectual Communication

Gemini, Libra, Aquarius

**Description:** A heart is pierced by three swords, against a backdrop of rain and storm clouds.

**Upright:** The Three of Swords represents betrayal, breakup, coming to terms with pain, conflict between the heart and the mind, confronting your sorrow, confusion, difficult truths, disappointment, divorce, emotional heartache, emotional pain, emotional release, emotional turmoil, emotional wounds, grief, harsh realities, heartbreak, loss, loss of a loved one, mental anguish, negative thinking, overwhelming emotional thoughts clouding judgement, painful experiences, painful realisations, rejection, sadness, separation, something important to you is now gone, sorrow, the end of a phase of life, the end of a relationship.

Face and process your emotions in order to heal. The feeling and acknowledging of pain is a necessary part of emotional recovery. Allow yourself time and space to process your emotions in order to move through the pain and eventually heal.

**Reversed:** The Three of Swords represents a need for further healing, a period of healing or recovery after emotional pain, avoiding dealing with pain, denial or suppression of painful emotions, and lingering emotional wounds.

The worst of the heartache is behind you and you are starting to move on. Lingering emotional wounds still need further healing, especially if you are holding on to the pain or avoiding dealing with it. You may be suppressing painful emotions or denying them altogether.

After you have grieved and mourned at the loss of something or someone, you may find yourself grieving at the loss of the sadness you have carried for something or someone all this time, as it is an indication that you are healing and moving forward.

**Symbolism:** The stormy sky represents sorrow and conflict that comes with emotional pain. The swords represent the sharpness of pain and the cutting nature of the truth, often suggesting betrayal or mental anguish.

**The Four of Swords**

Upright / Positive
- Clearing the mind
- Contemplation
- Emotional rest
- Healing
- Introspection
- Recharging

Reversed / Negative
- Delay in recovery
- Avoiding rest
- Burnout
- Drained energy
- Emotional unrest
- Exhaustion

Element: Air

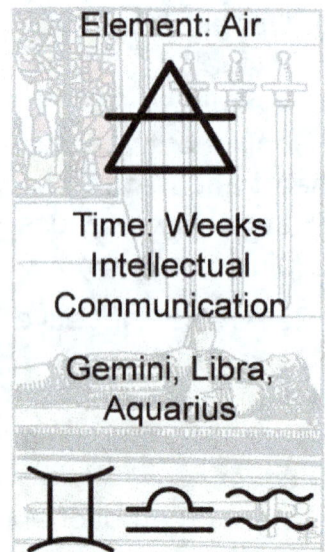

Time: Weeks
Intellectual
Communication

Gemini, Libra, Aquarius

**Description:** A coffin is adorned with an effigy of a prone figure of a knight in a state of prayer or meditation. Three swords are mounted on the wall while a fourth is mounted on the side of the coffin. A stained glass window above the knight depicts a scene of a blessing, with the word 'pax' depicted above the head of the figure on the left who is giving the blessing.

**Upright:** The Four of Swords represents a need for mental clarity, clearing the mind, contemplation, convalescence, distancing oneself to gain perspective, emotional rest, healing, introspection, meditation, mental clarity, mental rest, recharging mental and physical energy, recovery, recuperation, reflection, rejuvenation, rest, restoration, retreat, stepping back temporarily, taking a break, taking a step back, and withdrawal.

Rest and recuperation is needed in order to heal. Take a break from the mental and physical stresses of life. You are exhausted and overwhelmed and need to pause and regain your strength before moving forward. Introspection and meditation is needed for clarity and renewal.

**Reversed:** The Four of Swords represents a delay in recovery, avoiding rest, burnout, drained energy, emotional unrest, exhaustion, lack of mental clarity, lack of perspective, overworking, reluctant to relax, resisting rest, self-neglect, unwillingness to take time to recover.

You may be resisting rest or not taking the necessary time for healing, even though you may be feeling burnt out and exhausted. You are avoiding taking a break, and you are overworking yourself and neglecting the need for mental or physical recovery. There is only so much you can do before you need to switch off. You may be delaying rest and recovery for fear of what might emerge from your subconscious during such a period of introspection.

**Symbolism:** The three swords symbolise the hardships that the knight faced while he was alive, while the fourth represents the knight's singular focus and effort to overcome those hardships. The stained glass window above the knight represents a blessing, and fragmentation yet unity.

Above the head of the figure on the left who is giving the blessing, the word 'pax' is inscribed (Latin for 'peace') and represents the blessing of peace depicted in the image, also symbolising that the knight is now blessed and at peace.

**The Five of Swords**

Upright / Positive
- Cruel victory
- Conflict
- Loss of integrity
- Mental cruelty
- Unethical tactics
- Power struggles

Reversed / Negative
- Retreat from conflict
- Dishonesty
- Lingering negativity and tension
- Resolution of a conflict

Element: Air

Time: Weeks
Intellectual Communication

Gemini, Libra, Aquarius

**Description:** A man stands in the foreground holding two swords in his left hand, and standing one sword on the ground with his right hand. A further two swords lay on the ground, belonging to two figures who are standing in the background looking out to sea. It is the aftermath of a conflict or confrontation.

**Upright:** The Five of Swords represents a cruel victory, a win-at-all-costs mentality, altercations, arguments, being outmanoeuvred, being taken advantage of, betrayal, competitive situations turning ugly, conflict, confrontation, deceitful actions, defeat, disagreements, dishonesty, hollow victory, humiliation, lack of integrity, loss, loss of integrity, loss of respect, loss of trust, mental cruelty, negative consequences, outward success and inward guilt, power struggles, questioning the validity of victory, shame, tension, the cost of victory, underhand tactics, underhanded success, unethical tactics, victory at others' expense, winning but losing something more valuable.

Reflect on the situation and choose your battles carefully. Walk away from unnecessary fights to avoid further damage.

**Reversed:** The Five of Swords represents a retreat from conflict, attempting to move on from a situation, dishonesty, lingering negative effects of a dispute, lingering tension, resolution of a conflict.

You are trying to make amends or repair relationships after a disagreement. There may be unresolved feelings of betrayal and guilt.

**Symbolism:** The man in the foreground is holding the majority of the swords and he is smiling, looking pleased with himself. He has defeated the other two figures, and is possibly contemplating attacking them while their backs are turned.

The two men in the background are walking away defeated. They are unaware that the man in the foreground is considering attacking them again. They represent loss, melancholy, and defeat. The two swords on the ground belong to the two figures walking away, representing their defeat and loss. The water in the background represents the subconscious which the two figures in the background are looking at and reflecting upon.

## The Six of Swords

**Upright / Positive**
- A healing journey
- Movement towards a better place
- Moving on
- Personal development

**Reversed / Negative**
- Difficulty moving forward
- Mental or emotional stagnation
- Unwillingness to face changes

Element: Air

Time: Weeks
Intellectual
Communication

Gemini, Libra, Aquarius

**Description:** A group of people are in a boat crossing the calm waters. Six swords stand upright in the boat. They are headed towards a distant shore in the background.

**Upright:** The Six of Swords represents a healing journey, a necessary journey, emotional or psychological healing, escaping difficulties, finding calmer waters, finding a way to heal, healing, moving forward, moving on, moving past emotional pain, moving towards better days, pursuing personal development, recovery, recovery from past trauma, relocation or travel, seeking new perspectives, transition.

You are moving way from difficult times towards a more peaceful and stable future. It may be a physical move, an emotional shift, or a mental process of letting go.

Although the journey is not easy, it is necessary for your growth and well-being. Be assured that things are improving and you are on the right path. Embrace the change and trust that moving forward is the right path.

**Reversed:** The Six of Swords represents being stuck, difficulty moving forward, mental or emotional stagnation, obstacles or unresolved issues holding you back, resistance to change, unwillingness to face changes.

You may be resisting change or having difficulty moving on from a past situation. While you may be trying to move on, there are unresolved issues and obstacles slowing your progress and holding you back.

**Symbolism:** The crossing of calm waters represents the move away from chaos or turbulence to a more peaceful and stable place.

The distant shore symbolises hope, healing, and the promise of a new beginning. The swords in the boat represent the mental and emotional baggage that is being carried on the journey.

## The Seven of Swords

**Upright / Positive**
- Deception
- Dishonesty
- Sneaky tactics
- Getting away with something
- Broken trust

**Reversed / Negative**
- A desire to make amends
- Confessing guilt
- Regret
- Facing up to wrongdoing

**Element: Air**

Time: Weeks
Intellectual
Communication

Gemini, Libra, Aquarius

**Description:** A man is moving in one direction while looking in another. He is walking on his toes and carrying five of the swords while two remain standing in the ground.

**Upright:** The Seven of Swords represents acting in a self-serving way, an easy way out, an indirect or unconventional approach, avoidance of accountability, avoiding confrontation, avoiding the truth, betrayal, broken trust, carelessness, deceit, deception, dishonesty, escaping confrontation, evasion, getting away with something, hidden truth, leaving something behind, manipulative behaviour, recklessness, self-deception, sneaky behaviour, stealth, strategy overcoming obstacles, trickery, underhanded tactics, unethical means.

There is deception and dishonesty, and someone (maybe you) is avoiding the truth or using underhanded tactics to try and get away with something. Be careful of someone trying to deceive you, or deceiving yourself about something.

Strategic thinking, discretion, seeking clarity, and obtaining all the facts will bring this to light. Deceit and dishonesty can lead to negative consequences, especially in relationships or situations that require trust.

**Reversed:** The Seven of Swords represent a desire to make amends, confessing guilt or regret, deception and dishonesty exposed, facing up to wrongdoing, guilt, owning up to something, regret, someone covering their tracks, and truth coming to light.

The truth is coming to light. Deception and dishonesty will be exposed. Someone (maybe you) is ready to stop hiding the truth and face a situation openly. There is a desire to make things right or confess to wrongdoing, or someone may be covering their tracks to avoid being caught.

**Symbolism:** The man looking around tip-toeing forward while looking back represents furtive behaviour, secrecy, and sneakiness. His red shoes represent passion and that his emotions have outweighed his intellect.

The tents in the background represent civilisation. The five swords in his hands and two remaining in the ground represent carelessness and leaving evidence of his theft behind him.

**The Eight of Swords**

**Upright / Positive**
- Caged in one's thoughts
- A mental cage of one's own making
- Self-imposed limitations

**Reversed / Negative**
- Breaking free
- Confronting fears
- Dissolving illusions
- Gaining clarity
- Overcoming anxieties

Element: Air

Time: Weeks
Intellectual Communication

Gemini, Libra, Aquarius

**Description:** A woman stands bound and blindfolded surrounded by a cage of swords with water trickling around her feet. She appears to be trapped and hopeless. In the background stands a castle.

**Upright:** The Eight of Swords a sense of paralysis, anxiety, being restricted by one's own mindset, confinement, confusion, fear, feeling helpless or powerless, feeling trapped, frustration, imagining the worst, limitation, mental bondage, mental entrapment, mental struggles, negative thought patterns, negative thoughts, obscured truth, over thinking, pessimism, restrictions, and self-imposed limitations.

You are experiencing mental or emotional imprisonment. You may feel trapped, restricted or helpless, but a way out is possible. Your imprisonment may be self-imposed and created by fear. Re-evaluate your mindset and recognise that limitations might not be as insurmountable as you first thought.

**Reversed:** The Eight of Swords represents beginning to break free, confronting fears, dissolving illusions, gaining clarity, letting go of over thinking, liberating oneself from mental restrictions, moving towards mental freedom, overcoming anxieties, overcoming mental confusion, seeing a way out.

You are starting to break free from the mental restrictions or anxieties that have been holding you back. You are gaining clarity and beginning to see a way out of a difficult situation. Confront and overcome your fears or self-imposed limitations. You are ready to let go of negative over thinking and make decisive choices.

**Symbolism:** The bindings around the woman represent limitations in thought; however these bindings are visibly escapable, indicating that mental limits can be overcome through self-realisation. The eight swords around the figure represent a cage, as if she is imprisoned in their own thoughts, which represents a need for her to reclaim herself from self-delusion.

The woman's red clothing symbolises her passion and zeal. The water around the woman's feet represents the woman's connection to her subconscious. Although she is trapped, she still has the power of her mind available to set herself free. The castle represents a protective structure in stark contrast to the cage of swords around the woman which are of her own making.

**The Nine of Swords**

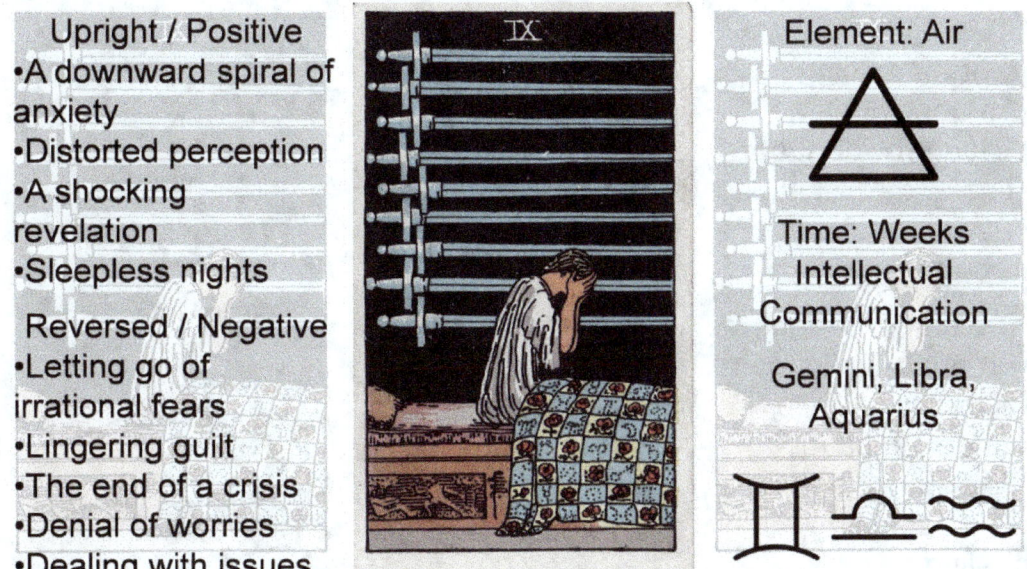

**Upright / Positive**
- A downward spiral of anxiety
- Distorted perception
- A shocking revelation
- Sleepless nights

**Reversed / Negative**
- Letting go of irrational fears
- Lingering guilt
- The end of a crisis
- Denial of worries
- Dealing with issues

Element: Air

Time: Weeks
Intellectual Communication

Gemini, Libra, Aquarius

**Description:** A figure sits up in bed unable to sleep, with the nine swords looming over them. The bed on which they are sitting is decorated with a carving depicting people fighting. The figure has awoken with a shocking revelation which has left them in disbelief. The quilt is decorated with roses and symbols of the zodiac.

**Upright:** The Nine of Swords represents a downward spiral of anxiety, anxiety, being trapped in one's own thoughts, distorted perception, distress, emotional turmoil, excessive worry and fear, guilt, harsh self-criticism, imagining worst-case scenarios, intense fears, intense worry, mental anguish, mental breakdown, mental distress, mental exhaustion, negative thoughts, nightmares, overblown worries, overwhelming thoughts, paranoia, regret, ruminating on past mistakes, self-blame, sleepless nights.

This is a period of intense mental and emotional distress and sleepless nights. A shocking revelation has left you in disbelief. Confront your fears or anxieties rather than allowing them to consume you. Distress is often exacerbated by the mind. Seeking help or finding ways to calm your thoughts can bring relief. Addressing the root of your worries is the way to break out of the downward spiral.

**Reversed:** The Nine of Swords represents avoiding or denying the full extent of worries, beginning to let go of irrational fears, finding ways to deal with issues, lessening of anxiety, lingering feelings of guilt or fear, the end of a crisis.

You are beginning to let go of irrational fears and are finding ways to deal with issues that have been keeping you up at night. It may be the end of a crisis or a period of intense emotional turmoil. There may still be lingering feelings of guilt or fear that need further attention. You may be in denial about the full extent of your worries, which may need more conscious effort to resolve.

**Symbolism:** The figure represents sleeplessness, despair, shock, and disbelief. The swords represent the figure's thoughts, worries, and anxieties standing out amidst the blackness of night and the subconscious. The carving on the side of the bed of people fighting represents conflict, which is figuratively unwelcome in a place designed for sleep. The roses on the quilt represent the harmony that has been disturbed by the figure's waking tension. The zodiac symbols on the quilt represent a divine plan which has brought about the figure's shocking revelation.

## The Ten of Swords

**Upright / Positive**
- A brutal ending
- An absolute low
- Hitting rock bottom
- The end of a chapter
- Transformation through pain

**Reversed / Negative**
- An opportunity for recovery
- Lingering pain
- Resistance
- The beginning of healing

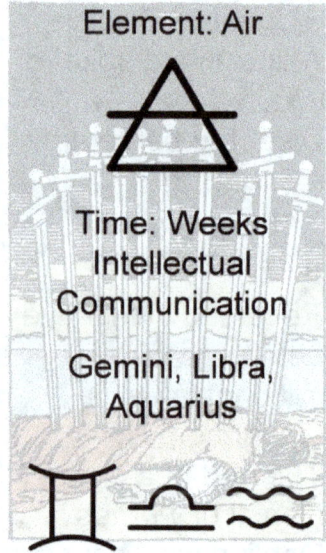

Element: Air

Time: Weeks
Intellectual
Communication

Gemini, Libra, Aquarius

**Description:** A man lies dead face down in a battlefield with ten swords standing up in his back.

**Upright:** The Ten of Swords represents a brutal ending, a destructive or painful ending, an absolute low point, being stabbed in the back, betrayal, deception, defeat, disillusionment, harsh conclusion, healing or recovery on the horizon, hitting rock-bottom, loss, overwhelmed by the weight of circumstances, painful endings, the end of a cycle, the end of a difficult chapter, and transformation through pain.

It is the culmination of a difficult and painful situation. You may feel mentally or emotionally defeated, but the worst is over. Acknowledge your pain, accept the loss, let go of the past. Make space for a new chapter. Now is the time to heal and start anew.

Let go of negative thought patterns that no longer serve you. It is the end of a cycle and the beginning of recovery, transformation, and healing. Release the past and prepare for something new.

**Reversed:** The Ten of Swords represents an opportunity for recovery, avoidance, lingering residual pain, moving on, resistance, the beginning of healing.

While the worst may still be lingering or there may be some residual pain, the worst of the experience is behind you. You are in the process of moving on from a traumatic event or emotional burden. Confront the pain and the reality of the situation in order to prepare yourself for the opportunity to recover and move forward.

**Symbolism:** The red cloth draped over the man represents passion and zeal, a representation of the figure's strength and courage to fight the battle he has fought. The dark sky represents the dark night of the soul in which the battle was fought.

The yellow sky underneath represents the coming morning and hoped for enlightenment. The still waters in the background represent the vast ocean, the stillness of the body, and a level of peace.

**The Page of Swords**

Upright / Positive
•A messenger of intellectual curiosity
•Thirst for knowledge
•Important conversations
•Mental agility

Reversed / Negative
•Acting impulsively
•Communication problems
•Conflict and gossip
•Misinterpretations

Element: Air

Time: Weeks
Intellectual Communication

Gemini, Libra, Aquarius

**Description:** The Page of swords stands holding up a sword in a vigilant or alert posture. He is observing something on the left that we cannot see, and he is ready for action.

**Upright:** The Page of Swords represents a learning curve, a messenger of intellectual curiosity, a new perspective, a phase of exploration, a sharp intellect, a thirst for knowledge, a watchful eye, asking questions, boldness, caution, communication, curiosity, developing ideas, eagerness to learn new things, exploration, gathering information, important conversations, mental agility, new ideas, observation, refining ideas, truth and clarity above all else, vigilance, willingness to engage with challenges, wit, youthful energy.

You may be gathering information or trying to understand something more deeply. You need to communicate your thoughts and ideas clearly and directly without hesitation.

Ask questions, seek the truth, and stay mentally alert. Be cautious in how you express yourself, avoid being too blunt or direct. Stay focused and clear-headed, even when faced with challenges or new information.

**Reversed:** The Page of Swords represents acting impulsively, communication problems, conflict, gossip, incomplete information, lack of clarity, lack of trust, misinterpretations, misleading information, misrepresentations, misunderstandings, rash decisions, and spying.

You may be dealing with a situation where information is incomplete, misleading, or being misrepresented. You or someone else is acting impulsively without considering the consequences, leading to rash decisions or conflict.

Spying and gossip leads to misunderstandings and lack of trust. Do more research, and be thoughtful about how you communicate.

**Symbolism:** The Page's feet imply movement to the right, whereas the Page is looking to the left, this represents the Page's agility and grace. He is capable of both defensive and evasive manoeuvres.

## The Knight of Swords

**Upright / Positive**
- Assertive action
- Boldness
- Bravery
- Determination
- Decisiveness
- Intensity and focus

**Reversed / Negative**
- Disorganisation
- Disruption
- Impatience
- Impulsiveness
- Recklessness
- Rash decisions

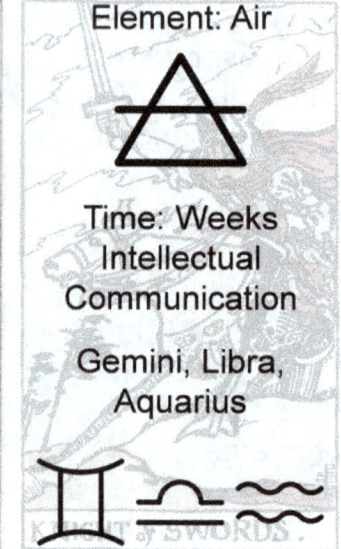

Element: Air

Time: Weeks
Intellectual
Communication

Gemini, Libra, Aquarius

**Description:** The Knight of Swords is galloping swiftly from right to left. The strong wind is blowing through the trees in the background, and through the red feather mounted on the Knight's helmet. He wears a red cloak over his armour. The ground from the right to left increases in altitude. The horse' reins are decorated with butterflies.

**Upright:** The Knight of Swords represents action, argument, assertive action, boldness, bravery, challenging the status quo, confrontation, courage, decisive steps, decisiveness, determination, dynamism, fast decision making, fearlessness, focused mindset, great speed, impatience, intellectual pursuit, intensity and focus, movement, moving ahead, quick action, recklessness, riding against the wind, swift action, swift movement, truth-seeking.

You are in a period of fast movement and focused action. You may be charging ahead with new ideas, projects, or pursuits, driven by the desire to achieve something and find answers. Be bold, assertive, and mentally sharp, but avoid rushing into decisions without thinking them through. Use your intellect and your words to push forward. Be mindful of the consequences of swift actions.

**Reversed:** The Knight of Swords represents disorganisation, disruption, impatience, impulsiveness, lack of clarity, over-hastiness, rash decisions, and recklessness.

Fast-paced energy has become reckless, impatient, and disorganised. You may be acting too hastily, causing disruption, or making decisions without looking at the bigger picture. There is confusion and a lack of clarity in your thoughts, which might lead to arguments or conflicts that could have been avoided. Someone in your life may be acting with aggression or impatience. Slow down, reassess your actions, and avoid rash or impulsive decisions.

**Symbolism:** The Knight symbolises dynamic action, charging forward like a gust of wind. The Knight's extensive armour represents deep preparation for what lies ahead.

The Knight's sword is drawn for battle. The white horse represents strength, energy, and purity of purpose. The butterflies on the horse's reins represent dynamism through metamorphosis. The trees blowing in the strong wind illustrate that the Knight is charging against the wind.

**The Queen of Swords**

Upright / Positive
- Clear communication
- Cutting through confusion and illusion
- Emotional resilience
- Impartiality
- Independence

Reversed / Negative
- Clouded judgement
- Confusion
- Dishonesty
- Distorted thinking
- Miscommunication
- Lack of clarity

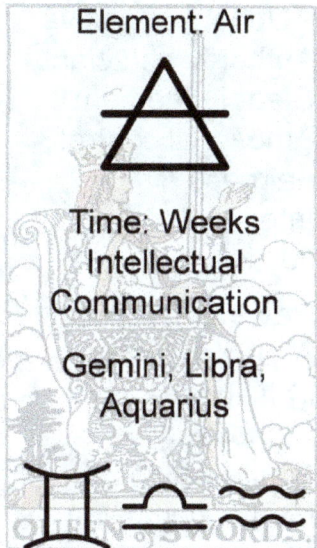

Element: Air

Time: Weeks
Intellectual Communication

Gemini, Libra, Aquarius

**Description:** The Queen of Swords sits on her thrown. In her right hand she is holding her sword pointing upwards while resting it on the arm of her throne. Her left hand is raised in a gesture that is both decisive in taking action and inviting. She wears a crown representing butterflies. Her throne is decorated with a cherub, a waxing and waning moon, and a butterfly.

**Upright:** The Queen of Swords represents a sharp mind, clarity, clear communication, clear judgement, cutting through illusion, emotional resilience, impartiality, independence, intellectual clarity, mental strength, objectivity, perceptiveness, self-sufficiency, truth-seeking, truth-telling, wisdom.

You are being called upon to make an important decision or communicate directly and clearly with others. You are being asked to embody the qualities of the Queen of Swords. Detach yourself from your emotions to gain a clear perspective.

**Reversed:** The Queen of Swords represents clouded judgement, confusion, dishonesty, distorted thinking, lack of clarity, and miscommunication.

You may be struggling to see the truth of a situation, or caught up in confusion, miscommunication, or dishonesty. Cut through confusion to see the truth. Someone who is overly critical or harsh with their words is being dishonest.

**Symbolism:** The Queen's sword represents a sharp intellect and ability to cut through confusion. Her left hand is open, suggesting a readiness to act decisively. The sword represents truth, intellect, decision-making, and communication. Pointing upwards, the sword represents preparedness, and readiness to take action when necessary. The throne represents authority, sovereignty, and control over intellect. The clouds symbolise mental processes, clarity, and overcoming confusion. The butterflies on the throne and crown symbolise transformation, adaptability, and intellectual growth. The crown represents wisdom, mastery, and authority over the mental realm. The empty space around the Queen indicates emotional detachment, mental focus, and clarity. The Queen's serene facial expression represents emotional control, objectivity, and clear-headedness. The cherub on her throne symbolises divine blessing and guidance. The two phases of the moon on the throne represent the beginning and ending of the cycle of the moon.

**The King of Swords**

Upright / Positive
- Authority and clarity
- Clear judgement
- Emotional control
- Fairness
- Integrity
- Justice

Reversed / Negative
- Abuse of power
- Falsehoods
- Dishonesty
- Manipulation
- Mental confusion
- Miscommunication

Element: Air

Time: Weeks
Intellectual
Communication

Gemini, Libra, Aquarius

**Description:** The King of Swords depicts the King seated on his thrown which is decorated with butterflies and the waxing and waning phases of the moon. He holds his sword in his right hand. The sky is clear apart from several clouds which are gathering in the background.

**Upright:** The King of Swords represents authority, clarity, clear judgement, communication, decision making, detachment, discipline, effective communication, emotional control, fairness, honesty, integrity, intellectual authority, intellectual mastery, justice, leadership, logic, mastery of the mental realm, problem-solving, skilled reasoning, strategic thinking, truth.

A situation requires clear and rational decision making. You may need to take on a leadership role or act with authority and wisdom. Focus on logic and objectivity to solve a problem, make a decision, or navigate the situation. Speak the truth and stand by your principles in the face of adversity.

**Reversed:** The King of Swords represents abuse of power, fallacies, falsehoods, intellectual dishonesty, lack of direction, lack of honesty, lack of transparency, lacking clarity, manipulation, mental confusion, miscommunication, misleading ideas, unfairness.

You may be dealing with someone who is using their intellect for manipulation or to control others where clarity and fairness are lacking. You are struggling to make decisions or are feeling overwhelmed by mental confusion and lack of direction. Confront misleading ideas, falsehoods, and fallacies, and be honest and transparent in your communication to seek clarity and cut through the confusion.

**Symbolism:** The sword represents the King's mastery of the mental and communicative aspects of life, making wise decisions, and speaking the truth with authority. The two phases of the moon on the throne represent the beginning and ending of the cycle of the moon. The butterflies on the throne symbolise adaptability, intellectual growth, and transformation. The crown symbolises authority, wisdom, and mental mastery. The calm sky in the background represents clear decisive action. The storm clouds gathering in the sky represent turbulent situations. Either way, the King remains resolute in his thrown, able to maintain his composure. The robes symbolise the King's regal authority, wisdom, and intellectual prowess.

## 7.2.4. Pentacles

The Suit of Pentacles (also called Coins, etc.) is associated with the material aspects of life, wealth, career, security, health, practical experiences, and all that is tangible. Pentacles are linked to the element of Earth, which represents the material world, money, possessions, work, and physical stability.

**The Ace of Pentacles**

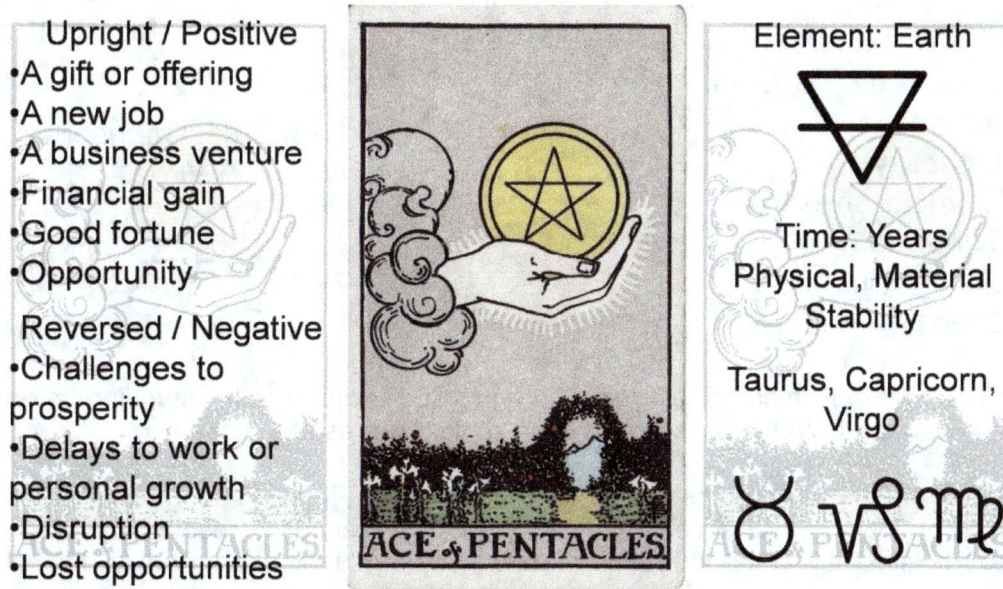

Upright / Positive
- A gift or offering
- A new job
- A business venture
- Financial gain
- Good fortune
- Opportunity

Reversed / Negative
- Challenges to prosperity
- Delays to work or personal growth
- Disruption
- Lost opportunities

Element: Earth

Time: Years
Physical, Material Stability

Taurus, Capricorn, Virgo

**Description:** The Ace of Pentacles depicts a hand appearing from a cloud holding a pentacle. In the background there is a well kept garden, and behind the hedge there is a mountain on the horizon.

**Upright:** The Ace of Pentacles represents a gift or offering, a new job, a business venture, financial gain, good fortune, investment, new beginnings, opportunities for wealth, potential for growth, practicality and grounded energy, security, stability, the material realm.

Seize new opportunities and start something tangible. Focus on practicality and invest in yourself. Build for the long term and be patient and grounded.

**Reversed:** The Ace of Pentacles represents challenges in achieving prosperity, delay in plans related to work, investments, or personal growth, disruption, failure to seize opportunities, fear of failure., feeling disconnected from practical pursuits, financial imbalance, financial instability, hesitation, missed opportunities, neglect of practical matters, potential that has not been fully realised, procrastination, short-term gains rather than long-term planning, and unexpected losses.

Don't ignore opportunities. Reassess financial goals and address financial instability. Avoid short-term focus. Focus on grounding yourself. Take action to overcome delays. Be careful with investments.

**Symbolism:** The hand from the cloud represents divine intervention. The Pentacle (Coin) symbolises material wealth. The garden or pathway suggests fertile ground for new beginnings and growth. The mountain in the background represents stability, long-term goals, and the idea of climbing toward higher achievements or success. The greenery and flowers symbolise growth, fertility, and the flourishing of new ideas or projects in the material world. The solid ground indicates stability, security, and a solid foundation from which to build future success.

## The Two of Pentacles

**Upright / Positive**
- Balance
- Adaptability
- Juggling priorities
- Time management
- Flexibility
- Decision-making

**Reversed / Negative**
- Imbalance
- Instability
- Financial stress
- Disharmony
- Losing control
- Chaos

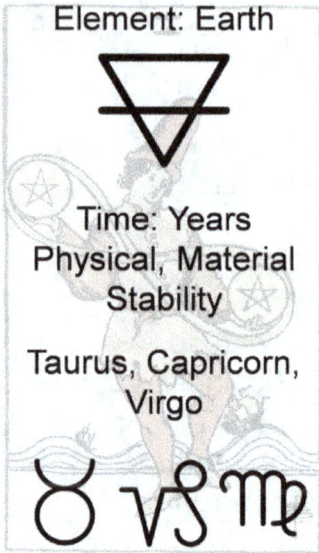

Element: Earth

Time: Years
Physical, Material Stability

Taurus, Capricorn, Virgo

**Description:** The Two of Pentacles depicts a figure juggling two pentacles, standing on one foot or in a dynamic, balancing pose. In the background are turbulent waves of the sea.

**Upright:** The Two of Pentacles represents balance, adaptability, juggling priorities, time management, flexibility, decision-making, change, fluctuating circumstances, resourcefulness, managing responsibilities, multitasking, stability through motion, keeping things in equilibrium, financial juggling, work-life balance.

Seize new opportunities that promise growth and prosperity, particularly in material or financial matters. Take practical, grounded steps toward manifesting your goals, focusing on creating a solid foundation for long-term success. Be patient diligent as you embark on new ventures, as well as a commitment to making tangible progress. Invest in yourself, whether through education, health, or financial planning, to ensure a secure and stable future.

**Reversed:** The Two of Pentacles represents imbalance, overwhelm, poor time management, neglecting responsibilities, instability, financial stress, difficulty juggling priorities, lack of adaptability, being unable to cope with change, disharmony, losing control, chaos, uncertainty, struggling to maintain balance.

Be cautious about missed opportunities or delays in material or financial matters. You are not fully embracing or recognising a valuable opportunity, either due to fear, hesitation, or distraction. Re-evaluate your goals and take practical steps to address any financial instability or lack of direction. Focus on long-term planning rather than seeking quick, short-term rewards. Avoid rushing into new ventures or investments without proper research and preparation, as there may be hidden risks or obstacles ahead. Reconnect with the foundational aspects of your life, ensuring that you are taking solid, grounded actions to move forward.

**Symbolism:** The central figure symbolises the ability to multitask and maintain equilibrium amidst competing demands. The two pentacles themselves signify duality, two aspects of life or resources that require balancing, such as finances, work, or relationships. The turbulent sea in the background represents fluctuating circumstances, challenges, or emotional upheaval. The infinity symbol suggests an ongoing cycle or flow, reinforcing the idea of continuous change.

**The Three of Pentacles**

**Upright / Positive**
- Collaboration
- Teamwork
- Mastery
- Skill development
- Craftsmanship
- Cooperation

**Reversed / Negative**
- Lack of collaboration
- Poor teamwork
- Disorganisation
- Lack of recognition
- Inefficiency
- Frustration

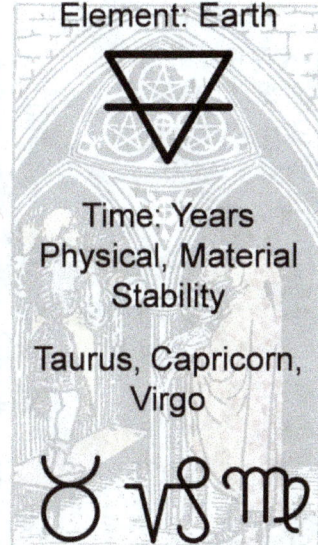

Element: Earth

Time: Years
Physical, Material Stability

Taurus, Capricorn, Virgo

**Description:** The Three of Pentacles depicts a skilled artisan or craftsman working on a project while collaborating with two others, highlighting teamwork, mastery, and the importance of combining skills and expertise. The figure is typically seen carving or constructing something with attention to detail, while two others, often represented as a patron or apprentices, look on, suggesting that collaboration and cooperation are key components of success. The surrounding imagery often includes architectural or intricate designs, symbolising the effort and dedication required to create something lasting and valuable.

**Upright:** The Three of Pentacles represents collaboration, teamwork, mastery, skill development, building something of value, craftsmanship, cooperation, recognition for hard work, learning from others, attention to detail, planning, shared goals, achievement through joint efforts, foundations of success.

Focus on collaboration and working with others to achieve a common goal, whether it's in a project, relationship, or career. Success will come from teamwork, dedication, and honing your craft. Seek guidance or mentorship, acknowledge, and celebrate your achievements as part of a collective effort.

**Reversed:** The Three of Pentacles represents lack of collaboration, poor teamwork, disorganisation, lack of recognition, working in isolation, inability to work with others, inefficiency, mistakes due to lack of skill or focus, lack of planning, feeling undervalued, frustration with group efforts.

Address any issues with collaboration or teamwork. If you are struggling with working alongside others or feeling unsupported, it's important to identify where communication or coordination is breaking down. Refine your skills or approach to ensure you're contributing effectively to a group effort. Avoid working in isolation, as seeking guidance and cooperation is essential for success.

**Symbolism:** The three figures represent collaboration and shared expertise, suggesting the need for diverse skills to achieve success. The architecture or detailed design background symbolises the effort and planning necessary to create something valuable, while the pentacles themselves signify material and practical success that comes from hard work and attention to detail. These symbols together underscore the importance of working together, honing your craft, and building a solid foundation for future success.

**The Four of Pentacles**

Upright / Positive
- Security
- Stability
- Possession
- Materialism
- Financial control
- Protecting resources

Reversed / Negative
- Greed
- Insecurity
- Fear of loss
- Lack of control
- Financial instability
- Hoarding

Element: Earth

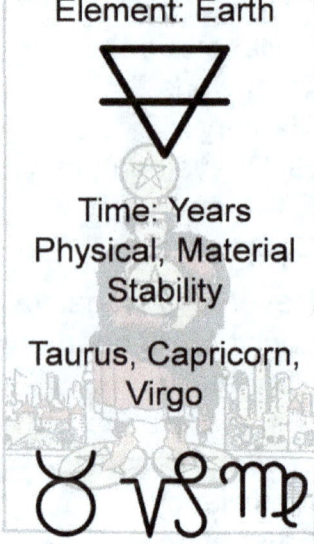

Time: Years
Physical, Material Stability

Taurus, Capricorn, Virgo

**Description:** The Four of Pentacles depicts a figure holding tightly to four pentacles, one atop their head, one in each hand, and one at their feet. The figure is sitting in a protective, guarded posture. The surrounding imagery includes a walled city.

**Upright:** The Four of Pentacles represents security, stability, possession, materialism, financial control, protecting resources, fear of loss, holding onto what you have, caution, conservation, financial stability, self-protection, accumulation, clinging to the past, fear of change.

Examine your relationship with material possessions, wealth, or security. While it's important to be financially stable and secure, you may be holding on too tightly to what you have, out of fear or possessiveness. Find a healthy balance between securing your resources and remaining open to new opportunities or changes. Let go of unnecessary attachments to material wealth and embrace the flow of life, recognising that true security comes from a broader sense of abundance, not from hoarding or clinging to the past.

**Reversed:** The Four of Pentacles represents greed, insecurity, letting go of possessions, fear of loss, lack of control, financial instability, excessive attachment to material wealth, hoarding, fear of change, financial mismanagement, letting go of fear, imbalance in security.

Release any unhealthy attachments to material wealth or possessions. If you're feeling insecure or overly focused on control, it may be time to reassess your priorities and let go of fears or behaviours that are holding you back. Embrace change and allow for new opportunities to flow into your life, rather than clinging to outdated financial structures or beliefs. Shift from a mindset of scarcity to one of abundance, where you feel more open and less protective over your material resources.

**Symbolism:** The figure's grasping posture suggests a fear of losing control or a desire to protect what has been accumulated. The walled city or barriers in the background emphasise a desire for security, yet also point to potential isolation, highlighting the tension between safety and confinement. The card also emphasises the symbolism of protection and conservation, suggesting a focus on stability but also cautioning against becoming too rigid or fearful of change.

**The Five of Pentacles**

Upright / Positive
- Financial hardship
- Poverty
- Loss
- Insecurity
- Isolation
- Being in need

Reversed / Negative
- Recovery from loss
- Finding support
- Overcoming isolation
- Ending a struggle
- Hope after adversity

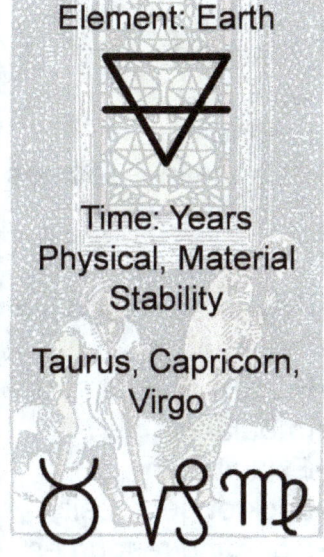

Element: Earth

Time: Years
Physical, Material Stability

Taurus, Capricorn, Virgo

**Description:** The Five of Pentacles depicts two figures, destitute or in a state of hardship, walking outside in the snow, passing by a church window that glows with warmth and light. The figures are dressed in tattered clothing. The five pentacles appear as part of the window's stained glass.

**Upright:** The Five of Pentacles represents financial hardship, poverty, loss, insecurity, isolation, feeling abandoned, struggle, exclusion, lack of resources, physical or emotional poverty, feeling unsupported, adversity, seeking help, being in need, exclusion from society.

Recognise that while you may be facing difficult times or financial struggle, help and support are available to you if you reach out. Do not isolate yourself in moments of need, as assistance may be closer than you think. Hardship is temporary, and you can find strength in asking for help, whether through emotional or financial support. Shifting your focus away from feelings of lack and toward potential sources of aid can help you overcome your difficulties.

**Reversed:** The Five of Pentacles represents recovery from financial loss, emerging from hardship, improved security, finding support, overcoming feelings of isolation, better health, ending a period of struggle, coming out of a difficult situation, regaining stability, lifting oneself out of poverty, finding hope after adversity.

Recovery is possible, and you are emerging from a period of hardship or struggle. Reach out for help if you haven't already, and take steps toward improving your situation. Healing is occurring, whether it's financial, emotional, or physical, and it's time to embrace a more hopeful outlook. If you've been feeling isolated, support is available to help you regain stability and security, but you must allow yourself to accept it and take the necessary steps toward recovery.

**Symbolism:** The two figures symbolise those experiencing struggle or exclusion, often showing them as vulnerable or in need. The snow and cold weather represent isolation, emotional or physical loss, and challenging times. The church window glowing with light indicates that help, both material and emotional, is nearby, but the figures may be unable to see it. The five pentacles on the window represent the potential for recovery and stability, suggesting that there is hope for change if one reaches out for assistance.

**The Six of Pentacles**

Upright / Positive
- Generosity
- Charity
- Kindness
- Balance in resources
- Financial support
- Fairness

Reversed / Negative
- Selfishness
- Inequality
- Imbalance
- Exploitation
- Lack of generosity
- Hoarding resources

Element: Earth

Time: Years
Physical, Material Stability

Taurus, Capricorn, Virgo

**Description:** The Six of Pentacles depicts a wealthy individual, holding a set of scales in one hand and handing out pentacles to two beggars or individuals in need. The beggars or recipients are shown in a state of humility or gratitude.

**Upright:** The Six of Pentacles represents generosity, charity, giving and receiving, balance in resources, financial support, fairness, equality, wealth distribution, sharing with those in need, gratitude, helping others, kindness, mutual support, harmony, justice in giving.

Practice generosity and fairness, whether by offering help to those in need or by being open to receiving assistance. Evaluate your resources and share them when possible, promoting a sense of balance and mutual support. Giving and receiving are equally important, and you should not be afraid to accept help if you are in a position to do so. Balance your efforts, act with kindness, and be fair in your dealings with others, ensuring that your actions align with principles of justice and equality.

**Reversed:** The Six of Pentacles represents selfishness, inequality, imbalance, one-sided relationships, exploitation, charity without fairness, stinginess, lack of generosity, unfair distribution, hoarding resources, feeling unappreciated, taking advantage of others, financial imbalance, lack of support.

Reflect on whether you are giving too much or too little, either financially or emotionally. Re-evaluate the dynamics of any relationships that may feel one-sided or exploitative. If you are hoarding resources or failing to share, practice generosity and fairness. Alternatively, if you are the one in need, it's time to ask for help or recognise the imbalance that exists in your life. Aim for fairness and ensure that any giving or receiving is done in a balanced and mutually respectful way.

**Symbolism:** The scales, symbolising balance, fairness, and justice, particularly in the distribution of resources. The pentacles themselves represent material wealth or resources, and the act of handing them out signifies generosity, charity, and the flow of abundance. The two beggars represent those in need, emphasising humility and the importance of receiving help.

**The Seven of Pentacles**

Upright / Positive
- Patience
- Assessment
- Reflection
- Evaluation
- Hard work paying off
- Progress

Reversed / Negative
- Impatience
- Lack of progress
- Disappointment
- Frustration
- Poor planning
- Lack of results

Element: Earth

Time: Years
Physical, Material Stability

Taurus, Capricorn, Virgo

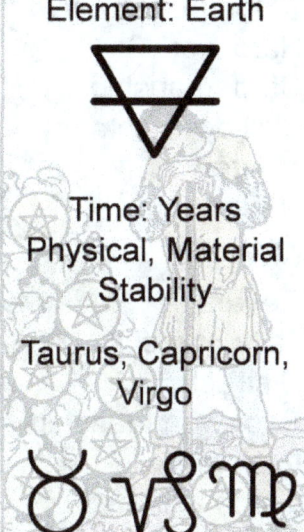

**Description:** The Seven of Pentacles depicts a figure standing before a bush or tree that is bearing pentacles. The figure looks contemplative, examining the growth of the plant and considering whether the effort invested is yielding the expected results.

**Upright:** The Seven of Pentacles represents patience, assessment, reflection, evaluation, hard work paying off, progress, perseverance, long-term investment, waiting for results, sowing seeds, persistence, slow growth, checking progress, thinking about the future, re-evaluating efforts.

Pause and assess the results of your efforts before moving forward. Patience is key, and that the rewards of your hard work may take time to manifest. Reflect on your progress, evaluate if your current approach is yielding the desired outcomes, and make adjustments if necessary. Growth is often slow, and persistence will eventually pay off if you stay dedicated and thoughtful in your actions.

**Reversed:** The Seven of Pentacles represents impatience, lack of progress, disappointment, frustration, poor planning, lack of results, feeling stuck, lack of reward for effort, reassessing goals, stalled progress, giving up too soon, unrealistic expectations, and dissatisfaction with results.

Reassess your approach if you're feeling frustrated or disappointed with the progress you've made. You might be rushing the process or having unrealistic expectations. If you're stuck, take a step back and consider whether your goals, planning, or effort need adjustment. It's time to give up on an endeavour that isn't producing the desired results, but do so with clarity and thoughtful consideration rather than out of impatience.

**Symbolism:** The pentacles symbolise material investments, growth, and long-term rewards. The tree or plant represents the nurturing and slow development of ideas, projects, or resources. The figure's contemplative posture emphasises reflection, assessment, and patience, suggesting a moment to evaluate whether the current path is leading to fruitful results.

# Tarot  07 The Tarot Deck

**The Eight of Pentacles**

Upright / Positive
- Hard work
- Craftsmanship
- Skill development
- Mastery
- Dedication
- Focus

Reversed / Negative
- Lack of focus
- Distractions
- Poor workmanship
- Lack of skill
- Complacency
- Unfinished projects

Element: Earth

Time: Years
Physical, Material Stability

Taurus, Capricorn, Virgo

**Description:** The Eight of Pentacles depicts a figure focused on their craft, diligently working on carving or crafting a series of pentacles. The figure is sat at a workbench in a quiet space, deeply immersed in their task. The surrounding imagery includes several pentacles that have already been completed, illustrating progress and mastery.

**Upright:** The Eight of Pentacles represents hard work, craftsmanship, skill development, mastery, dedication, focus, persistence, learning, improvement, attention to detail, routine, productivity, building expertise, commitment to goals, refining abilities, apprenticeship.

Focus on honing your skills and dedicating yourself to the task at hand. Embrace a mindset of continuous improvement, learning, and practice, whether it's a project, career, or personal goal. Success comes through consistent effort and paying attention to the details. Be patient and disciplined in your work, and take pride in the progress you are making. If you're looking to improve or master something, now is the time to put in the hard work and build your expertise.

**Reversed:** The Eight of Pentacles represents lack of focus, distractions, poor workmanship, lack of skill, complacency, rushing through tasks, unfinished projects, lack of motivation, repetitive work without growth, feeling stuck, lack of improvement, lack of dedication, cutting corners.

Evaluate whether you're putting in enough effort or attention to your work or goals. If you're feeling distracted or disillusioned, it might be time to reassess your approach or focus on developing your skills further. Be warned against rushing through tasks or cutting corners, as it will only hinder your growth. Take the time to refine your craft and ensure that you're truly dedicated to improving. If you've become complacent or are facing a lack of motivation, find ways to reignite your passion and commitment to your goals.

**Symbolism:** The Eight of Pentacles features pentacles as symbols of material resources, wealth, and the work required to achieve them. The figure's focused posture and workbench suggest diligence, craftsmanship, and skill development. The eight completed pentacles represent progress and mastery, while the unfinished pentacle symbolises ongoing work and the pursuit of perfection.

# The Nine of Pentacles

**Upright / Positive**
- Abundance
- Financial independence
- Self-sufficiency
- Success
- Luxury and comfort

**Reversed / Negative**
- Financial insecurity
- Dependence on others
- Excess or overindulgence
- Insecurity

**Element: Earth**

Time: Years
Physical, Material Stability

Taurus, Capricorn, Virgo

**Description:** The Nine of Pentacles depicts a woman standing in a lush garden, surrounded by ripe fruit and beautiful plants, with a falcon perched on her arm. She is dressed in luxurious clothing. The nine pentacles are displayed behind her. She appears at peace and content, enjoying the fruits of her labour and the comfort of her achievements, with no need for external support.

**Upright:** The Nine of Pentacles represents abundance, financial independence, self-sufficiency, success, luxury, comfort, enjoyment of rewards, self-reliance, personal accomplishment, material well-being, harvest, stability, confidence, fulfilment, enjoying the fruits of labour.

Take pride in your achievements and enjoy the rewards of your hard work. Appreciate the abundance and comfort that you've created through your efforts. Self-reliance and personal fulfilment are important. True success comes from being secure in your own abilities and standing firm in your independence. Take time to enjoy the peace and luxury that comes with hard-earned success, and recognise that you have built a solid foundation for yourself.

**Reversed:** The Nine of Pentacles represents financial insecurity, dependence on others, lack of independence, dissatisfaction with material success, excess or overindulgence, superficiality, inability to enjoy rewards, feeling unfulfilled, lack of self-worth, insecurity, poverty mindset.

Assess your sense of independence and fulfilment. If you're feeling dissatisfied or unfulfilled, it may be time to re-evaluate your goals and what truly brings you happiness. You may be focusing too much on material wealth without appreciating the deeper aspects of success, such as personal growth and inner peace. You may need to find a balance between enjoying your material success and ensuring that you're also nurturing your emotional and spiritual well-being. If you're overly reliant on others, this card encourages you to reconnect with your own strength and self-sufficiency.

**Symbolism:** The Nine of Pentacles features the nine pentacles, symbolising material wealth, accomplishment, and the successful completion of a project or endeavour. The garden represents abundance, fertility, and a life of luxury and comfort, while the falcon symbolises mastery, control, and personal power. The woman's attire represents dignity and self-sufficiency, while her calm and peaceful expression conveys a sense of contentment and harmony with her environment.

## The Ten of Pentacles

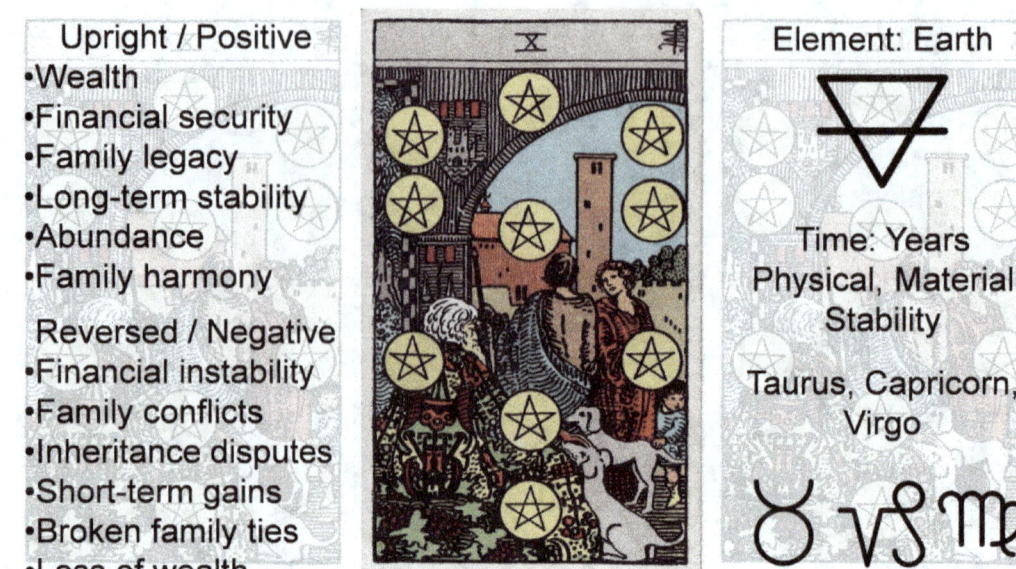

**Upright / Positive**
- Wealth
- Financial security
- Family legacy
- Long-term stability
- Abundance
- Family harmony

**Reversed / Negative**
- Financial instability
- Family conflicts
- Inheritance disputes
- Short-term gains
- Broken family ties
- Loss of wealth

**Element: Earth**

Time: Years
Physical, Material Stability

Taurus, Capricorn, Virgo

**Description:** The Ten of Pentacles depicts a family scene, where multiple generations are enjoying the benefits of wealth and abundance, often in a prosperous home or estate. In the foreground, a couple of older figures are surrounded by their children and grandchildren, with two dogs at their side.

**Upright:** The Ten of Pentacles represents wealth, financial security, family legacy, long-term stability, inheritance, abundance, family harmony, generational wealth, home, legacy building, lasting success, tradition, loyalty, prosperous foundation, community.

Focus on building long-term security and stability in your life, particularly in terms of family, finances, and legacy. Create a solid foundation for future generations, whether through wealth, values, or traditions. Community, family, and shared success is important. Your efforts today will ripple out to benefit those who come after you. Nurture relationships, ensuring that your resources are wisely managed, and contributing to the well-being of your loved ones for years to come.

**Reversed:** The Ten of Pentacles represents financial instability, family conflicts, inheritance disputes, short-term gains, lack of long-term planning, broken family ties, loss of wealth, materialism, neglecting family traditions, fleeting success, mismanagement of resources.

Pay attention to any potential conflicts or instability within your family or financial matters. Be warned against focusing too heavily on short-term gains at the expense of long-term security. You may need to re-establish balance or rebuild fractured relationships, especially with family members or in community settings. If you're facing financial instability, carefully manage your resources and re-evaluate your priorities. Reflect on whether your actions align with the values and legacy you wish to leave behind, and ensure that your wealth and family ties are nurtured for lasting stability.

**Symbolism:** The Ten of Pentacles features the ten pentacles prominently, symbolising wealth, abundance, and the culmination of material success. The family represents generational ties, tradition, and the continuation of legacies, whether through financial inheritance or shared values. The house or estate signifies stability, security, and the foundation upon which future generations will build. The dogs symbolise loyalty and familial connections, while the older couple represents wisdom and the rewards of a lifetime of hard work. The younger generation emphasises the passing of wisdom and wealth to the next cycle of family, underscoring themes of continuity and lasting legacy.

# The Page of Pentacles

**Upright / Positive**
- New beginnings
- Curiosity
- Learning and study
- Practicality
- Ambition
- Opportunity

**Reversed / Negative**
- Lack of focus
- Missed opportunities
- Procrastination
- Shallow approach
- Immaturity
- Easily distracted

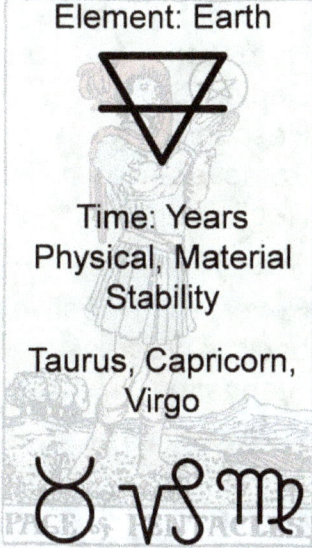

Element: Earth

Time: Years
Physical, Material Stability

Taurus, Capricorn, Virgo

**Description:** The Page of Pentacles depicts a young figure, a student or apprentice, holding a single pentacle in their hands, studying it intently. The figure is dressed in practical, earthy clothing, standing on a fertile, green landscape.

**Upright:** The Page of Pentacles represents new beginnings, curiosity, learning, studying, practicality, ambition, opportunity, diligence, manifestation of ideas, setting goals, growth, focus, attention to detail, laying foundations, starting a new project, financial opportunities, exploring new skills.

Approach new opportunities with curiosity, dedication, and a focus on learning. Invest time in studying, researching, or acquiring new skills that will help you build a solid foundation for future success. Take practical steps toward manifesting your goals and focusing on the details that will lead to long-term growth. Now is a good time to start new ventures or projects, particularly those that require persistence and a steady, methodical approach.

**Reversed:** The Page of Pentacles represents lack of focus, missed opportunities, procrastination, shallow approach, lack of follow-through, immaturity, lack of discipline, being easily distracted, overconfidence, unpreparedness, inability to manifest ideas, unrealistic goals, lack of commitment.

Reassess your approach if you feel distracted or if you have started something but lack the dedication to follow through. It may be a sign to slow down and focus on the task at hand, ensuring that you are adequately prepared and grounded before moving forward. Avoid being overly ambitious or rushing into new ventures without proper planning. It is important to be realistic, committed, and disciplined if you wish to achieve your goals, rather than getting caught up in distractions or failing to put in the necessary effort.

**Symbolism:** The pentacle in the Page's hands represents material wealth, opportunities, and the tangible manifestation of ideas into reality. The young figure symbolises the beginner's mindset, fresh opportunities, and the eagerness to learn and grow. The green landscape signifies potential, fertility, and new beginnings, while the practical clothing reflects groundedness, practicality, and focus. The studious posture of the Page emphasises attention to detail, diligence, and the thoughtful approach required to succeed.

**The Knight of Pentacles**

Upright / Positive
- Hard work
- Dedication
- Responsibility
- Perseverance
- Realiability
- Methodical approach

Reversed / Negative
- Lack of progress
- Stagnation
- Laziness
- Irresponsibility
- Procrastination
- Scattered efforts

Element: Earth

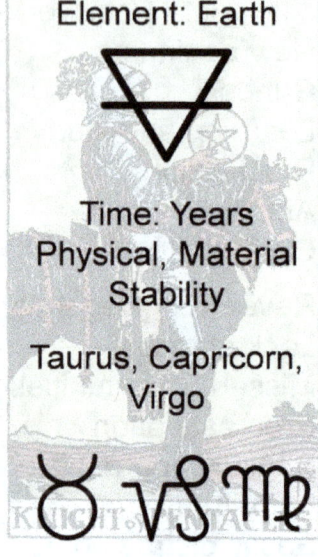

Time: Years
Physical, Material Stability

Taurus, Capricorn, Virgo

**Description:** The Knight of Pentacles depicts a knight on horseback, holding a pentacle firmly in his hand, with a focused and determined expression. The knight rides through a vast, open landscape. Unlike the other knights who may be depicted in motion, the Knight of Pentacles is often shown at a steady pace.

**Upright:** The Knight of Pentacles represents hard work, dedication, responsibility, perseverance, reliability, methodical approach, attention to detail, patience, discipline, trustworthiness, steady progress, focus on long-term goals, commitment, routine, determination, practical solutions.

Stay focused, disciplined, and patient in your efforts to achieve your goals. Take a methodical and steady approach, focusing on the long-term vision and not getting distracted by immediate rewards or shortcuts. Success will come through persistence, consistency, and attention to detail. Avoid rushing through tasks, and instead, work diligently, following through on commitments and responsibilities. Trust the process and know that your hard work will eventually pay off if you remain steady and reliable.

**Reversed:** The Knight of Pentacles represents lack of progress, stagnation, laziness, irresponsibility, procrastination, lack of focus, scattered efforts, impatience, avoiding responsibility, being overly cautious, lack of discipline, missing opportunities, failure to follow through.

Reassess your level of commitment and whether you are putting in enough effort or being too cautious. Be warned against stagnation and procrastination. If you're feeling unmotivated or if things have come to a halt, it may be time to re-engage with your goals or approach them from a different angle. It's time to refocus, find motivation, and regain your discipline in order to move forward.

**Symbolism:** The pentacle in the Knight's hand represents material wealth, stability, and the grounded nature of the journey ahead. The horse symbolises power, energy, and the ability to move forward with steadiness. The knight's armour signifies protection, resilience, and preparedness, while the steady pace of the horse reflects the methodical, unhurried approach required for success. The open landscape emphasises the journey and long-term goals, suggesting that this card is about dedication to a process that may take time to bear fruit.

**The Queen of Pentacles**

Upright / Positive
- Nurturing
- Abundance
- Practicality
- Financial security
- Groundedness
- Responsibility

Reversed / Negative
- Neglecting responsibilities
- Financial instability
- Overindulgence
- Neglecting self-care
- Excessive worry

Element: Earth

Time: Years
Physical, Material Stability

Taurus, Capricorn, Virgo

**Description:** The Queen of Pentacles is depicted as a nurturing, grounded woman sitting on a throne, holding a pentacle in one hand while the other rests on her lap. She is surrounded by a lush environment, often with animals or plants. The queen's attire is luxurious yet practical. She has a calm, attentive demeanour.

**Upright:** The Queen of Pentacles represents nurturing, abundance, practicality, financial security, groundedness, caring, motherly energy, responsibility, resourcefulness, home life, stability, self-sufficiency, prosperity, business acumen, domestic harmony, wealth, fertility.

Cultivate a balanced life, focusing on both material success and emotional well-being. Be resourceful and take practical steps toward achieving your goals while nurturing the people and environment around you. You may need to focus on creating a secure and loving home, developing your financial security, and embracing your nurturing side. Care for yourself while caring for others, ensuring that you maintain harmony between your personal and professional life.

**Reversed:** The Queen of Pentacles represents neglecting responsibilities, financial instability, overindulgence, insecurity, lack of balance, being overly focused on material wealth, feeling ungrounded, neglecting self-care, excessive worry, lack of nurturing, burnout, isolation, overly protective.

Pay attention to areas in your life where you may be neglecting your responsibilities, whether in terms of your finances, home life, or self-care. Restore balance and ensure that you're not overindulging or focusing too heavily on material concerns at the expense of emotional or physical well-being. Take a step back, reassess your priorities, and make sure that you're nurturing yourself as well as others. Be warned against becoming overly controlling or protective in a way that isolates you from others.

**Symbolism:** The pentacle represents material wealth, security, and the ability to manifest abundance. The queen's throne symbolises authority, stability, and mastery in her domain. The lush environment around her, often filled with animals or plants, reflects her connection to nature and fertility, as well as her ability to create harmony and abundance in her surroundings. Her practical and luxurious attire demonstrates her ability to balance comfort with responsibility. The nurturing energy she radiates is a symbol of her maternal, caring qualities that ensure the well-being of others.

## The King of Pentacles

**Upright / Positive**
- Wealth
- Success
- Financial security
- Authority
- Stability
- Responsibility

**Reversed / Negative**
- Instability
- Greed
- Overindulgence
- Lack of planning
- Materialism
- Misuse of power

Element: Earth

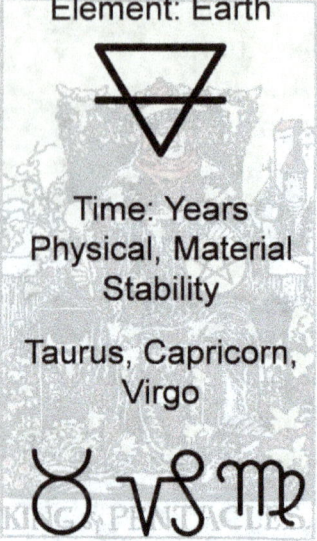

Time: Years
Physical, Material Stability

Taurus, Capricorn, Virgo

**Description:** The King of Pentacles is depicted as a mature, regal figure seated on a throne adorned with bulls. He holds a pentacle firmly in one hand, while the other rests on the arm of his throne. He is dressed in fine, rich clothing, with a calm demeanour.

**Upright:** The King of Pentacles represents wealth, success, financial security, authority, stability, responsibility, mastery of the material world, groundedness, abundance, leadership, practical wisdom, trustworthiness, discipline, strong work ethic, protective, reliable, long-term planning, entrepreneurship, prosperity.

Embrace your practical side and take a grounded, disciplined approach to your finances, career, and long-term goals. Use your wisdom and experience to create stability and abundance in your life. Be responsible with your resources and take the time to plan for the future. You have the ability to be a leader in your own domain. Trust in your ability to make sound decisions and build lasting success.

**Reversed:** The King of Pentacles represents financial irresponsibility, instability, greed, overindulgence, lack of planning, materialism, arrogance, misuse of power, neglect of responsibilities, poor leadership, untrustworthy, lack of discipline, failure to commit, insecurity, short-term focus, and impracticality.

Reflect on whether you are taking a reckless or short-sighted approach to your financial and material life. Reassess your priorities, focusing less on immediate gratification and more on long-term stability. You need to curb materialistic tendencies and ensure you are being responsible with your resources. You need to restore balance in your leadership or management style, being careful not to misuse your influence or power. Reconnect with your sense of discipline and plan more effectively for your future.

**Symbolism:** The pentacle held by the King symbolises material wealth, stability, and the ability to manifest abundance through hard work and wisdom. The bulls on the throne represent strength, determination, and a deep connection to the earth, highlighting his solid and unwavering foundation. The throne itself signifies authority and mastery, while the rich clothing reflects both the material wealth he has accumulated and his ability to live in abundance. The calm demeanour of the King symbolises maturity, wisdom, and experience.

# 8. Divination

Tarot reading is a form of divination, a practice of seeking knowledge, gaining insight, or obtaining guidance about the divine forces that shape our lives, the unknown, the future, or a specific query or question.

Questions asked can include: *Who am I?, When is the best time to do ...?, What can I do to support myself while ...?, What is the best choice between ... and ...?, How can I be a better ...?, How can I best overcome the obstacle of ...?, What is standing in the way of my ...?, What can I do to help ...?, What is the next step I need to take to achieve ...?, What do I need to know about ...?*

### The Querent
The person who wishes to have their query answered is called the 'Querent'. Before a tarot reading, the Querent focuses on a question, situation, or area of life they want guidance on. It can be specific or open-ended, but the more focused the question, the more specific the guidance might be.

### The Reader
The person performing the reading is called the 'Reader'. They may be the same person as the Querent, performing a reading for themselves. The Reader shuffles the Tarot deck while focusing on the question or intention.

Once the cards are drawn, the Reader interprets their meanings based on their positions in the spread and their relationships to each other. While tarot card meanings are rooted in traditional symbolism, Tarot readers also rely heavily on intuition. As they interpret the cards, they may feel certain insights or intuitive impressions, guiding their interpretation of how the cards relate to the Querent's situation.

### The Cards
The symbolism and imagery on the cards is believed to tap into the subconscious mind, intuition, or spiritual energies, offering clarity on questions or situations. After shuffling, cards are drawn and placed in a spread (a pattern or arrangement of cards). Shuffling is believed to mix the energies of the cards and the person asking the question. Each card has symbolic meanings that can shift depending on its position in the reading.

### The Reading
The reading is generally aimed at offering insight rather than predicting a fixed future. It's seen as a tool for reflection, helping the Querent gain clarity, new perspectives, or direction. A tarot reading can highlight potential outcomes, challenges, strengths, or paths based on the energy surrounding a situation at the time of the reading.

### The Spreads
There are a number of different spreads that can be used, depending on the complexity of the question being asked. From the one card question, to complex and elaborate spreads of many cards.

### The Double Card Method
Rather than drawing single cards for each stage of the spread, another method is to keep the Major Arcana and Minor Arcana separate, and then draw one card from each pile for each stage. This method gives an added layer of complexity and detail which expands the meaning of the reading.

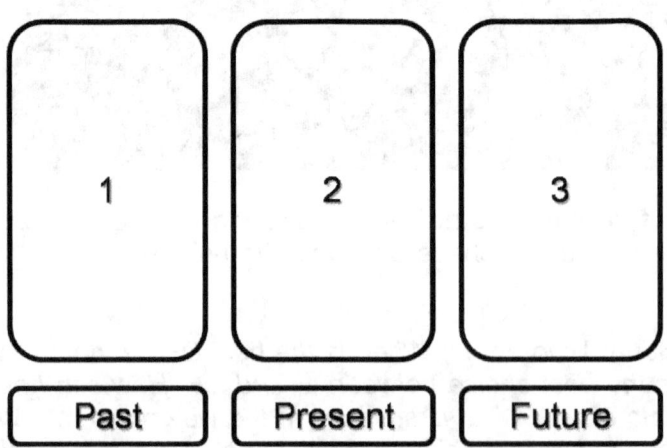

Fig 1. A three stage reading with single cards

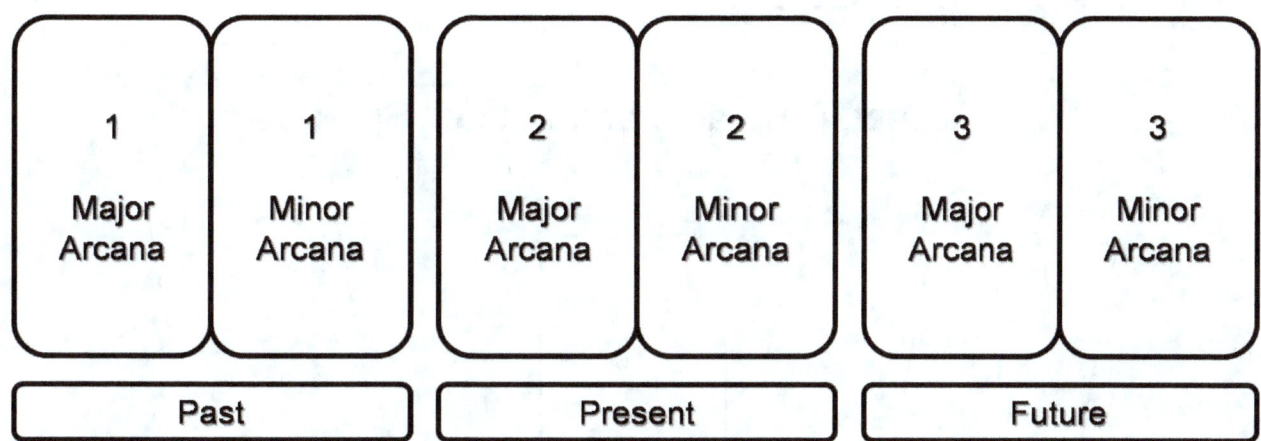

Fig 2. The same three stage reading as previous, but with doubled-up cards from both the Major and Minor Arcana for each stage.

## 8.1. One Card Reading: Yes / No Question

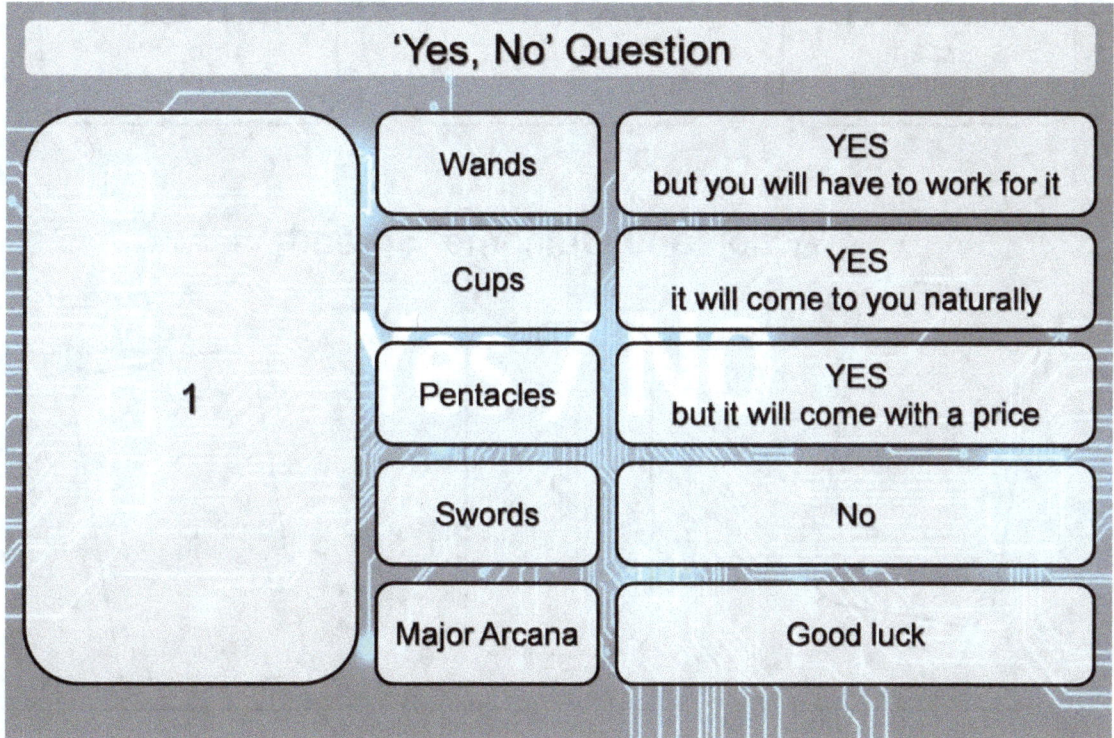

## 8.2. Three Card Spreads

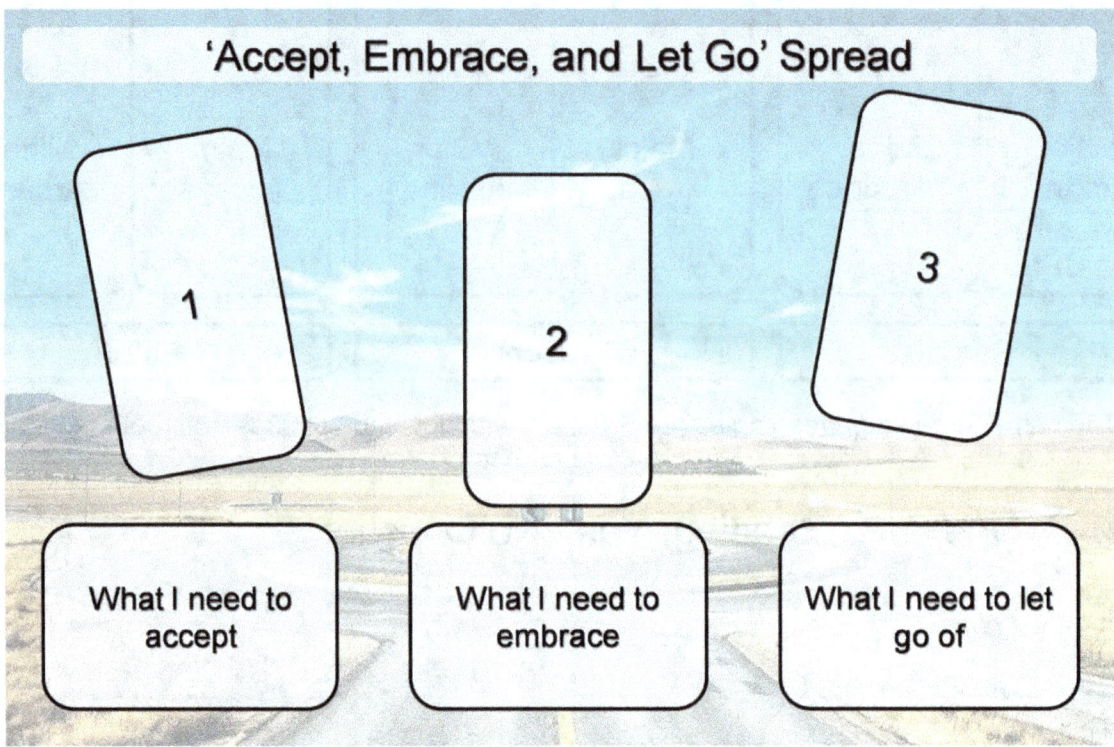

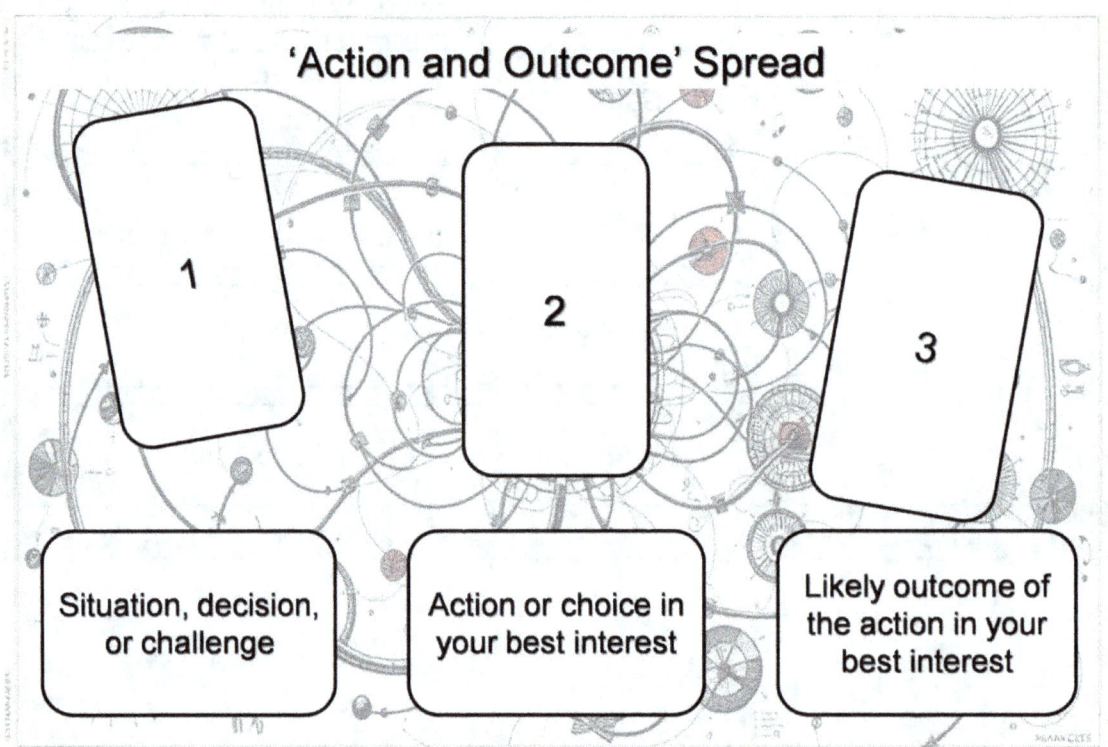

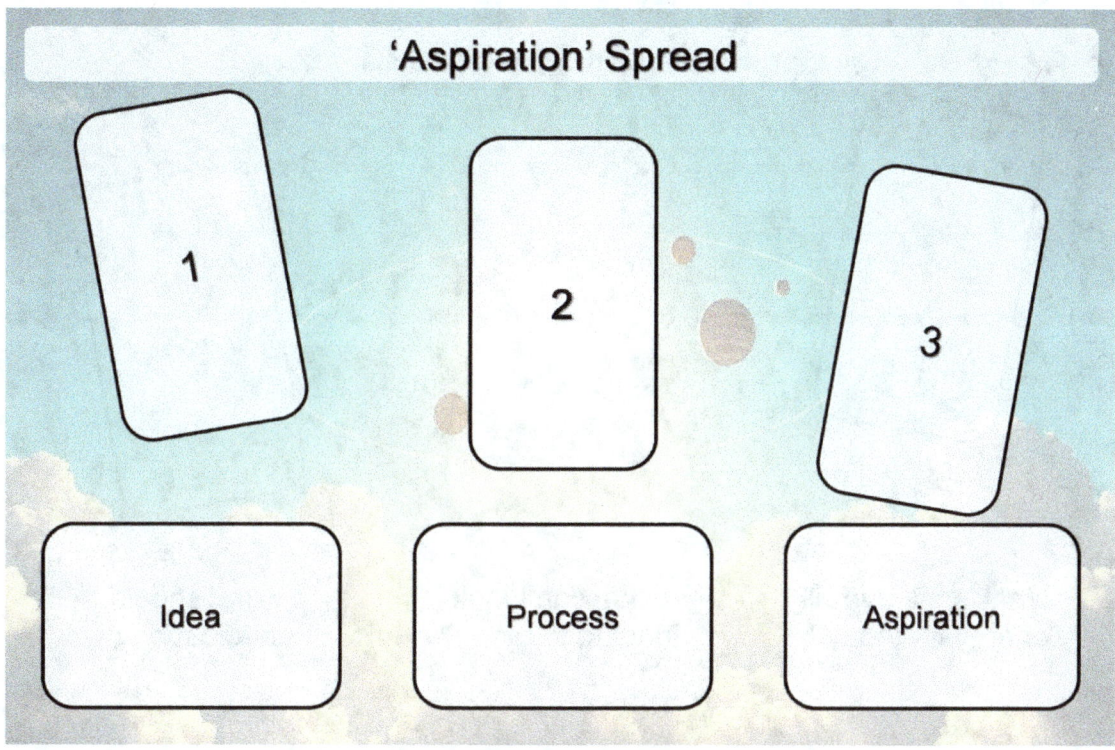

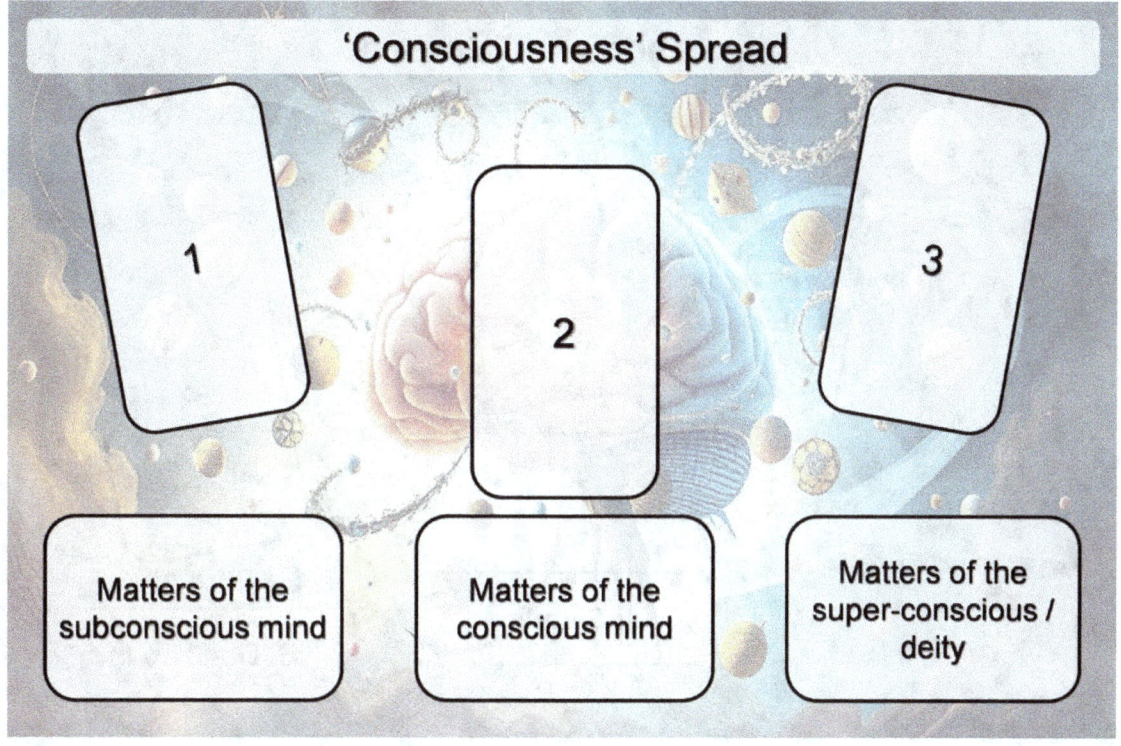

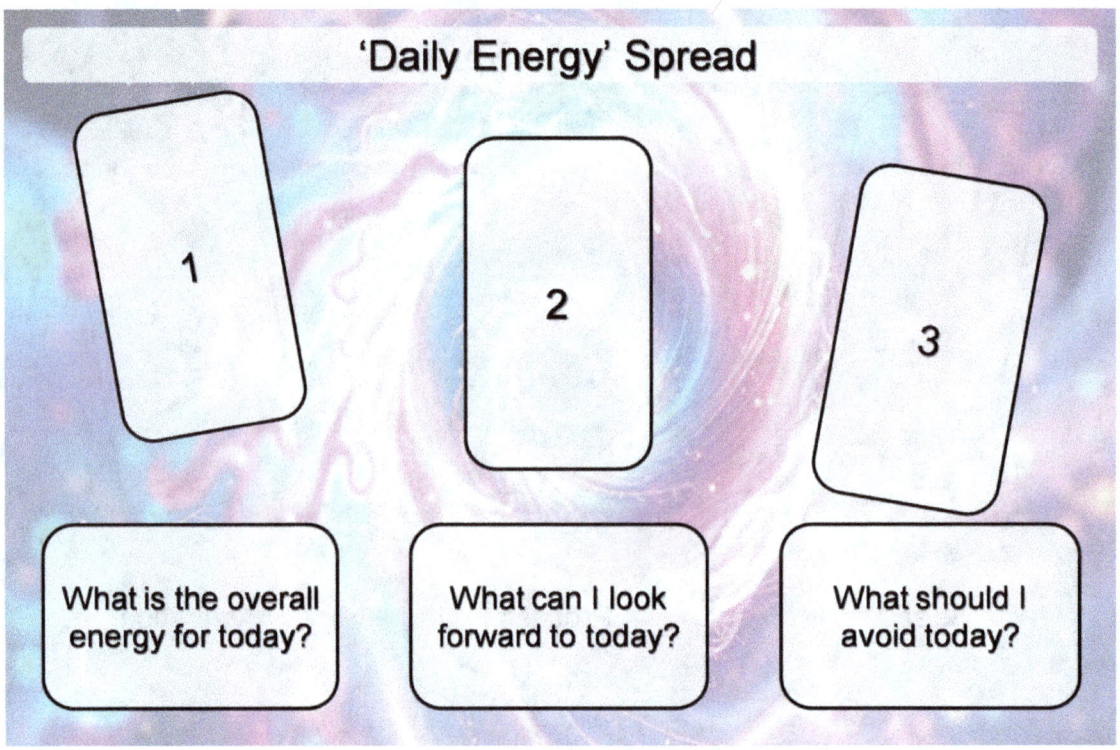

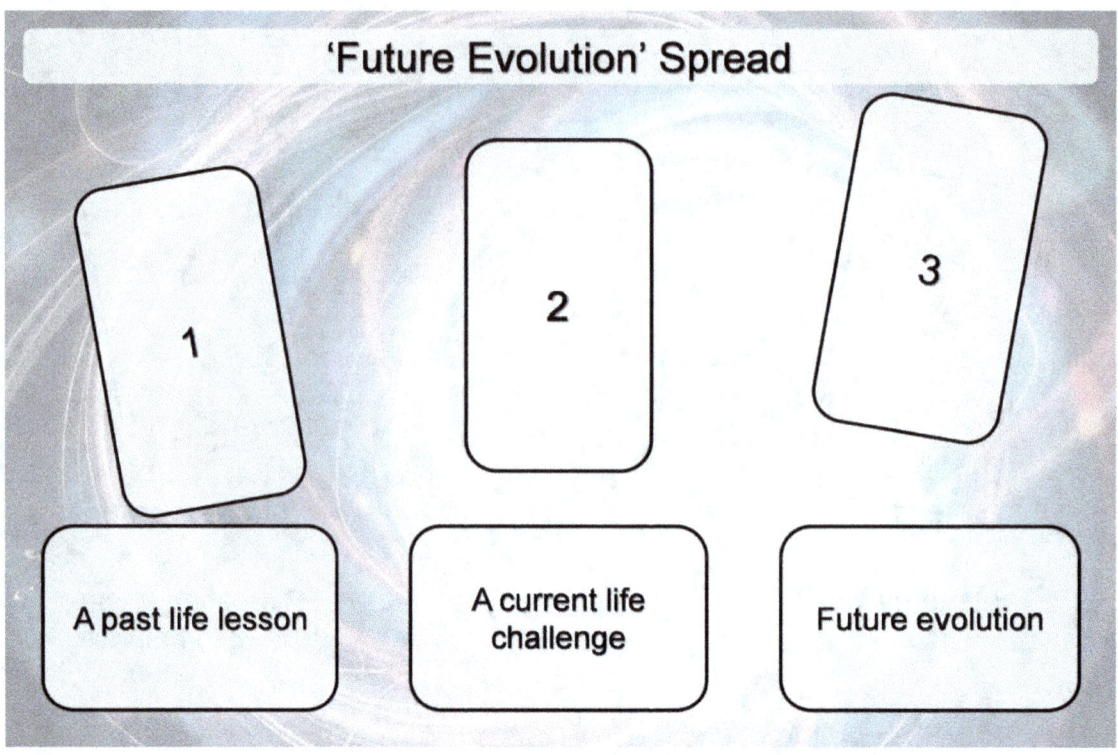

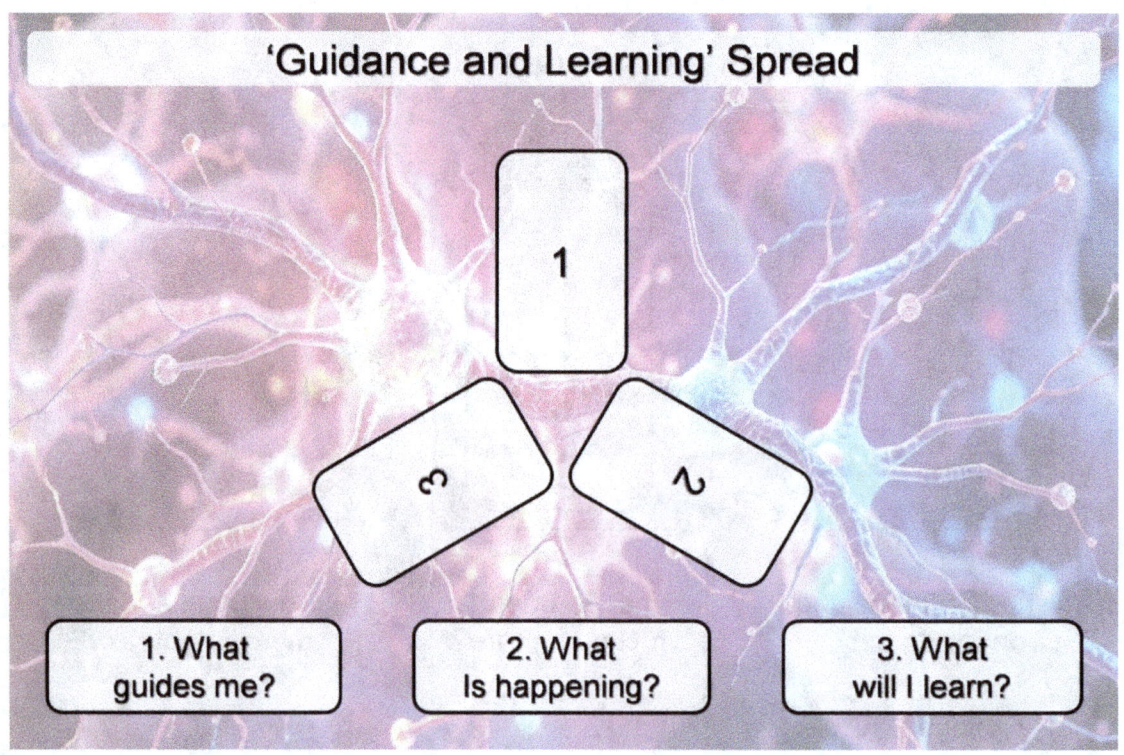

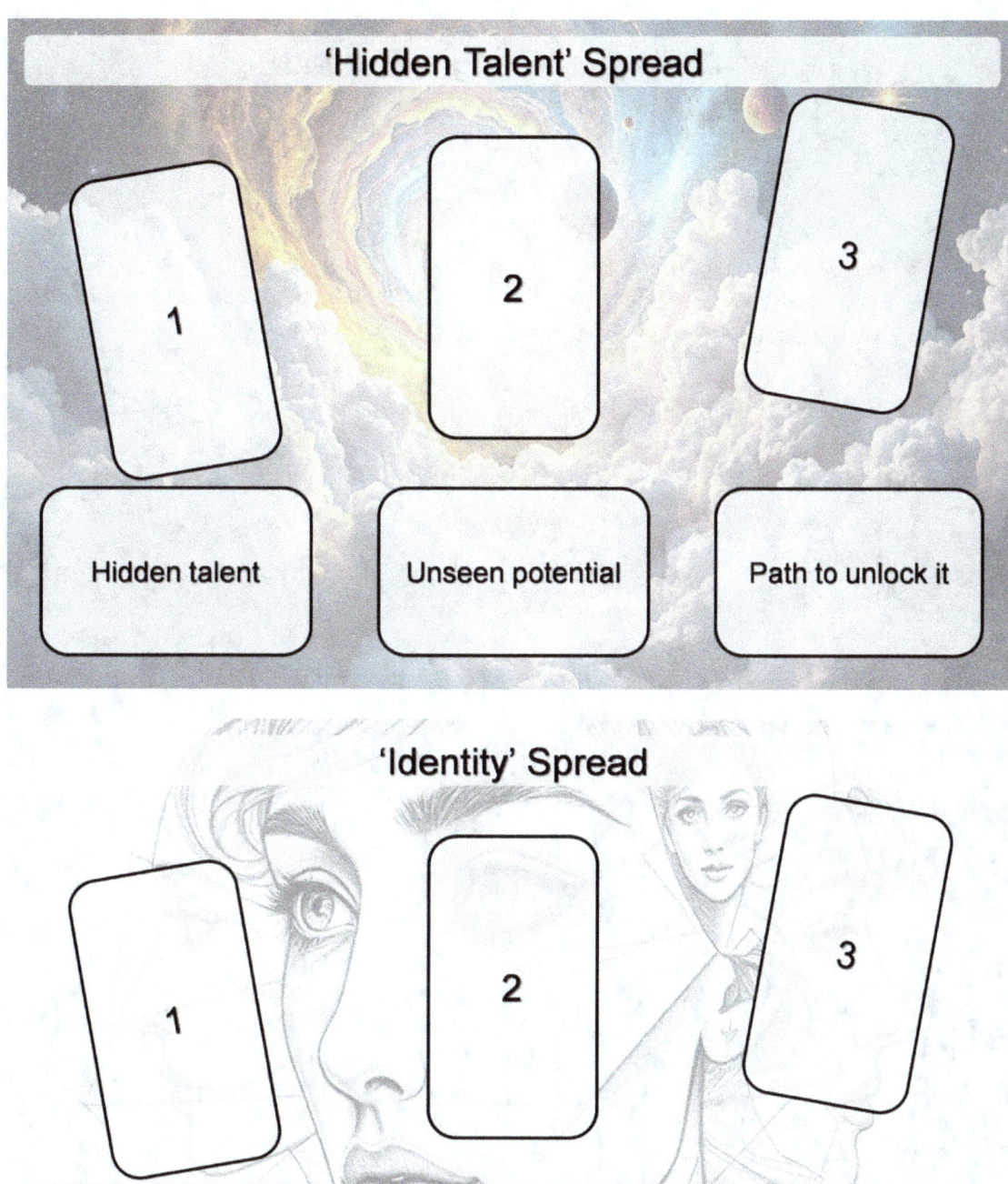

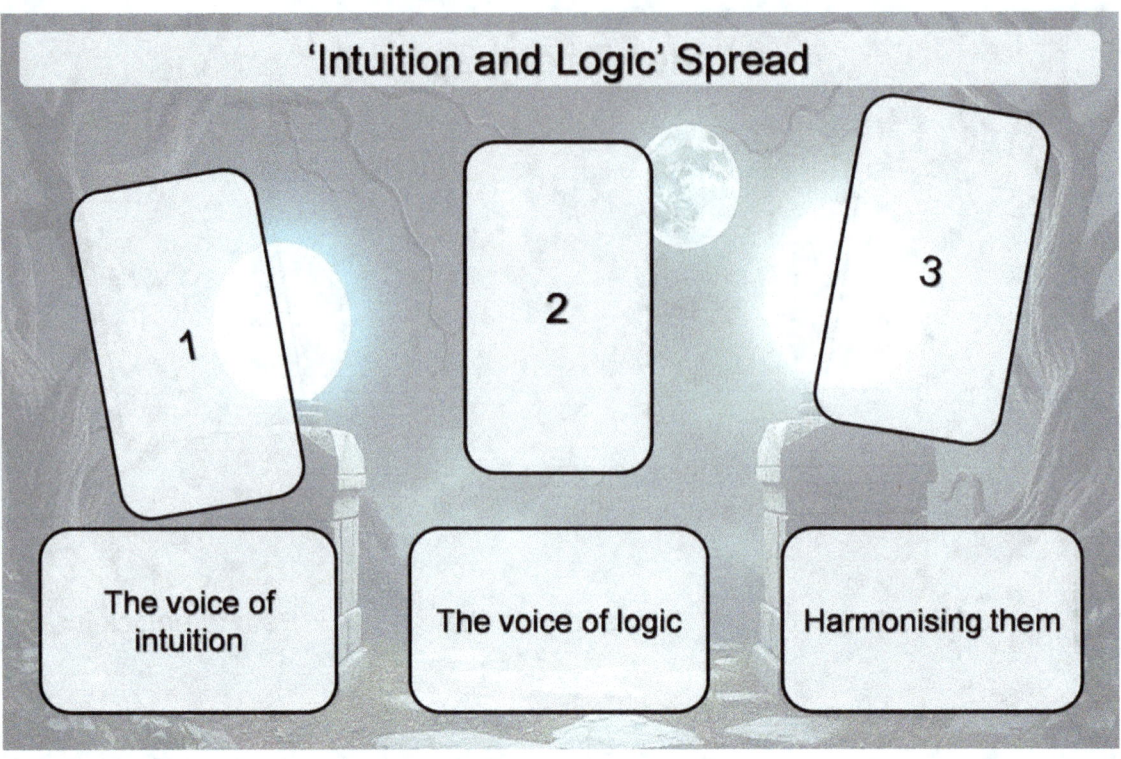

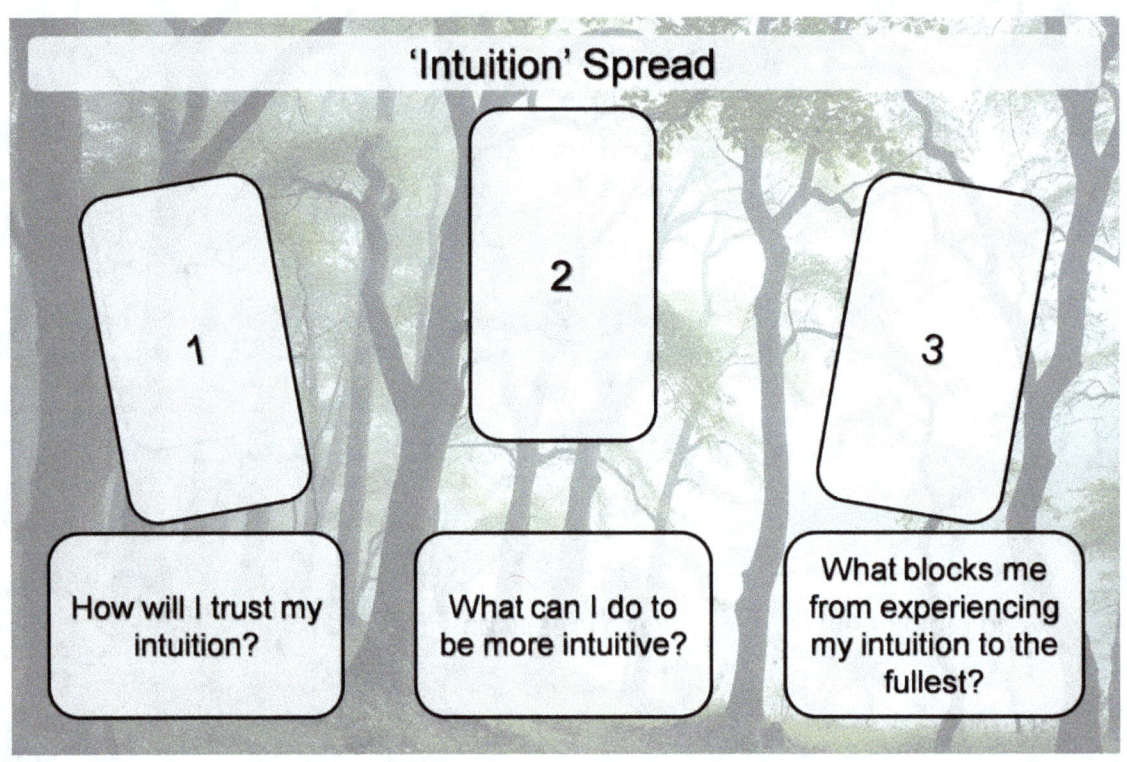

Tarot  08 Divination

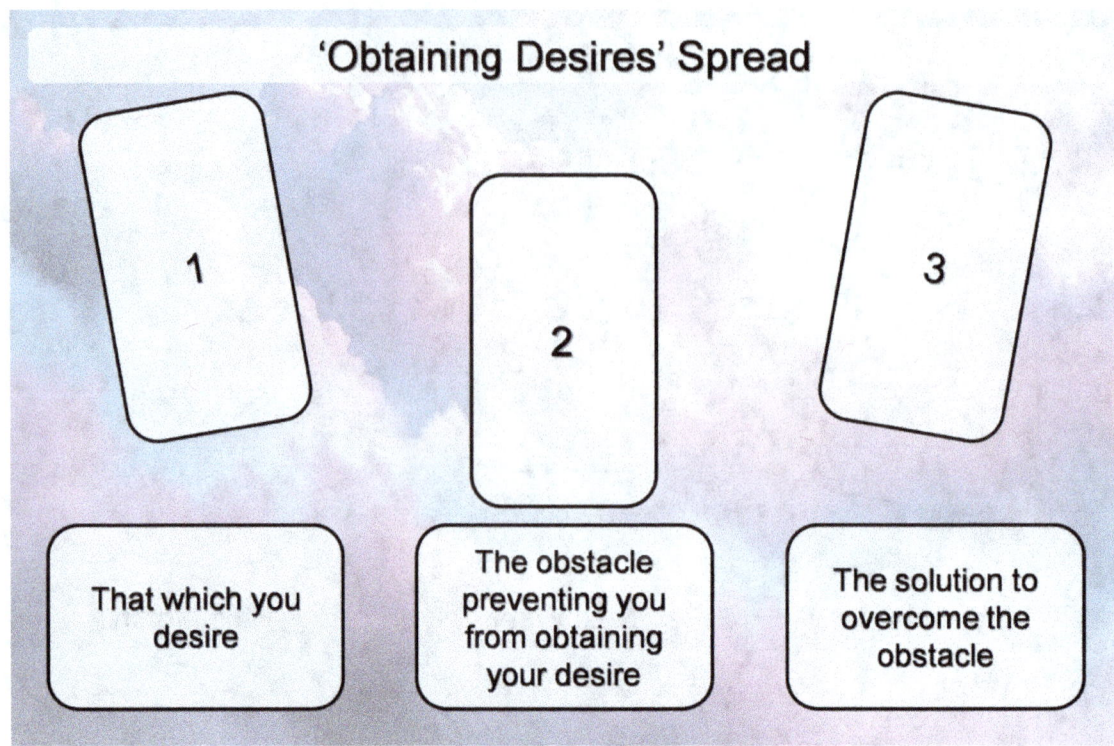

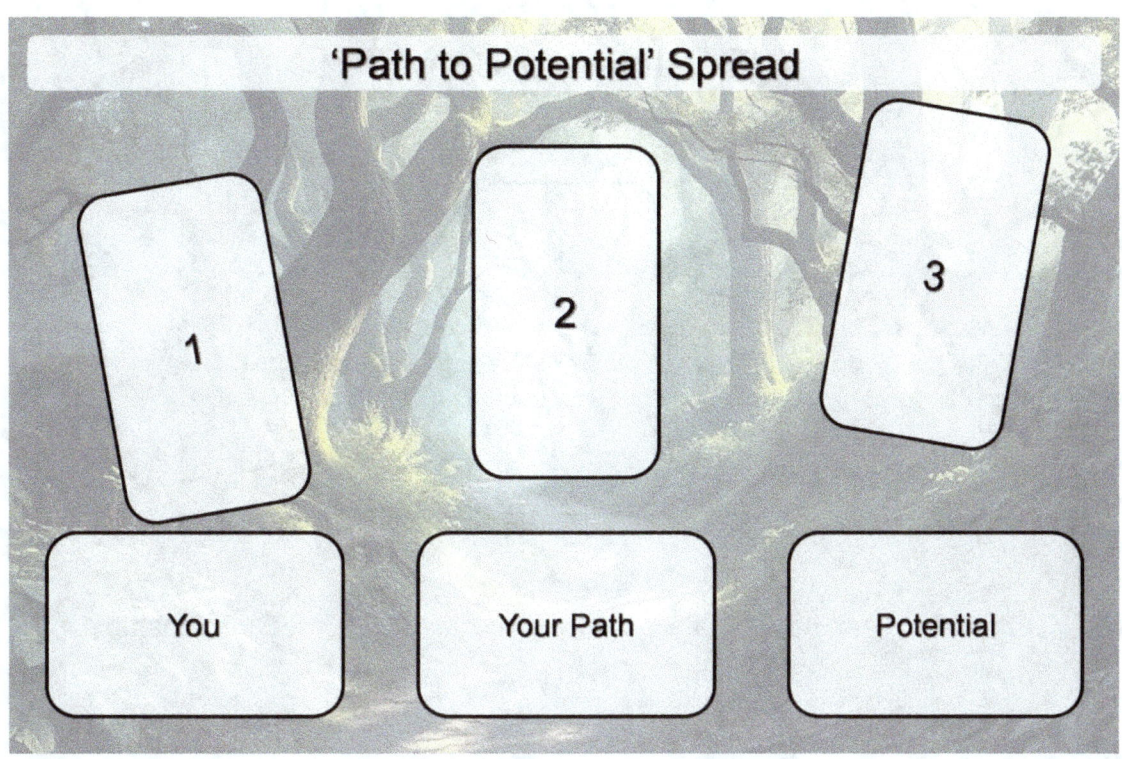

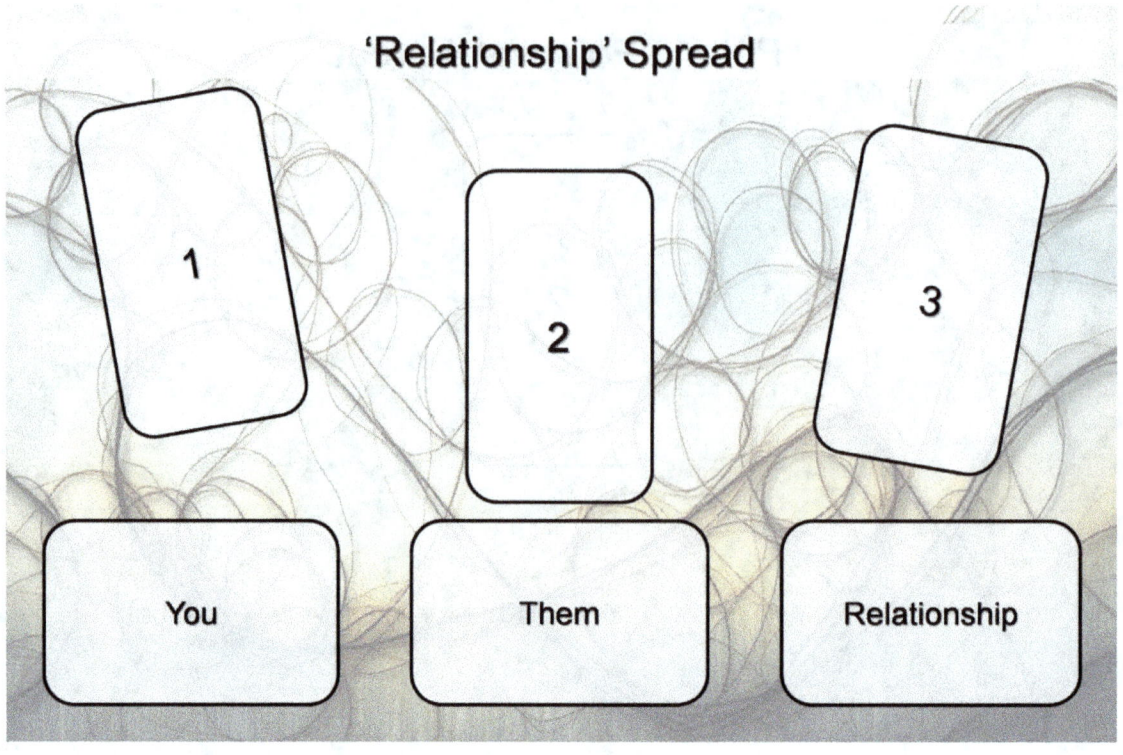

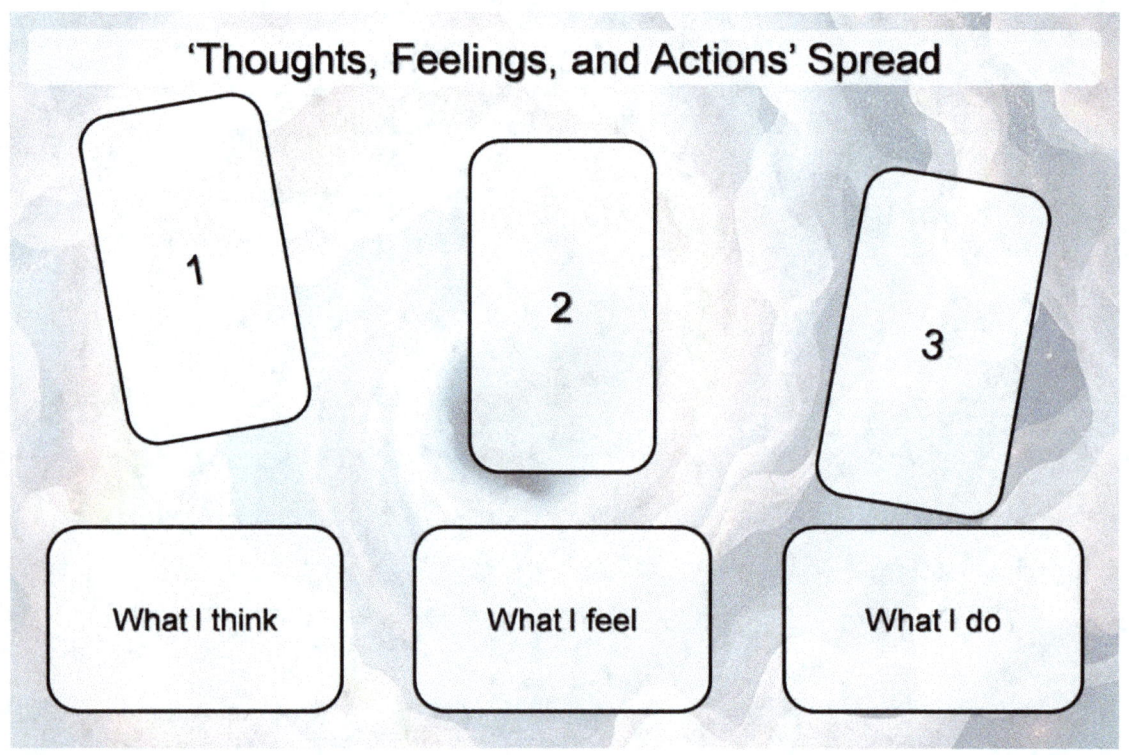

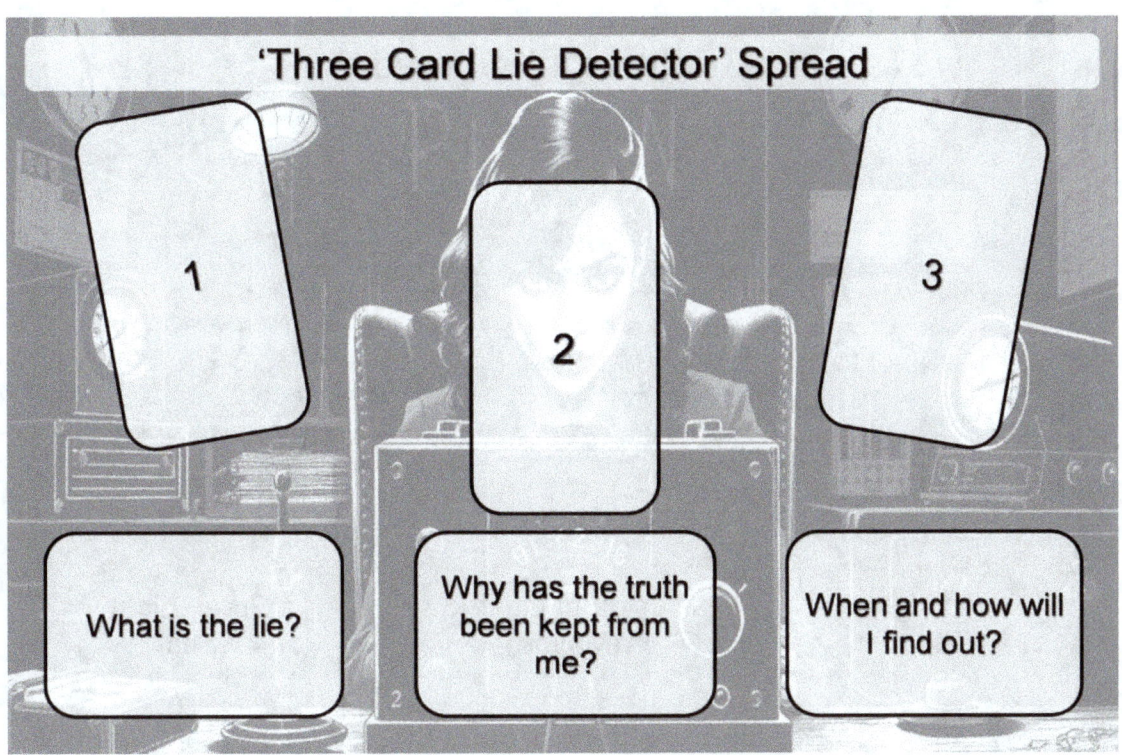

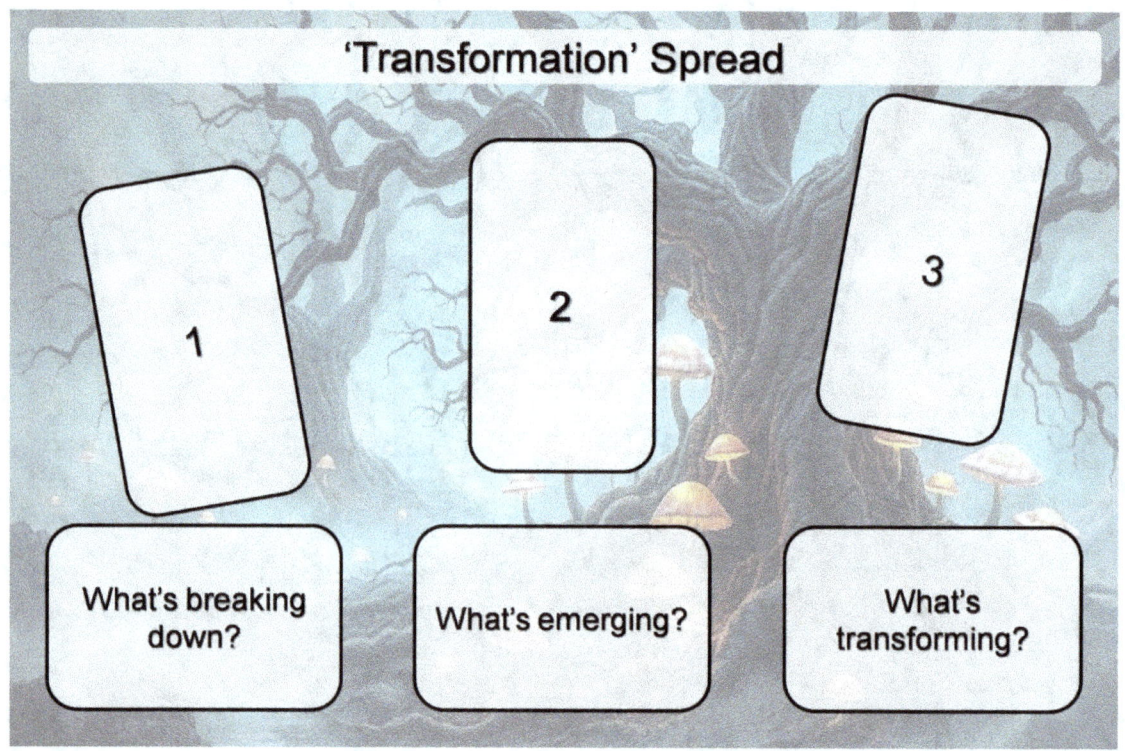

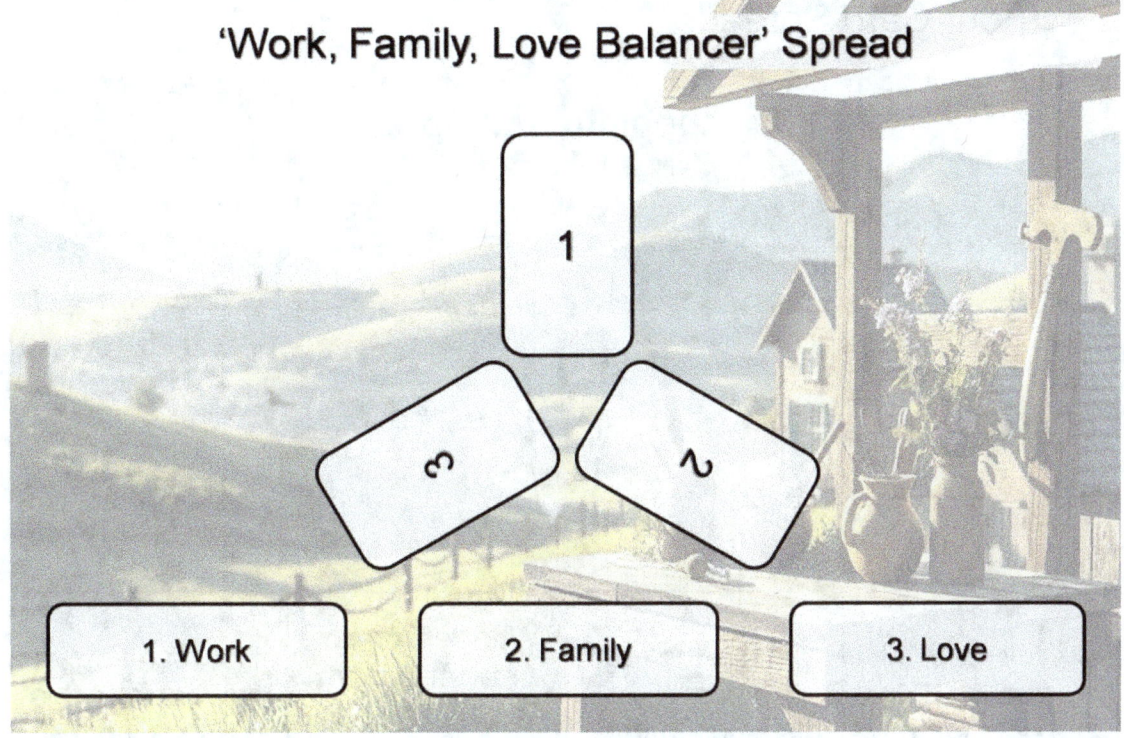

## 8.3. Four Card Spreads

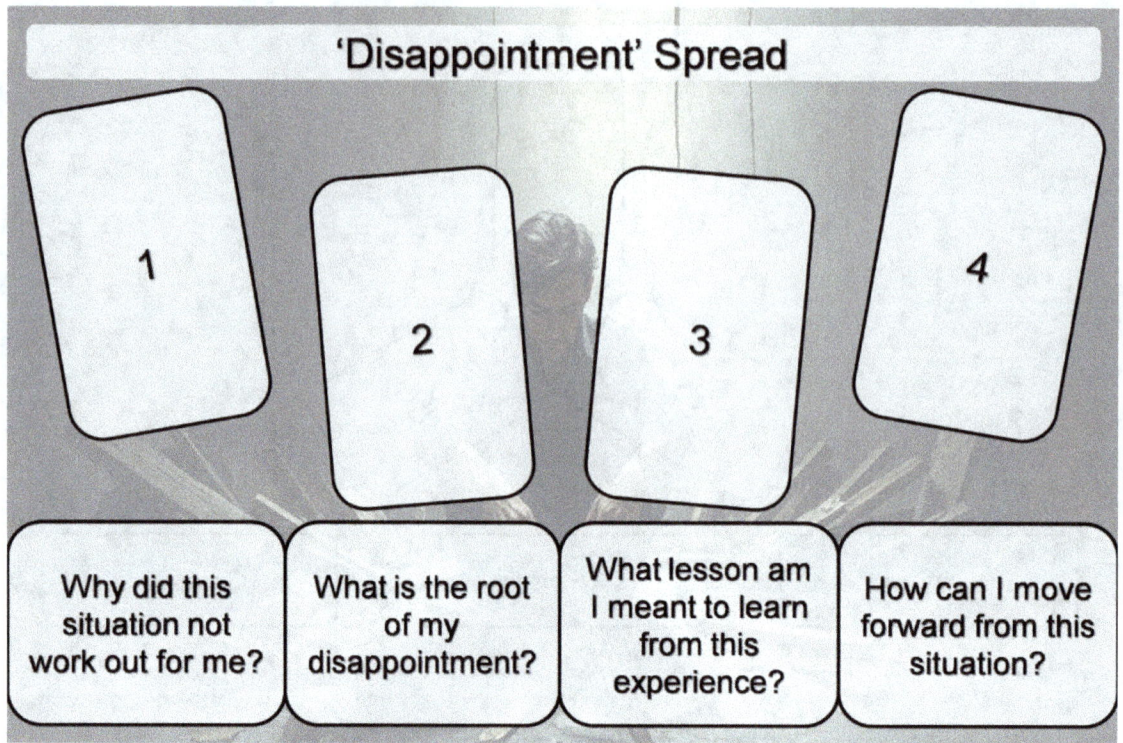

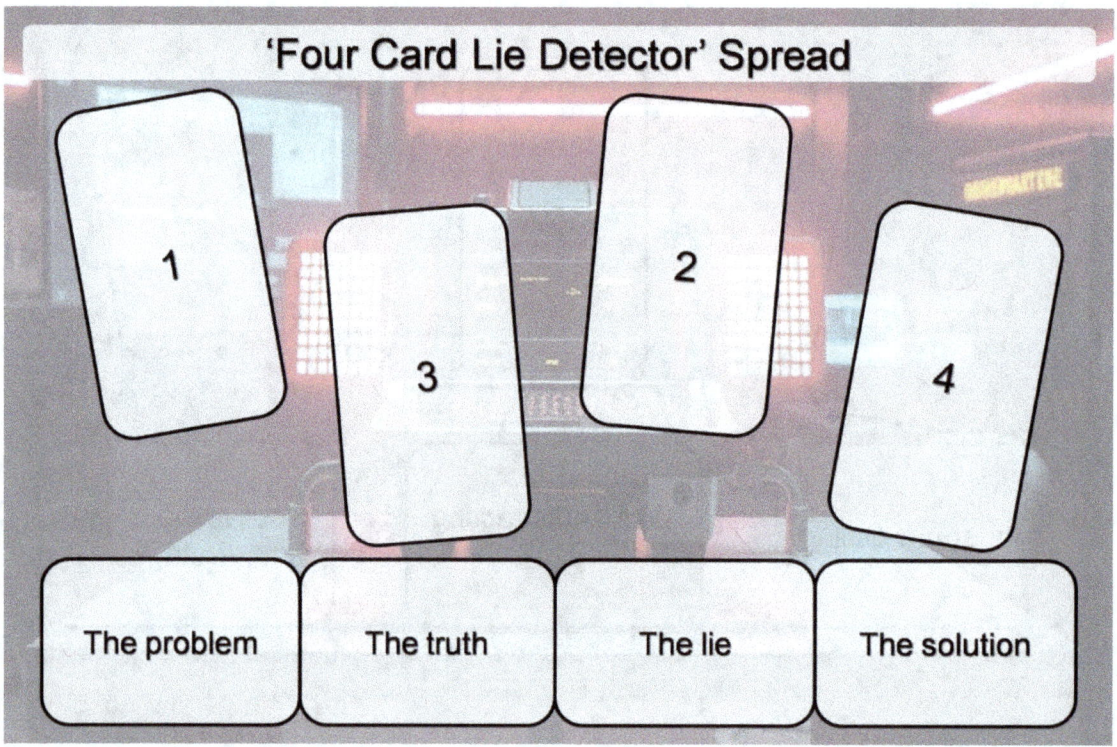

## 'Hidden Truth' Spread

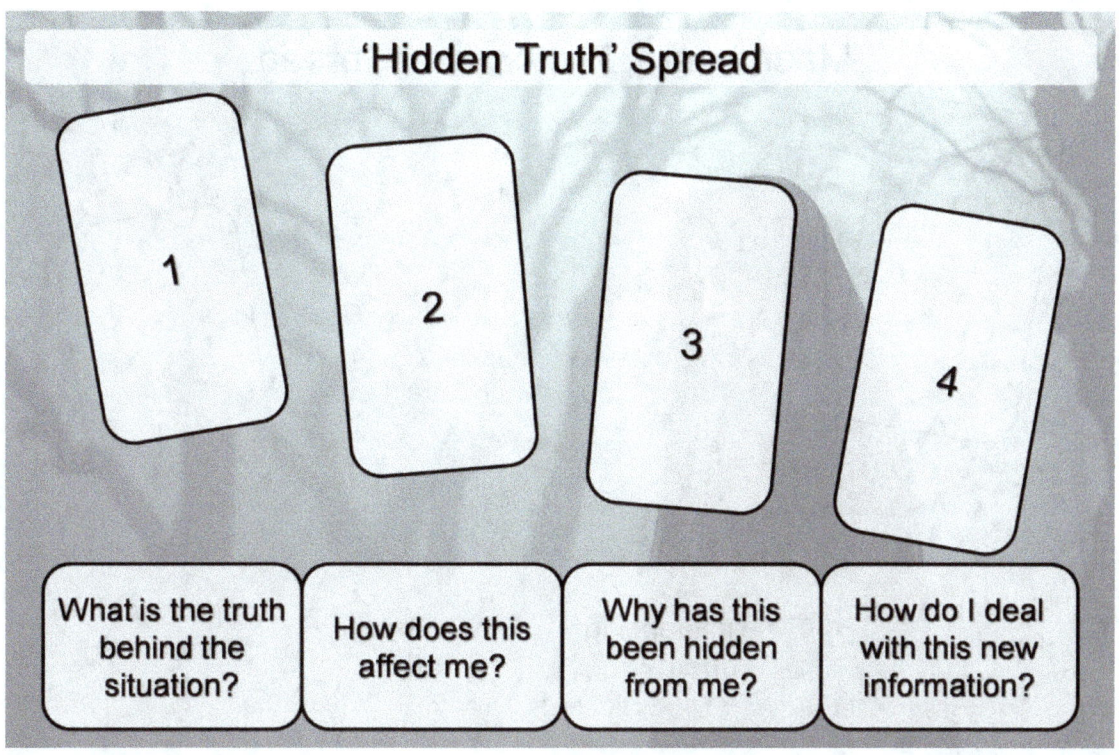

## 'Let Go And Grow' Spread

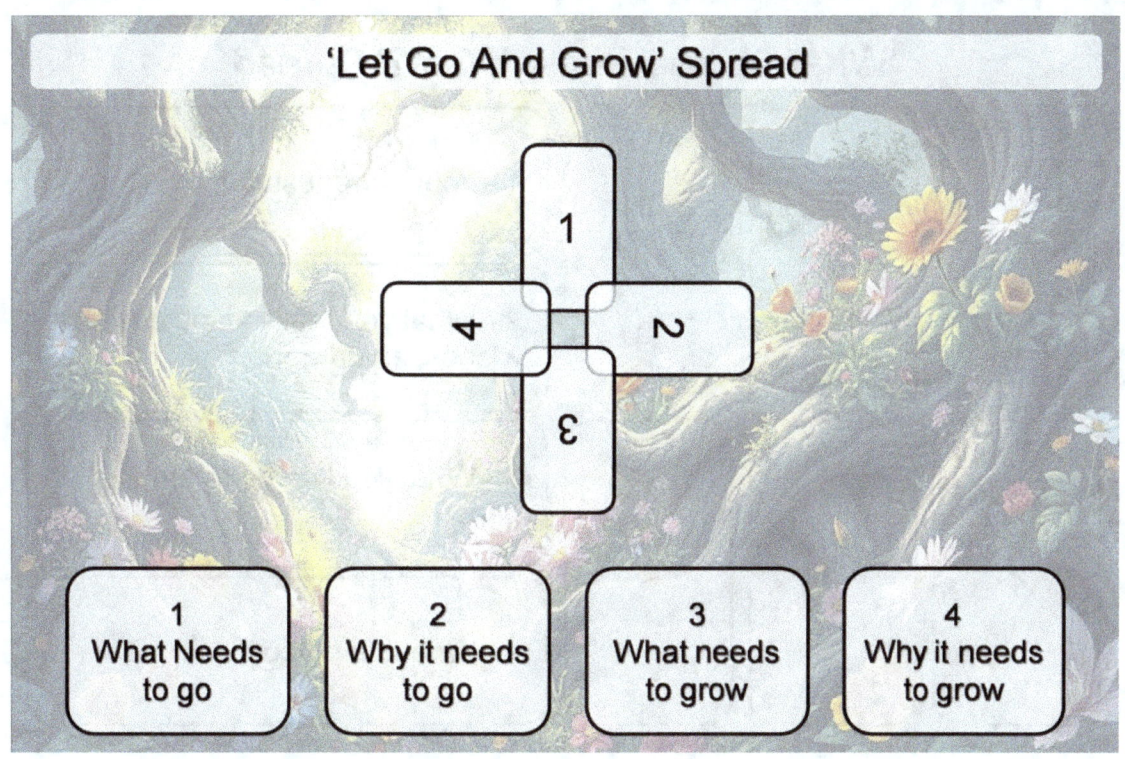

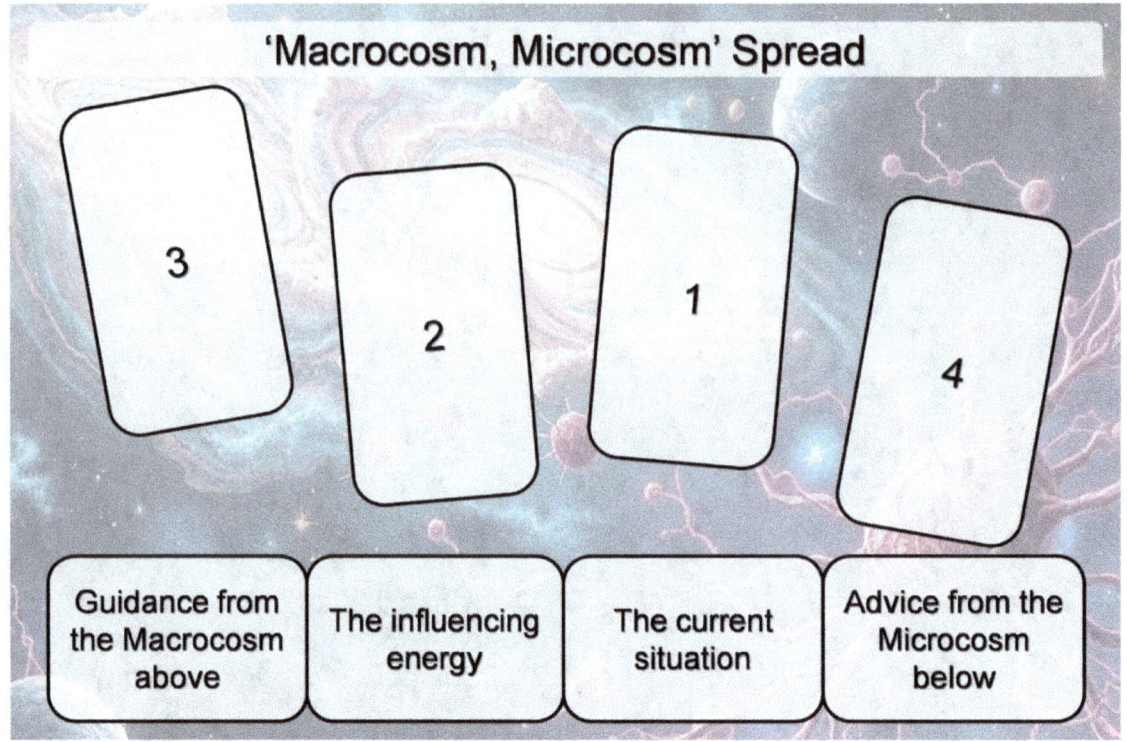

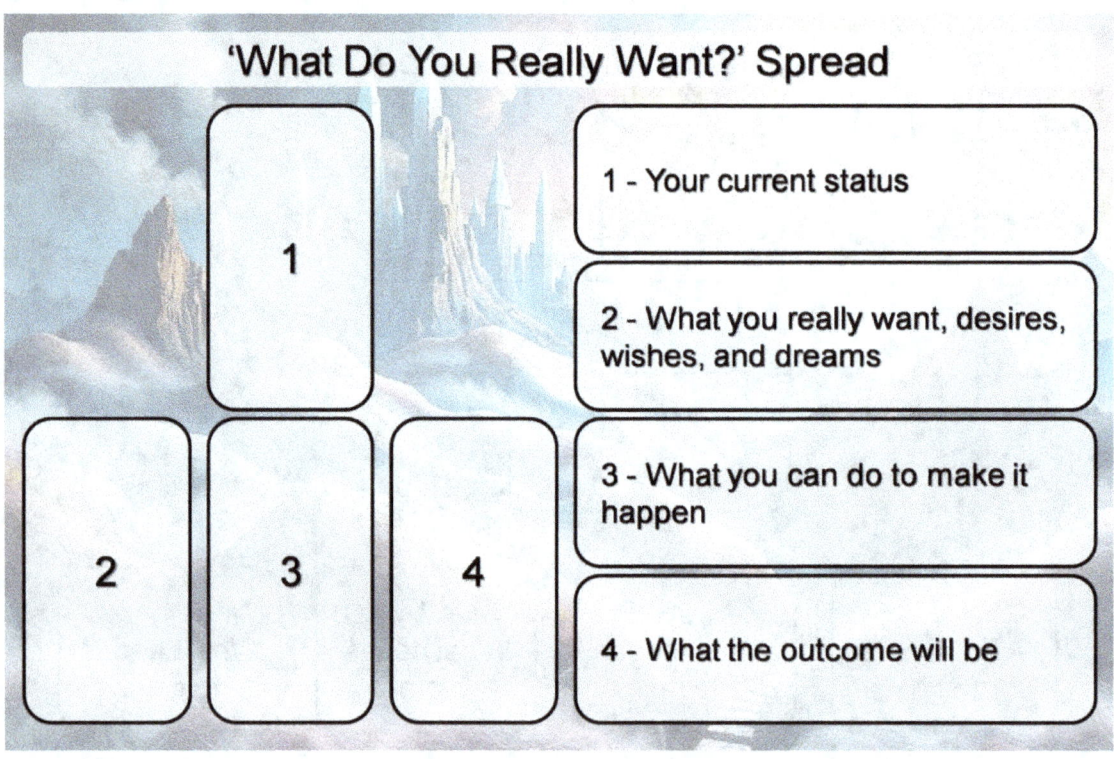

## 8.4. Five Card Spreads

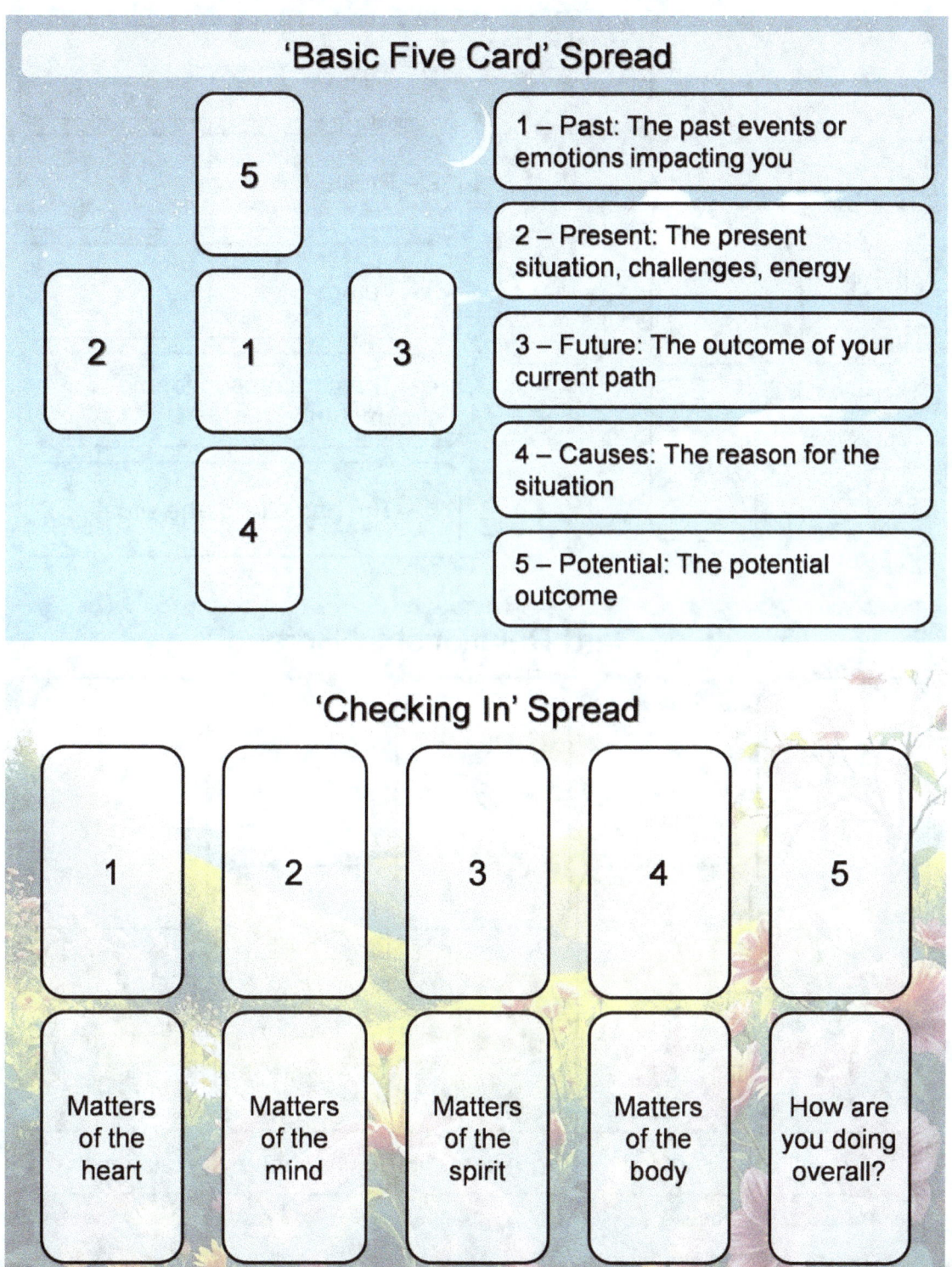

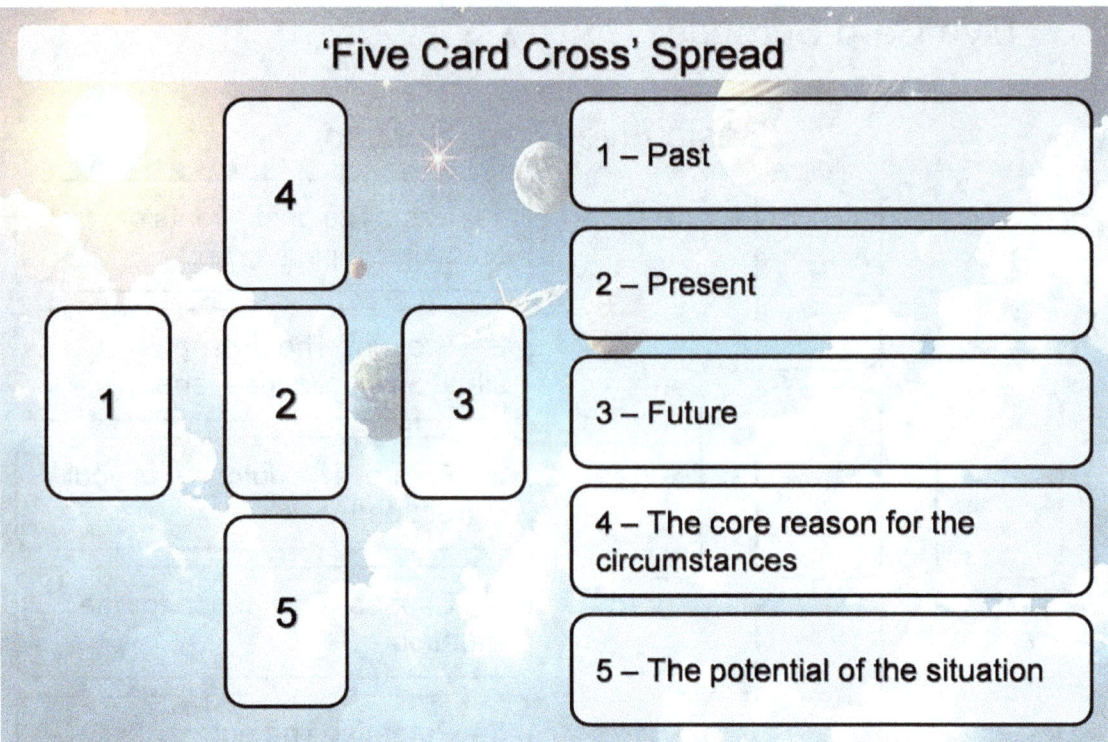

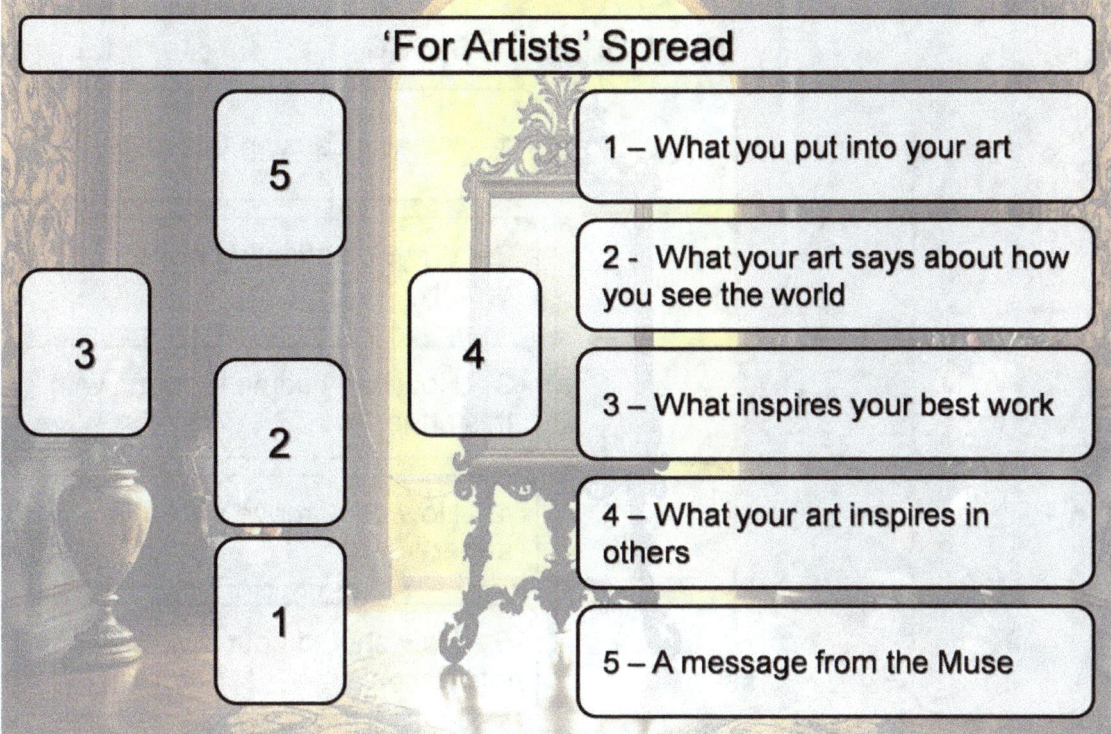

## 'Inner Anger' Spread

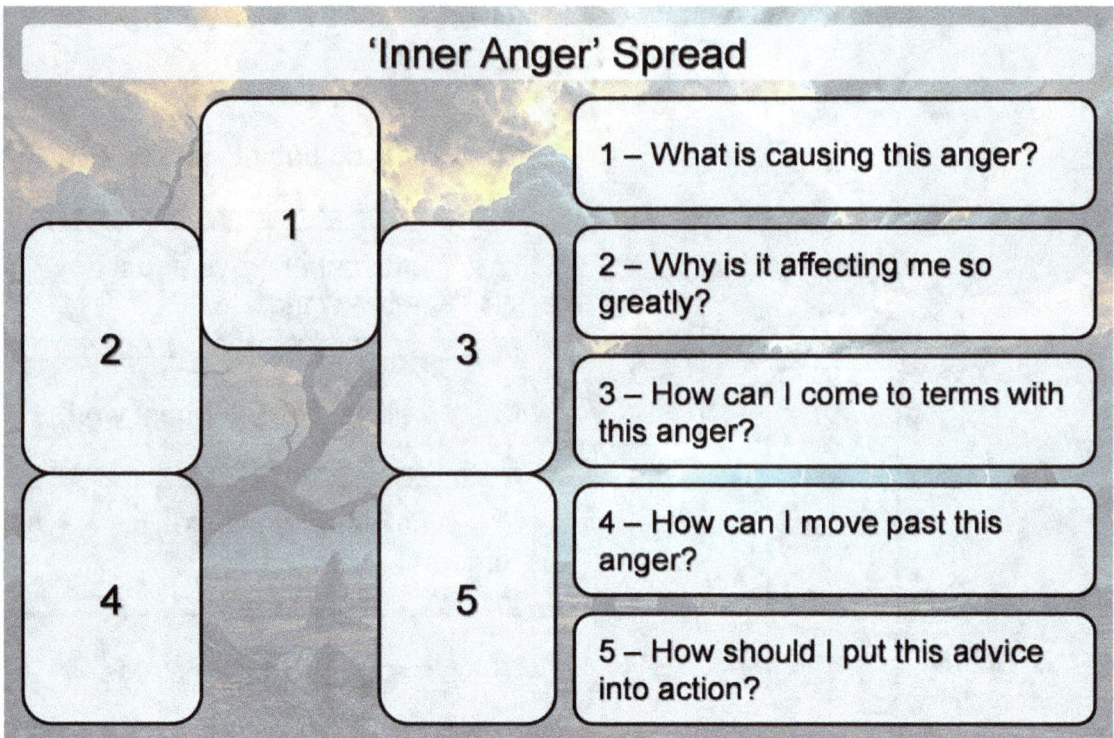

1 – What is causing this anger?

2 – Why is it affecting me so greatly?

3 – How can I come to terms with this anger?

4 – How can I move past this anger?

5 – How should I put this advice into action?

## 'Motivation' Spread

1 – Where is my lack of motivation coming from?

4 – How can I sustain my motivation?

2 – What lesson do I need to learn?

5 – What do I need to focus on?

3 – How can I learn this lesson?

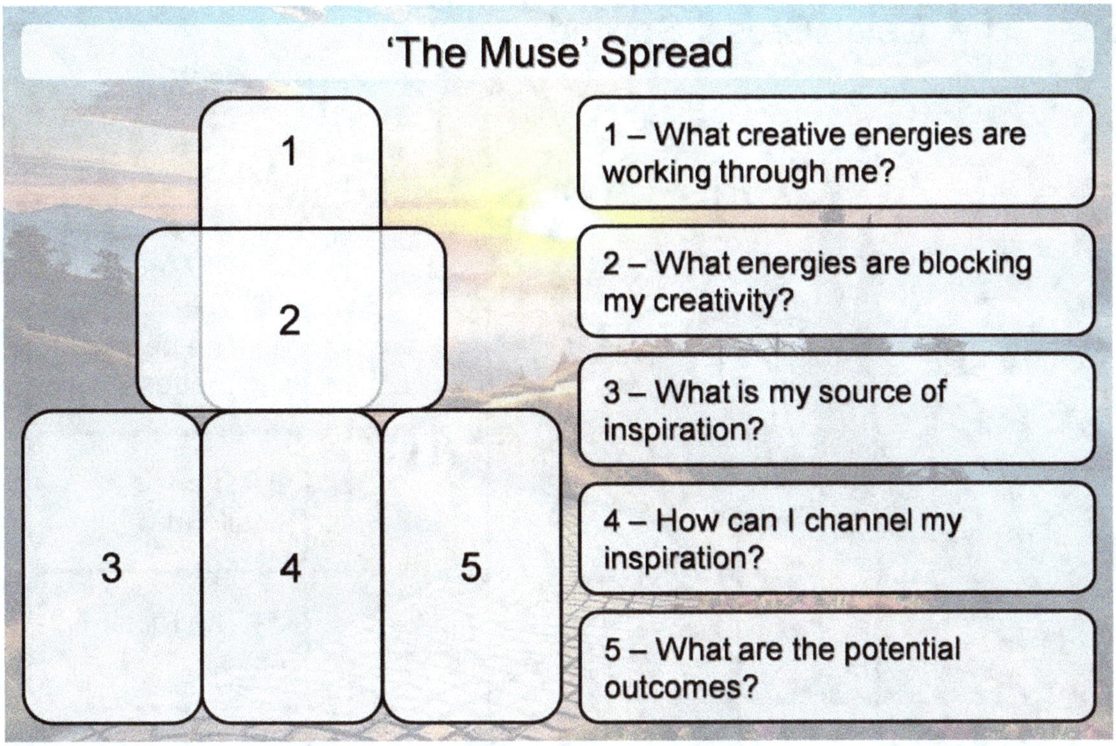

Tarot    08 Divination

## 'The Muse' Spread

1 – What creative energies are working through me?

2 – What energies are blocking my creativity?

3 – What is my source of inspiration?

4 – How can I channel my inspiration?

5 – What are the potential outcomes?

## 'Traditional Five Card' Spread

1 - Past

2 - Present

3 - Future

4 - Obstacles

5 - Moving Forward

163

## 8.5. The 'Celtic Cross' Spread

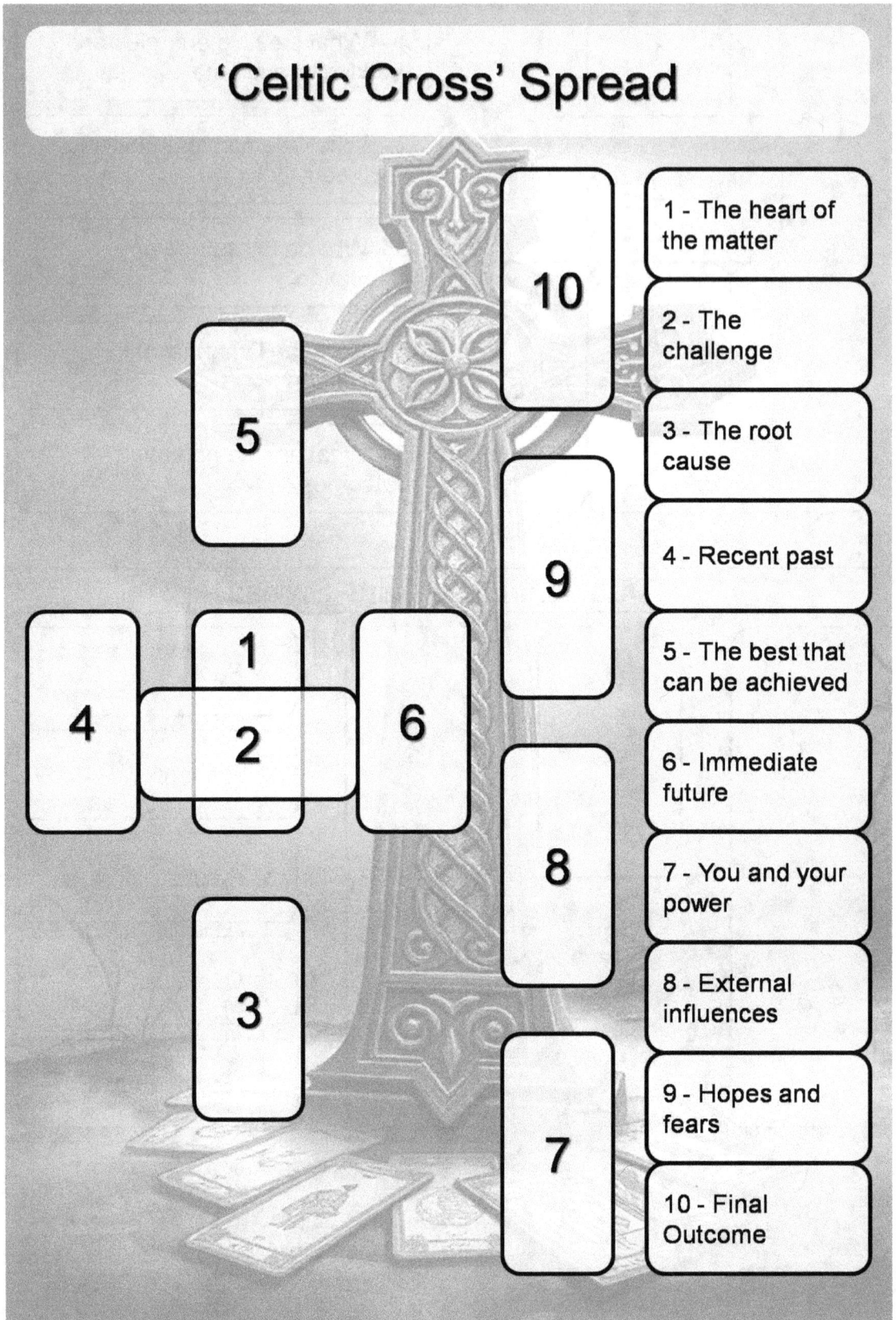

# 9. Magic

People are drawn to Tarot in many different ways and for many different reasons. There are a number of potential benefits to working with tarot, such as a greater sense of self-reflection, personal growth, clarity in decision-making, enhanced intuition, creative expression, emotional healing, empowerment, confidence, spiritual growth, mindfulness, problem-solving, improved communication, increased self-awareness, and stress relief.

Tarot cards are often used as a tool for self-discovery, empowerment, and manifestation. While they are most commonly associated with divination, they can also serve as a powerful medium for personal magical practices.

## Setting Intentions

Tarot cards can help focus energy toward a specific intention or desire. Before a ritual or spell, you might select cards that represent your goals or intentions. Lay out cards in a spread that represents your desired outcome, and then meditate on their symbolism. By focusing your energy on these images, you align yourself with your intent.

## Spells and Rituals

You may wish to incorporate tarot cards into your rituals. You might choose to burn a card that represents something you wish to banish, like The Devil for addiction or The Tower for chaos, or keep a card with you that represents something you wish for, like The Sun for success or The Star for hope.

You can also use cards from specific suits depending on what you are working on. For matters of emotions and intuition, use cards from the Suit of Cups. For matters of intellect and communication, use cards from the Suit of Swords. For matters of creativity and passion, use cards from the Suit of Wands. For matters of material wealth and health, use cards from the Suit of Pentacles.

## Meditation and Visualisation

Select a card that represents a quality you wish to manifest, and meditate with it. Focus on the symbolism, colour, and energy of the card to draw it into your life. A more advanced technique involves using the tarot cards as a path-working tool, where you 'step into' the image on the card and explore its symbolism in a meditative state. This can be used to gain insight into a situation or challenge.

## Affirmations and Empowerment

You can draw a single card daily to inspire a magical affirmation. For example, if you draw The Magician, you might affirm, "I have all the tools I need to manifest my desires", or "I am in control of my reality". Cards can serve as reminders of your strengths and qualities. You can lay out cards like The Emperor (for confidence and control) or The Chariot (for determination and forward movement) as a way of enhancing your personal power.

## Journaling and Self-Reflection

You can use tarot as a tool for self-reflection and magical journaling. Record your readings, which cards were drawn, and how they relate to your goals. Over time, the cards you draw and the insights you gain will inform and direct your magical workings. If you're facing resistance or obstacles in your magical practice, draw a card to identify the source of the blockage. For instance, The Hanged Man can suggest the need for surrender or a change in perspective.

## Manifestation

Tarot cards can enhance manifestation spells by symbolically representing the outcome. For instance, if you're working on a money spell, you might include The Wheel of Fortune or The Ten of Pentacles to attract abundance. During a manifestation meditation, you might use cards to focus your intentions, visualising the imagery as you imagine your desired outcome becoming a reality. For example, if you wish for love, focus on The Lovers or The Two of Cups.

**Protection Magic**

Cards like Strength, The High Priestess, or The Hermit can be used in protective spells or to call upon inner strength. You can use these cards to create boundaries, ward off negative energies, or enhance your personal shield of protection. For situations where you want to bind negative influences or individuals, you can use The Devil or The Ten of Swords in a binding spell, symbolising the release of toxic patterns.

**Healing and Transformation**

The tarot can be used to focus on healing, whether physical, emotional, or spiritual. Cards like The Star or The Ace of Cups can be invoked to bring about rejuvenation and healing energy. Tarot's transformative imagery, such as The Death card (representing endings and rebirth), can help you release old patterns, beliefs, or relationships that no longer serve you, aiding in personal growth.

## 9.1. General Advice

**Choose a Deck That Resonates With You**

There are countless tarot decks, each with their own artwork, style, and energy. The traditional Rider-Waite-Smith deck is a popular choice for beginners because it has very clear symbolism, but do explore other decks to find one that resonates with your personal aesthetic and intuition.

Some decks are designed around specific themes, such as nature, mythology, or astrology, etc., so choose one that aligns with your interests. The right deck will feel like it 'clicks' with you, even if you're just drawn to the artwork or imagery.

A pirate themed tarot deck by Carrie and Lucas Amodio, Illustrations by Liz Harper, published by Schiffer, 2009, author's collection.

**Practice Daily**

Draw one card a day, reflect on its meaning and how it might relate to your current situation or mindset. You don't need to do a full reading, just spend a few minutes connecting with the card and noting any feelings or thoughts it inspires.

**Trust Your Intuition**

While it's helpful to learn traditional interpretations of the cards, tarot is ultimately a tool for your intuition. When looking at a card, take a moment to tune into your feelings and thoughts about it. The images, symbols, and colours on the card might inspire insights that go beyond textbook meanings.

Try to let your intuition guide you when reading the cards. What does the imagery remind you of? What emotions or thoughts arise? The more you practice this, the stronger your intuition will become.

**Respect the Cards**

Some people like to keep their tarot decks in a special bag or box, or even "cleanse" the cards regularly by using methods like smudging with sage, or leaving them in the moonlight. Treat the cards with respect, as they are a tool for divination and spiritual insight.

When you use the cards, create a sacred space, even if it's just for a few minutes. You can do this by focusing your intention or by lighting a candle, clearing your mind, or saying a small prayer. This helps you connect to the energy of the cards in a more meaningful way.